EMPOWERING HISPANIC FAMILIES: A CRITICAL ISSUE FOR THE '90s

EDITED BY MARTA SOTOMAYOR

Family Service America
11700 West Lake Park Drive
Milwaukee, Wisconsin 53224

P9-DFI-709

Copyright © 1991
Family Service America
11700 West Lake Park Drive
Milwaukee, Wisconsin 53224

Library of Congress Cataloging-in-Publication Data

Empowering Hispanic families: a critical issue for the '90s /
  edited by Marta Sotomayor.
    p. cm.
  Includes bibliographical references.
  ISBN 0-87304-243-3 (pbk.)
  1. Hispanic Americans — Families. I. Sotomayor, Marta.
  E184.S75E47 1991   91-584
  362.84'68073 — dc20

Printed in the United States

Contributors

Elena Bastida
Associate Professor
Department of Sociology
Pan American University
Edinburg, Texas

Herman Curiel
Associate Professor
School of Social Work
University of Oklahoma
Norman, Oklahoma

Mario De La Rosa
Social Science Analyst
National Institute on Drug Abuse
Administration for Mental Health,
Drug Abuse and Alcohol
Public Health Service
Rockville, Maryland

América Facundo
Private Practice
Amherst, Massachusetts

Joseph S. Gallegos
Director of Social Service
and Gerontology Programs
University of Portland
Portland, Oregon

Alejandro García
Professor
School of Social Work
Syracuse University
Syracuse, New York

Genaro Gonzalez
Associate Professor

Department of Psychology
Pan American University
Edinburg, Texas

Rumaldo Juárez
Director
University of Texas System
Edinburg, Texas

Manuel R. Miranda
Assistant Director
National Institute on Aging
National Institutes of Health
Public Health Service
Bethesda, Maryland

Frank F. Montalvo
Director of Field Practicum
Worden School of Social Service
Our Lady of the Lake University of
San Antonio
San Antonio, Texas

Juan Ramos
Deputy Director for Prevention
and Special Projects
National Institute of Mental Health
Administration for Mental Health,
Drug Abuse and Alcohol
Public Health Service
Rockville, Maryland

Arturo T. Río (d. 1990)
Formerly Research Assistant
Professor
School of Medicine
University of Miami
Miami, Florida

Contributors

Daniel A. Santisteban
Project Director
Spanish Family Guidance Center
Research Assistant
School of Medicine
University of Miami
Miami, Florida

Fernando I. Soriano
Assistant Professor
Department of Behavioral Sciences
School of Dentistry
University of Missouri–Kansas City
Kansas City, Missouri

Marta Sotomayor
President and CEO
National Hispanic Council on Aging
Washington, D.C.

José Szapocznik
Professor of Psychiatry and
Director of Spanish Family Guidance Center
School of Medicine
University of Miami
Miami, Florida

Contents

Foreword

Juan Ramos

The impact of patterns of social service provision—and their structuring, financing, and evaluation—on culturally diverse populations has received considerable attention from scholars and human service practitioners in recent years. Increasing recognition is being given to the need to develop multicultural human services and to increase the understanding of the cultural aspects of patient care.

The meaning of cultural competence is sought by a growing number of professionals, agencies, and institutions; becoming culturally competent is a developmental process that is beginning to be seen as part and parcel of professional competence. Discourse on these issues will become even more important as we advance through the 1990s. Specifically, the dramatic increases and changes in the Hispanic population in the United States will bring new and exciting challenges to the human service infrastructure, including public and private social welfare agencies and training institutions.

The challenge to the helping professions is to examine the impact and consequences of their policies and processes on culturally and linguistically diverse populations such as Hispanic Americans and to find ways to change the social service infrastructure so that it can respond appropriately to their growing needs.

A major component of the human service infrastructure that traditionally has been overlooked in the change process is the authorizing bodies that deal with accreditation of facilities providing inpatient and residential care, accreditation of educational institutions and specialized training, licensing and certification, and the approval of diagnostic and assessment tools used by the helping professions. These factors significantly influence the services provided by the helping professions; all will need to be reviewed and revamped to reflect the needs and special characteristics of the diverse Hispanic populations that in the past have not been given their due consideration. As experience indicates, present policies and procedures have enormous impact, mostly negative, on culturally and linguistically diverse populations in that they do not generally incorporate criteria representative of these groups.

The usual approach to changing the social service enterprise has been to focus on programmatic components of the infrastructure, disregarding the value assumptions on which they are based, thus maintaining and perpetuating the social contract that legitimizes them. Reevaluating and reforming the value base of the infrastructure require enormous efforts. However, reevaluation and changes are crucial if the cause of justice is to be advanced. Inaction or avoidance of self-examination on the part of human service professionals is extremely costly to members of culturally disadvantaged population groups who are in need of services based on fair and appropriate assessment tools and accreditation requirements and procedures.

Recognizing the negative impact of the value base of the human services infrastructure and how that infrastructure negatively affects various minority population groups, we can begin the process of overhauling the infrastructure according to a different set of assumptions. Although such work will require considerable effort and time, it is imperative that the reform process include several key tasks. Retraining helping professionals through continuing education, changing and improving the effectiveness of the service delivery system as it pertains to culturally and linguistically diverse populations, adding multicultural content to certification and licensing examinations, and including multicultural criteria in the accreditation process are all essential to improving services for minority clients. Such changes require ongoing commitment as well as a passion for justice on the part of professionals and institutions.

Discourse about the service needs of the Hispanic population is long overdue and should be conducted in a spirit of openness, justice, and understanding. Much work needs to be done. The chapters in this book will help inform and guide this discourse and provide a significant knowledge base for understanding the strengths of the Hispanic population, for whom the family is central and crucial to their well-being. The authors of the various chapters work within the framework of social justice, articulating their professional judgments on behalf of all Americans. Their discussions reflect professional experience evolving from various settings, geographical regions, disciplines, and bodies of knowledge in an effort to trigger a reexamination of current policies and practices.

The goal of this book is ambitious: to ameliorate the symptoms, consequences, and outcomes generated by a human services system that remains almost immune to any discourse on its effectiveness with multicultural populations and that is surrounded by walls of indifference and ethnocentrism. The infrastructure of this system needs to be challenged; strategies must be designed to open the process to evaluation and to important work that is currently being done. We look forward to the time when services will be provided by licensed or certified helping professionals who have passed examinations with sections on multicultural content and who have been trained in accredited programs that incorporate multicultural content as required by accreditation criteria. We also look forward to the time when treatment facilities will have to meet accreditation standards and criteria that incorporate multicultural content.

We believe that Hispanic helping professionals will recommit themselves to providing leadership in collaboration with the Hispanic community and others to set goals and objectives for the 1990s and beyond. Our message to human service professions and institutions is that the helping processes must be reexamined so that populations that have been excluded from society may be included. To do less is to continue to support harmful social patterns that are ethnocentric, undemocratic, and paternalistic. We must work together, utilizing new perspectives and new knowledge to shatter the walls of indifference and ethnocentrism and to create a better society for all people.

National Institute of Mental Health
Washington, D.C.

Introduction

Marta Sotomayor

It has been two decades since *La Causa Chicana* (Mangold, 1972) was published by the Family Service Association of America, now Family Service America. That book represented a period of reflection for a group of Chicanos active in the civil rights movement, a time of reevaluation of values that brought profound social and political changes to the nation. Representing a variety of disciplines, the authors reflected on the meaning and context of their participation in a social change movement and its impact on their communities. The book had a clear message: to promote social justice and to reaffirm that access to health and social services is a right rather than charity. The authors sought to raise the level of awareness of the helping professions regarding the role that ethnicity, race, language, and culture play in the Latino definition of reality. It was assumed that such understanding would bring about changes in the helping professions and, by extension, improve the well-being of this population group. The present book is an effort to go beyond the issues posed by Chicanos in the 1970s. Most of the issues evident at that time are still a matter for concern, although some have been ameliorated. In addition, new issues and concerns have arisen that affect a larger, more diverse, complex population.

Hispanics in the Past Two Decades

Since *La Causa Chicana* was published, a lot has happened regarding issues of justice and equality as they pertain to Hispanics. There has been dramatic population growth of Hispanics as a result of immigration from every Latin American country. In chapter 1, Genaro Gonzalez reviews the history of Mexican migration since the early 1920s and ponders whether the outcome for new immigrants will be the same as it was for early immigrants. Although the reasons for migrating then and now are the same, the new immigrant waves add significant dimensions to the experience of the second, third, fourth, and even fifth generations of Mexican Americans, or Chicanos, in this country. In the United States, all the different Hispanic subgroups have come together under the banner of "Hispanidad" to examine historical realities, sort the good from the bad, seek solutions to ameliorate the immigrant experience, and forge a new future. For Hispanics, their countries of origin and the constant movement back and forth to the homeland help to solidify and revitalize culture and language in the United States. Thus, this immigrant group is different from others in that strong cultural and linguistic, and thus emotional, bonds transcend geographical and political boundaries.

In chapter 2, Alejandro García examines a number of demographic variables and their interconnections to describe the current and future status of Hispanics in the United States. The increasing number of single-parent Hispanic families and the growing population of Hispanic women entering the work force signal a future need for social and health care services. Because of their tremendous growth rate and the diminishing birth rate of the majority society, the well-being of this society depends on the well-being of this one group, for Hispanics will constitute the bulk of the growth in the labor force in the next two decades (Johnston & Packer, 1987).

Latino populations' limited access to social and health care services presents problems for which effective solutions have yet to be found. Debate on the topic of low service-utilization rates reflects two different but interrelated views. One focuses on factors characteristic of the Hispanic population, such as lack of acculturation into the majority culture and lack of skills to negotiate large helping systems. The other point of view focuses on factors that are related to the way society and institutions are organized. It is argued that discrimination, insensitivity of service providers to cultural and linguistic differences, and agency policies and procedures discourage accessibility to services and are barriers that keep service-utilization rates down.

The new wave of immigrants poses challenges and dilemmas to service providers. Because the populations are so multifaceted and complex, no single helping approach and/or theoretical perspective is adequate for understanding and solving problems. Cultural borrowing, shock, and conflict; bilingualism and biculturalism; acculturation; assimilation; and adaptation must continue to be explored for their usefulness in developing helping approaches that are appropriate to meet the needs of these populations. Issues of poverty, the underclass, colonialism, racism, and powerlessness continue to surface. Forced migration as a result of economic and political dislocation, whether promoted by civil war, outside political interference, or internal mismanagement of resources, have created tremendous stress on entire communities as well as on the supportive institutions of these immigrant groups. And the family, like other institutions, has suffered. The socioeconomic and political forces that have stimulated recent Latin American migration accompany the sojourner to this country, and their negative effects surface in the family, the school, the church, and the community.

The authors of chapters in this volume discuss social and political forces that exacerbate the vulnerability of Hispanic populations and place them at high risk. Poverty, AIDS, substance abuse, and discrimination based on color, age, and gender are some of the problems addressed in this book. These problems undermine the basic institutions of society regardless of cultural traditions or place of origin. Mario de la Rosa (chapter 3) and Fernando Soriano (chapter 4) discuss the problems of substance abuse and AIDS, both of which are prevalent in the entire society. However, the incidence of these devastating social and health problems, with their accompanying socioeconomic and emotional ramifications, are disproportionately high among Latinos. The threat that they pose to the family as a cultural value, as an institution, and as a primary nurturing and supportive resource is immeasurable, and finding viable solutions to these crises is a matter of urgency for the entire society.

Educational problems experienced by Hispanic children constitute a crucial issue of concern. Perhaps no other issue so well illustrates the conflicts experienced by new immigrants as well as those who have been here for several generations. Herman Curiel (chapter 5) describes Hispanic parents' sense of powerlessness to make a difference in their children's education, which in turn exacerbates the children's internal conflicts created by cultural dilemmas. The author discusses bilingual education as an effective tool to improve the life chances of Latino children. Inherent in bilingual education is the recognition that language reflects culture and defines reality. However, the proponents of the English-only movement see bilingualism as a threat to the unity of society.

In that one of the main functions of the educational system is to perpetuate the culture over time, it is not surprising that promotion of another cultural perspective is perceived as undermining that basic function.

In chapter 6, Frank F. Montalvo discusses acculturation and assimilation *vis-à-vis* the use of skin color and physiognomic features to classify and reward individuals in a society that is stratified according to race and color. His discussion highlights how the politics of color, culture, and language determines self-identity. Discrimination among Hispanics based on color shade is a topic that is not often publicly discussed, despite the fact that it is an integral part of the ethos of the conquered and colonized experience of most Hispanics. The hierarchy of influence and privilege in colonized Latin America was based on color, ultimately leading to the political, economic, social, and psychological dilemmas faced by Hispanics today. In Latin America, as in this country, light skin color continues to go hand in hand with privilege, influence, and access to life opportunities. Thus, discrimination based on color is not a new experience for Hispanics when they cross the border. For most Hispanics, opportunity continues to be tied more to skin color than to country of origin or language.

The Hispanic Family

For most Hispanics, the family continues to be the most important resource for coping with life's stresses, regardless of length of time in the United States, social class, religious preference, or geographical area of residence. In chapter 7, América Facundo describes the great variability found among Puerto Rican families, pointing out that issues related to national ethnic identity, language dominance, variability in adherence to values and belief systems, available economic resources, educational background, and migration patterns need to be considered in clinical interventions.

In his analysis of the Hispanic family, Montiel (1975) concluded that although the make-up of the family varies substantially among and within Hispanic subgroups, some values and cultural attributes are shared. For example, closely knit extended families are an advantage and cultural value for Hispanics. Reciprocal help among members and across generations has been considered the main support in managing stresses of daily life and in coping with discrimination. Traditionally, the Hispanic family has been described as an interdependent and interactive kin network that allows for mutual and reciprocal help among its members. The

Hispanic extended family differs from that of the dominant white majority in two main aspects: for the dominant society, the extended family is seen as a kin system organized along consanguinal rather than conjugal lines, consisting of a network of subfamilies often residing in the same household. For most Hispanics, the extended family includes relationships other than those defined by consanguinal and/or conjugal lines.

Zuniga-Martinez (1979) describes Mexican culture as being family oriented and the family as being extended and intradependent. She found that Mexican Americans, like their counterparts in Mexico, maintain the primacy of the family as a cultural tradition in the *barrios* (neighborhoods) of the United States. Kin live next door, on the same block, or within a short walking distance of one another, forming supportive intradependent relationships. But urbanization, poverty, discrimination, and lack of access to adequate housing have combined to force some families to reside in a single household. In many cities, for example, Washington, D.C., this situation has reached crisis proportions and is the rule rather than the exception. It is reported that sometimes two or three immigrant families from El Salvador, consisting of up to 18 individuals, share a one-bedroom apartment because they cannot afford adequate housing (*Hispanic*, 1990).

Family Support

Past research (Kluckhohn & Strodbeck, 1961; Clark, 1959; Rubel, 1966) and more recent research (Fitzpatrick, 1971; Sotomayor, 1973; Bastida, 1979) dealing with aging among Hispanic populations point out that Mexican Americans and Puerto Ricans are more closely involved with local kin groups than is the majority society. Mizio (1974) asserts that the emotional and financial support that Puerto Ricans receive from their families influences their well-being. According to Valle and Martinez (1980), the aid that Hispanic families provide to members is critical to their survival. Sabogal and Marin (1987) studied the effects of acculturation on attitudes toward the family among 452 Hispanics. They found that despite differences in national origin, family support appeared to be the most essential dimension of Hispanic familism. The authors noted that the perception that family support would be available when needed did not diminish with the level of acculturation. The protective function of family support in preventing stress or in mitigating its impact was also examined by Vega and Kolody (1985). The findings from data collected from 635 white non-Hispanics and 533 Mexican Americans seemed to support the results reported by Keefe, Padilla, and Carlos (1979) and others that family support systems provide a buffer against the development of stress in Mexican Americans.

The findings from the above studies also support the notion that the extended family is a vital social support system that reserves a special role for certain family members, such as elders. Torres-Gil and Negm (1980) suggested that the socioeconomic barriers encountered by the Mexican American elderly may make them more dependent on their natural support networks than their white counterparts. Latino elderly and their families commonly help each other. According to Sotomayor (1973), Miranda (1980), and Maldonado (1979), the reciprocal supportive relationship that exists between older Hispanics and their families serves as a source of mutual support and/or protection, especially during times of crisis. Valle and Martinez (1980), Valle and Mendoza (1978), and Keefe et al. (1979) also found that helping interaction is essential to the well-being of family members. In chapter 8, Manuel Miranda explores family supports for the Hispanic elderly in the midst of social forces that have undermined the family. He believes that the ability to identify potential risk factors and develop therapeutic intervention strategies lies in the ability to mobilize social support networks that mediate potential risk factors. Insight into preventive techniques appropriate to the culture and language of Hispanics can be gained by examining these significant interactional processes.

Other views exist on this subject. Croach (1972) suggested that the extended Hispanic family may be a myth. Maldonado (1979) raised questions about the irreversible effects of modernization and growing family mobility on family values that can change the role and status of the elderly within their own family units. Laurel (1976) found younger Mexican Americans departing from traditional roles with regard to caring for elderly parents. And Markides, Boldt, and Ray (1986), in an ethnic comparative study in Texas, found that older Mexican Americans are not more likely than are older Anglos to be cared for by their own family network.

Thus the debate continues as to whether the traditional supports of the Hispanic family have been irrevocably eroded. Most of the studies of the Hispanic family address Mexican American and Puerto Rican families; little information is available on other Hispanic subgroups. Little empirical evidence substantiates the assumption that longstanding traditional supportive and reciprocal family relationships have changed. On the contrary, the family emerges as the most important support network available to Latinos and as such must be recognized and supported by the helping professions.

Hispanic gerontologists, in particular, have studied the traditional caregiving role of Hispanic families. Available data indicate that Latino women, like women in the majority society, become the primary caregivers for the elderly. And just as women in the majority society live longer than men, so do Hispanic women. Elena Bastida and Rumaldo Juárez point out in chapter 9 that despite these important and fundamental facts, most studies tend to report the demographic characteristics of the Hispanic elderly in general and do not note gender differences. Their chapter profiles this population based on a decade of research. Their results indicate that elderly Hispanic women are not more isolated from peer relationships, as has been assumed, and that they have the same, and sometimes more, sources of support as Hispanic men in the samples the authors studied. The incidence of depressive symptoms, in addition to alienation in regard to self-esteem and life satisfaction among older Mexican American women, raises significant questions for future research. In chapter 10, Joseph S. Gallegos asserts that culturally relevant services for Hispanic elderly persons must consider the role of family and its changing structure on their well-being. If services for the elderly are not accessible, the burden of care will inevitably fall upon the rest of the family, which is already burdened. Action must be taken to support and strengthen the family and enable its potential for mutual help.

In chapter 11, Arturo T. Río, Daniel A. Santisteban, and José Szapocznik discuss family therapy perspectives that are suited to the experience of the Latin American immigrant. Szapocznik pioneered the search for family-focused interventions that respond to the needs of the Hispanic family, focusing on the family's ability to react to crisis. Specifically, he has sought to identify family therapy approaches that address issues arising from family disorganization as expressed in delinquent behaviors and substance abuse. This chapter builds on his prior work and demonstrates the effectiveness of brief structural family therapy. Such research enables us to identify interventions that will be helpful in influencing the Hispanic family's material, structural, and moral resources in order to assist its members in coping with life stresses. Of particular importance is the identification of interventions that strengthen the family's role in linking members with other societal support networks.

Support and Resource Exchange Networks

Because of Hispanic families' vulnerability, support networks and resource exchange networks are very important. Mutual exchange, collective and collaborative efforts, egalitarian relationships, and equitable resource distribution play key roles in supporting Hispanic families (Cox, 1989; Goodstein, 1983). Support and resource exchange networks share common characteristics, the most important being that they tend to be not for profit, emphasize informal arrangements, and facilitate the exchange of various goods and/or services, particularly during times when resources are scarce (Sarason & Lorentz, 1979). The primary goal of such informal support groups is to assist members to move toward greater competency so that they can cope with and improve their daily life. Equally as important, participation in such groups helps members to participate in the restructuring of society in general (Cox, 1989), an important issue for new immigrants as well as minorities of color in general.

Goodstein (1983) states that human service networks perform some of the functions of resource exchange networks. However, they must also establish linkages between human service agencies, facilitate communication among the different community groups, eliminate interagency boundaries, and assess community resources and target them to assist those who are vulnerable in the community. Thus, human service networks can play a key role in helping the Hispanic family achieve greater competence in the performance of its traditional functions.

Resource Exchange Networks among Hispanics

Historical records of Mexican Americans describe support and exchange resource networks that supported and strengthened the family during the European colonization of the Southwest. Mutual-aid societies, or *sociedades mutualistas*, flourished in the Hispanic Southwest at the turn of the century, serving as primary sources of economic and social support. They were established by a population group that suddenly found itself dispossessed when the United States entered its territories. The values of unity, work, education, faith, and brotherhood (*hermandad*) guided their activities. My study (Sotomayor, 1973) of a Denver barrio revealed that one in five of the elderly reported belonging to a mutual-help society at the time of the interview, with a significant number stating that they had belonged to similar organizations in the past, some of which were no longer in existence. Most of these organizations had disability, burial, and widows' benefits as well as protective components. For example, members might be educated on ways to confront employment and wage discrimination.

Rivera (1984) examined the history of four *sociedades* that have survived to date: the *Alianza Hispano Americana* in Arizona; the

Sociedad Progresista Mexicana in California; the *Sociedad Proteccion Mutua de Trabajadores Unidos* in Colorado, Utah, and New Mexico; and the *Union Protectiva de Santa Fe* in New Mexico. Rivera highlighted five characteristics of these organizations: organizational continuity, or staying power, over time; their flexibility and capacity to perform a variety of functions and to meet the needs of their members; their capacity to reflect and express the sociopolitical climate and concerns of the times; their effectiveness in developing community and organizational linkages and networks; and their potential for becoming alternative resources for self-help and for channeling resources. Rivera's study also pointed out that social service providers lack knowledge of these societies and thus neglect a resource with the potential to support and improve the well-being of basic institutions among Hispanics, such as the family.

In his work on support and resource exchange networks among Mexicans and Mexican Americans, Velez (1983) proposes that the development of such informal systems of exchange is an attempt to reduce the stress and uncertainty of their lives. *Confianza* (mutual trust) is the "glue" that holds reciprocal exchange relationships together. This notion is further expanded to include *confianza en confianza* (trusting mutual trust) a degree of trust that commands *respeto* (respect). Indeed, *confianza* and *respeto* are accepted as the basis for all social relationships and guide the rules and procedures through which they are structured and ordered. Thus, to be meaningful and lasting, social participation must reflect trust, trust in mutual trust, and respect.

Significantly, these constructs shape the expectations of the group's social reality. They converge to form support and resource exchange networks that reflect cultural values and traditions and that enable Latinos to cope with present and future problems. Modern examples of these associations are the self-help advocacy organizations that grew out of the civil-rights movement and in many cases expanded into more formal service-delivery agencies during the 1970s and 1980s. Thus it is not surprising that Hispanics do not work well with human service networks characterized by seemingly contradictory rules and procedures and staffed by personnel who are often insensitive to their cultural values and traditions.

A Framework for Family Interventions

The challenge to helping professionals as they seek to address and meet the needs of Hispanic populations is to find tools of understanding that address both the environmental and the internal factors that affect Hispanics' well-being. The problems of the family cannot be viewed separately from those of society (Gore, 1978). A simple relationship has been noted between socioeconomic factors, particularly poverty, and first admissions to state mental hospitals, alcohol abuse, auto accidents, cirrhosis of the liver, heart disease, functional disorders, infant mortality, crime, and suicide (Brenner, 1973; Seidman & Rapkin, 1983).

At the emotional level, poverty leads to self-blame, which is usually followed by a sense of powerlessness. Demoralization, often expressed in lack of motivation or the inability to act on one's own behalf, follows (Liem & Rayman, 1982; Frank, 1973). These forces combine to form powerful deterrents to action, which in turn perpetuates low self-esteem. Powerlessness and the subsequent inability to believe in the possibility of change preclude people's ability to mobilize local helping resources (Lerner, 1986).

Liem and Rayman (1982), in their efforts to assist the unemployed, found that in areas where unemployment rates are high, community dysfunction is as common as is individual dysfunction. Not only was the group of unemployed workers and their families Liem and Rayman studied unfamiliar with local helping resources, but most of them found human and health care service providers uniformly unresponsive to their needs. This population felt they were excluded from community resources and turned to their families and relatives for help.

Economic conditions and social dislocation are significant stressors that produce a full range of emotional disabilities. This leads some to view psychiatry as an arm of the social system, one that largely functions to patch up ruptures resulting from economic and social circumstances rather than individual dysfunction (Brenner, 1973; Harwood, 1977). It is now widely accepted that stress associated with socioeconomic and political conditions cannot be treated exclusively by using traditional medical and person-focused methods (Liem, 1983).

Empowerment

The theme of competence, as it relates to ameliorating the stress resulting from socioeconomic and political factors and their negative impact on families, individuals, and communities, is repeatedly discussed in the literature dealing with empowerment of minority neighborhoods (Biegel, 1984). Empowerment has two main components, *capacity* and *equity*. Capacity is the ability of the community to use power to solve problems and to promote equity in the distribution of available resources. In effect, empowerment is the process by which individuals and communities gain mastery over their lives. The concept of empowerment has been expanded to include the creation of community-based services that are adequate, acceptable, and affordable; empowerment can mean giving individuals and groups an opportunity to choose from an array of services that meet their perception of need (Ossofsky, 1985).

In appealing to a paradigm of mastery within the community, the concept of empowerment touches issues of power and authority at every turn. Power is held by the individual who initiates change, with or without the consent of the individual who responds to the change. On the other hand, authority is part of all human relationships; it accomplishes its ends by gaining the assent of those over whom it is exerted, thus evoking in them a sense of control and mastery. The concept of authority assumes that self-help and mutual help are inherent in the helping relationship. To gain control over someone's life, the individual or community must accept the responsibility to act on that person's behalf.

To be meaningful, profound, and lasting, empowerment must be initiated and experienced by those who see themselves as powerless. In reality, one cannot empower someone else. However, others can strengthen and support individuals who view themselves as powerless. Empowerment occurs by enhancing strengths, promoting the development of the skills necessary to mobilize resources, and/or providing the necessary resources. In working with Hispanics, self-help and mutual help are critical elements in helping individuals and families cope with their environment. Empowerment allows these various populations to seek affirmation through traditional cultural values.

The chapters in this volume are written with a historical perspective while also looking toward the future. As Genaro Gonzalez might say, they are written with both "hindsight" and "foresight." Many Hispanics referred to the 1980s as the "decade of the Hispanic," thinking that population growth alone would bring desired changes. Today, however, many question whether anything has changed appreciably. Currently, experts speak of the "decade of Latinos." This does not reflect a capricious change of labels or mere wordplay; rather it reflects the reevaluation of the values and symbols of Hispanic/Latino culture. In the ongoing process of reaffirming identity, we scan the environment for symbols that reflect and affirm who we are, discarding those values and symbols that are no longer useful. Thus in this volume Hispanic and Latino are used interchangeably.

I appreciate the assistance of Dr. Mario de la Rosa, who contributed to the literature search for this article.

References

Bastida, E. (1979). *Family integration and adjustment to aging among Hispanic American elderly*. Unpublished doctoral dissertation, University of Kansas.

Biegel, D. (1984). Help seeking and receiving in urban ethnic neighborhoods: Strategies for empowerment. *Prevention in Human Services, 3*(2/3), 119–144.

Brenner, M. H. (1973). *Mental illness and the economy*. Cambridge, MA: Harvard University Press.

Clark, M. (1959). *Health in the Mexican American culture*. Berkeley, CA: University of California Press.

Cox, E. O. (1989). *Empowerment of the low-income elderly through group work*. New York: Haworth Press.

Croach, B. (1972). Aged and institutional support: Perceptions of older Mexican Americans. *Journal of Gerontology, 27*, 524–529.

Fitzpatrick, J. P. (1971). *Puerto Rican Americans: The meaning of migration to the mainland*. Englewood Cliffs, NJ: Prentice-Hall.

Frank, J. D. (1973). *Persuasion and healing*. Baltimore, MD: Johns Hopkins Press.

Goodstein, L. (1983). Consultation to human service networks. In S. Cooper & W. Hodges (Eds.), *The mental health consultation field* (pp. 205–220). New York: Human Sciences Press.

Gore, S. (1978). The effect of social support in moderating the health consequences of unemployment. *Journal of Health and Social Behavior, 19*, 157–165.

Harwood, A. (1977). *Rx: Spiritist as needed: A study of a Puerto Rican community mental health resource*. New York: John Wiley.

Hispanic. (1990, May), Washington, DC.

Johnston, W. B., & Packer, A. E. (1987). *Workforce 2000: Work and workers for the twenty-first century*. Indianapolis, IN: The Hudson Institute.

Keefe, S., Padilla, A., & Carlos, M. (1979). The Mexican American extended family as an emotional support system. *Human Organization, 38*(2), 144–152.

Kluckhohn, F., & Strodbeck, F. (1961). *Variations in value orientations*. Chicago: Row, Peterson and Company.

Laurel, N. (1976). *An intergenerational comparison of attitudes toward the support of aged parents: A study of Mexican Americans in two South Texas communities*. Unpublished doctoral dissertation, University of Southern California, Los Angeles.

Lerner, M. (1986). *Surplus powerlessness*. Oakland, CA: Institute for Labor and Mental Health.

Liem, R. (1983). *Unemployment: Personal and family effects*. Unpublished manuscript, Boston College.

Liem, R., & Rayman, P. (1982). Health and social costs of unemployment: Research and policy considerations. *American Psychologist, 37*, 1116–1123.

Maldonado, D. (1979). Aging in the Chicano context. In E. E. Gelfand & A. J. Kutzik (Eds.), *Ethnicity and aging: Theory, research and policy* (pp. 175–183). New York: Sprague.

Mangold, M. M. (Ed.). (1972). *La Causa Chicana*. New York: Family Service Association of America.

Markides, K., Boldt, J., & Ray, L. (1986). Sources of helping and intergenerational solidarity: A three generation study of Mexican Americans. *Journal of Gerontology, 41*, 506–511.

Miranda, M. (1980). The family natural support system in Hispanic communities: Preliminary research notes and recommendations. In R. Valle & W. Vega (Eds.), *Hispanic natural support systems: Mental health promotion perspectives* (pp. 25–33). Los Angeles: State of California Department of Mental Health Publications.

Mizio, E. (1974, February). The impact of external systems on the Puerto Rican family. *Social Casework, 55*, 7–15.

Montiel, M. (1975). The Chicano family: A review of research. *Social Work, 18*, 22–31.

Ossofsky, J. (1985, April). *Empowering older persons.* Presented at the National Council on the Aging Annual Conference, San Francisco.

Rivera, J. A. (1984). *Mutual aid societies in the Hispanic Southwest: Alternative sources of community empowerment.* (DHHS Grant No. 121A-83). Washington, DC: U.S. Government Printing Office.

Rubel, A. (1966). *Across the tracks: Mexican Americans in a Texas city.* Austin, TX: University of Texas Press.

Sabogal, F., & Marin, G. (1987). Hispanic familism and acculturation: What changes and what doesn't. *Hispanic Journal of Behavioral Science, 9*, 397–412.

Sarason, S., & Lorentz, E. (1979). *The challenge of the resource exchange network.* San Francisco: Jossey-Bass.

Seidman, E., & Rapkin, B. (1983). Economics and psychosocial dysfunction: Toward a conceptual framework and prevention strategies. In R. Felner, L. Jason, J. Moritsugu, & S. Faber (Eds.), *Preventive psychology.* New York: Pergamon Press.

Sotomayor, M. (1973). *A study of Chicano grandparents in an urban barrio.* Unpublished doctoral dissertation, School of Social Work, University of Denver.

Torres-Gil, F., & Negm, M. (1980). Policy issues concerning the Hispanic elderly. *Aging, 3*, 3–5.

Valle, R., & Martinez, M. (1980). Natural networks of elderly Hispanics of Mexican heritage: Implications for mental health. In M. Miranda & R. Ruiz (Eds.), *Chicano aging and mental health.* (DHHS Publication No. [ADM] 81-952). Rockville, MD: National Institute of Mental Health.

Valle, R., & Mendoza, L. (1978). *The elderly Latino.* San Diego, CA: Campanile Press.

Vega, W., & Kolody, B. (1985). The meaning of social support and the mediation of stress across cultures. In W. Vega & M. Miranda (Eds.), *Stress and Hispanic mental health: Relating research to service delivery* (pp. 48–75). (DHHS Publication No. 85-1410). Washington, DC: U.S. Government Printing Office.

Velez, C. (1983). *Bonds of mutual trust.* New Brunswick, NJ: Rutgers University Press.

Zuniga-Martinez, M. (1979). *Los ancianos: A study of the attitudes of Mexican Americans regarding support for the elderly.* Unpublished doctoral dissertation, Brandeis University.

1

Hispanics in the Past Two Decades, Latinos in the Next Two: Hindsight and Foresight

Genaro Gonzalez

In attempting to predict issues that affect Hispanics in the future, several factors must be taken into account. First, *uncertainty* makes it difficult to visualize the future. Population groups do not function in a social vacuum; they are influenced by external events. Minority groups are especially vulnerable to social, cultural, and political influences. Even less risky predictions, such as projecting demographic changes within the Hispanic community, require one to make major assumptions. In an age in which technological innovations can transform society in the space of a generation, predictions of even the near future may be rendered obsolete. For example, technological breakthroughs in the next few years could make many jobs in the low-skills service sector obsolete, which in turn would affect Spanish-speaking immigrants who enter the United States with limited job skills.

Despite these difficulties, one can make educated guesses. Inferences, though, are most useful when one has some basis of comparison. Prediction, at its best, is part science and part art. It is difficult to anticipate future trends and issues even when a historical reference point is available; it becomes nearly impossible without one. For this reason, only those issues that have an historical precedent in the Hispanic experience will be discussed in this chapter. For instance, the emergence of Hispanics as the largest minority group in the United States promises to affect American society in significant ways. This phenomenon is explored elsewhere in the book. However, it is not addressed at great length here because the past few decades do not provide us with an equivalent experience at the national level. Rather, issues such as the growth of the Hispanic population are woven into other themes, for example, prejudice, that are anchored in history. In other words, this chapter addresses questions such as how issues of prejudice will be affected by growth in the Hispanic population and how such issues and phenomena will affect their acculturation and future immigration policies.

A second prerequisite for the choice of topics was that the topics in some way overlap, even though such overlap may not be obvious. The link between acculturation—a high-stress variable—and mental health is one example of such overlap, and the relationship between mental health and prejudice is another. Prejudice, in turn, is linked to acculturation to the extent that Hispanics who adhere to mainstream values are less likely to encounter prejudice (Ramirez, 1977). These interrelationships will be examined in greater detail throughout the chapter.

Although researchers may feel more comfortable investigating concerns that traditionally have been dealt with by their respective disciplines, they must examine groups or cultures from a number of perspectives in order to develop an authentic and useful view of the Hispanic population.

Thus the major purpose of this chapter is to consider issues from various disciplines and show how these themes and concerns coincide. Four overlapping issues are discussed: prejudice, mental health, acculturation, and immigration. In each area, existing research has been examined for clues to future trends. Too often, though, in the existing literature these issues are relegated to "appropriate" disciplines, and few attempts have been made to integrate the findings by means of a multidisciplinary perspective to provide insights into the Hispanic community. Psychologists may focus on mental health, anthropologists on acculturation, sociologists on prejudice, demographers on immigration. These issues should not be treated as discrete topics to be studied in isolation. Rather, researchers need to study how they interact and affect one another. Thus, whenever possible, the focus of this chapter is on research that has attempted to address issues that go beyond the scope of traditional disciplines.

Even the above restrictions, however, would have produced an unwieldy chapter. Thus this chapter concentrates on a particular Hispanic population. Because Mexican Americans constitute the largest Hispanic group in the United States, they were selected to represent how certain issues may affect them and, by implication, other Hispanic communities. It should be remembered, however, that considerable diversity exists among the various Hispanic communities (Gann & Duigan, 1986). For this reason, issues that affect Mexican Americans are targeted, with consideration of how these issues have manifested themselves in the recent past and might manifest themselves in the near future; in addition, the possible implications of these issues for other Hispanic groups are discussed.

As the chapter title suggests, the Hispanic/Latino population is in a state of transition—exiting this century with one name (Hispanics) and entering the next century with another (Latino). A certain ambivalence surrounds this change. Specifically, one might ask whether a change of labels is more cosmetic than substantive. This issue will be explored in a later section of the chapter. For now, the terms "Hispanic" and "Latino" as well as "Chicano" and "Mexican American" will be used interchangeably throughout the chapter. Many authors insist on using one label, either for the sake of consistency or for ideological reasons. Moreover, many Hispanics/Latinos may prefer one label over the other. Does the designation of a particular label matter? Yes and no. Arriving at an appropriate label for a group has both trivial and serious consequences. These, too, will be discussed later.

Prejudice

In one of the first attempts at a comprehensive outline of Latino mental health, Padilla and Ruiz (1973, 1976) cited a number of high-stress indicators that affect the psychological well-being of Hispanics. Some of these, such as poverty, are more obvious than are others, such as prejudice and discrimination. The latter are usually considered important insofar as they create obstacles for the economic advancement of minorities.

Recently, as Hispanics and other minorities have shifted their agenda somewhat from the plight of the poor and its concomitant emphasis on civil rights and equal opportunity toward a concern with an emerging minority middle class, the war on prejudice has lost its moral locus. One nationally known Hispanic politician even went so far as to state that prejudice was no longer an issue for Hispanics. Prejudice, he seemed to suggest, was passé. Although this observation may be a politically astute maneuver for courting mainstream votes, recent research indicates that prejudice is not a thing of the past (Ramirez, 1977). Many people assume that because institutionalized discrimination against minorities has been greatly reduced since the civil-rights era, so too has prejudice. But prejudice refers primarily to a cognitive as opposed to a strictly behavioral phenomenon, although the conative dimension (i.e., discrimination vs. racism) is certainly one part of prejudice (Aronson, 1977). Thus, although prejudice involves mental processes, its consequences can be quite real.

In the 21st century, Hispanics will emerge as the country's largest minority. In many parts of the nation, they will constitute a majority in their own right. Thus a major concern is how these increased numbers will affect issues of prejudice.

One approach attempts to translate these increased numbers into political clout. Some view the Hispanic community as a body of voters whose participation in the political process will lead to the breaking down of economic and social barriers, including prejudice and discrimination. Although Latino leaders hope this will occur, reality may fall quite short.

To begin with, one must question the assumption that Hispanics will reach consensus on a variety of issues. Mexican Americans differ from Cuban Americans on a number of demographic dimensions (Portes & Bach, 1985), and each group's social and political agenda reflects distinct priorities. For instance, Mexican Americans as a group are younger and poorer than Cuban Americans, and although the dropout rate is a critical concern among Mexican Americans, it is not among Cuban Americans. Assigning a rubric or common label to individuals with certain shared characteristics does not mean that their political behavior will be the same or even similar.

In addition, voter participation among ethnic groups with a large immigrant population has traditionally been disappointing. As noncitizens, recent immigrants cannot vote and are therefore powerless to influence electoral outcomes. Moreover, many Latino immigrants may come from countries without a tradition of participatory democracy and thus may lack the incentive to become citizens. Finally, any illegal immigrants who may want to become voting citizens cannot do so. All of these arguments, therefore, question the assumption that greater numbers in the Hispanic community will translate into greater political opportunities, which in turn would mitigate or eliminate prejudice.

A disproportionate increase of Latinos in the near future may also jeopardize their participation in other spheres of society, ranging from the interpersonal to the political realm. An increase in the numbers of Hispanics may lead to increased contact with other ethnic groups, but as Sherif (1966) points out, more contact does not necessarily lead to decreases in prejudice or discrimination. In fact, higher visibility may increase the apprehension of non-Hispanics who view Hispanics as a threat to the "American" way of life. It may also increase tensions with other minority groups, such as African Americans, some of whom may perceive Hispanic demands for equal opportunity as infringing upon their opportunities.

This is not to suggest that Hispanics would be better off if their numbers were not increasing. Rather, even though opportunities exist, so do potential problems; that is, an increase in the Latino population may aggravate old problems and create new ones. In order to exploit the opportunities, one must anticipate and confront the problems.

Immigration

Acuna (1988) has pointed out various aspects of the Mexican American experience that make it appreciably different from the experiences of other immigrants in the United States. The patterns of Mexican migration into the United States are one such aspect. Other ethnic groups have experienced mass migration to this country, with clear historical demarcations, as a result of war or famine elsewhere ("push" factors) or America's need for labor during war or economic expansion ("pull" factors). After "push/pull" factors were mitigated, the number of immigrants entering the country decreased dramatically. This phenomenon, coupled with geographical separation from the mother country, has allowed most American ethnic groups to assimilate steadily into the mainstream population so that by the third generation, or even sooner, the group is well on the way toward cultural integration.

However, such has not been the case with Mexican Americans, the largest subgroup of Hispanics, or, for that matter, with Cuban Americans, the third largest group (Portes & Bach, 1985). By and large, Mexican Americans who are second generation or older can trace their roots in this country to the Mexican Revolution of 1910. During this period, an estimated one million Mexicans fled Mexico to find agricultural, industrial, and railroad jobs in the United States. However, unlike other immigrant populations, Mexicans continued to migrate to America throughout the remainder of the century (except during the Great Depression, when thousands of Mexican Americans and Mexicans in the United States were deported). Traditionally, Mexicans have served as a cheap source of labor during this country's periods of prosperity. These periods sometimes coincided with nativist movements wherein reluctance to allow Asian and other nonwhite immigrants into the United States led to the perception of Mexican Americans as the lesser of two evils. As a result, Mexican immigration patterns tend to be cyclical.

To complicate the picture, many persons of Mexican descent have lived in the American Southwest since the 1600s, when Mexico was a Spanish colony. By the time the territory was ceded to the United States following the Mexican American War (1846–1848), many Mexican families had lived in the area for generations. In this sense, the claim by many Chicanos that Hispanics were in the Southwest before Americans is correct. However, the size of this original Mexican American population was miniscule compared with the number of Mexicans who would arrive during the Mexican Revolution. In addition, immigration and prejudice have often dovetailed in the Southwest. Recent Mexican immigrants often encountered prejudice from settled Mexican Americans as well as from the Anglo community. Thus, as Acuna (1988) states, the cyclical nature of Mexican migration has not only kept Mexican Americans from following assimilation patterns similar to those of other ethnic groups, it has also resulted in an ongoing conflict between the settled Mexican American community and new arrivals.

Thus the past indeed becomes prologue. To the extent that documented and undocumented immigration will continue well into the 21st century (the Immigration Reform and Control Act of 1986 notwithstanding), intraethnic prejudice will increasingly become a reality for Hispanics. Moreover, increased opportunities as a result of the erosion of discriminatory barriers may widen the gap between "haves" (Hispanics who have been in the United States for several generations) and "have-nots" (recent immigrants). Even if programs are implemented to facilitate the transition for immigrant families, one must be prepared to deal with possible resistance from members of the more settled Hispanic community, who may resent what they perceive as preferential treatment that was denied them and their ancestors.

Immigration has become a vitally important issue in the past few years, not simply because Americans, including Hispanics, are concerned with the number of Latino immigrants entering this country. Much of the resistance to immigration revolves around the perception, however erroneous, that the new immigrants are uneducated, unskilled, or unmotivated and thus are prime candidates for welfare and other entitlement programs.

In his review of research on Mexican American culture, Buriel (1984) explained how investigators have often portrayed Mexican Americans as the victims of their own culture. Poverty, an alarming high school dropout rate—all problems great and small—have traditionally been laid on the doorstep of a damaged (and damaging) parent culture. Such explanations, of course, conveniently absolve mainstream America of blame. To the extent that the privations of Hispanics are seen as the result of anomalies in their own culture, the dominant group is vindicated. If one believes that the traditional culture is at fault, then the apparent solution is to wean individuals from it. In essence, this describes both the goal and process of acculturating Hispanics. The rationale for acculturation is the premise that the "traditional" culture is counterproductive to educational and economic advancement.

Buriel's article questions this assumption and reexamines data from previous research, particularly investigations that subscribe to the "damaging parent culture" model. He points out that some of these studies have, in fact, patently ignored or minimized findings that contradict the assumption that traditional Mexican American values impede economic and educational advancement and that immigration contributes to the overall socioeconomic decline of this group. Buriel also cites less well-known research that supports his thesis that traditional Mexican American values promote achievement. One cannot help but consider whether these studies received less attention because they contradicted or questioned the implicit biases of social thought in the past few decades.

Buriel focuses on several key areas: economic success, educational achievement, and social pathology. In each area, he cites evidence that Mexican Americans who are influenced by their traditional culture are more likely to advance socially and economically and less likely to fall into deviant behavior patterns. Thus traditional cultural values may help insulate first- and second-generation Chicanos from the vicissitudes of minority status, whereas the educational and income levels of the more acculturated generations actually decline. Acculturation, Buriel argues, undermines traditional strengths, such as family support, leaving few alternative resources in its place. He concludes by pointing out that Mexican immigrants are a vital link in the cultural ecology of the Chicano community in that they replenish and reinforce those traditional values that permit the individual to progress. Buriel profiles a Mexican immigrant quite different from the stereotypical one our society has created. He describes the immigrant as an individual who tends to be more educated and more motivated than those who choose not to emigrate—in short, a person whose assets are Mexico's loss and our gain.

To the extent that much of Latin America will continue to experience economic and political instability in coming years,

Hispanic immigration will occupy an increasingly large role in our national agenda in the 21st century. For this reason, research that reexamines negative assumptions about immigration and focuses on the contributions that immigrants make to American society should be heeded and encouraged. Nonetheless, research of this sort itself raises unanswered questions, such as how applicable are the findings to changing times? For instance, even if Mexican and other Latin American immigrants bring with them a high level of motivation, their skills may not be sufficient for success in a high-technology workplace. Although a willingness to work hard may have paid off for earlier generations of immigrants, physical labor or industrial jobs may soon be scarce or obsolete.

The conclusion that third-generation Mexican Americans may earn even less than their second-generation counterparts needs more careful analysis. Buriel attributes this to less acculturation in the latter; the second generation earns more because it subscribes to traditional Mexican American values that encourage initiative. However, an equally plausible explanation may be that discrimination faces applicants for white-collar, managerial positions, which acculturated Hispanics are more likely to seek. Indeed, Poston and Alvirez (1973) concluded that the economic gap between Anglo and Mexican American workers widened with increased levels of education. In other words, years of college may result in diminishing returns for Hispanic professionals. Thus, the social structure rewards Hispanic initiative in the blue-collar job market, but entrance into the white-collar domain may be viewed as trespassing.

To the extent that greater numbers of Mexican Americans and other Hispanics will be moving into the professional realm, the issue of prejudice and unequal salaries is likely to become increasingly important. Just as important will be the fates of those at the other extreme—immigrants with high hopes and good intentions but who are ill prepared to compete in an increasingly complex world. Their vulnerabilities must not be exploited in a way that destroys their cultural traditions, a significant resource for all Mexican Americans. Destruction of the traditional culture could result in a growing Hispanic underclass in the years to come. Simply to believe that their traditional values will somehow see them through is not enough.

Acculturation

Acculturation is perhaps the most critical issue for Hispanics in general and Mexican Americans in particular. An ethnic group can exist only insofar as its members share a common identity. To the extent that acculturation may erode common values and substitute mainstream attitudes and behaviors in its place, the future of Hispanic culture depends on how Latinos are able to balance their participation in both social and cultural spheres.

Keefe and Padilla (1987) argue that the term ethnic identity has, in fact, been used confusingly and with operational ambiguity. They maintain that ethnicity is a complex social and psychological phenomenon consisting of at least two basic components: cultural awareness and ethnic loyalty. Their research shows that whereas cultural awareness tends to decline with acculturation of succeeding generations of Mexican Americans, the degree of ethnic loyalty or identity may even increase in the face of diminishing cultural awareness.

Why this phenomenon occurs is not yet fully understood. Perhaps first-generation Hispanics take their intact ethnic identity for granted, whereas third-generation members may lack specific aspects of this identity (e.g., language). To overcome their perceived deficits, they may compensate by becoming overtly loyal to their ethnic roots. Or perhaps discrimination by the mainstream culture has different effects on the generations. First-generation immigrants may explain discrimination on the basis of their being different and thus attempt to shed their ethnic identity or affiliation. In later generations, however, continued discrimination is more difficult to explain, which may cause later generations to embrace the very identity that society uses to stigmatize them, despite the fact that they may lack cultural awareness.

Keefe and Padilla's work has important implications for future research on acculturation of Hispanics. Theory in the past decades has emphasized a bipolar, albeit unidimensional, approach; that is, investigators began questioning the legitimacy of categorizing culturally dissimilar groups as marginal or dysfunctional. In place of these categories, they offered other constructs such as acculturation and biculturalism. Thus acculturation can be mapped along a bipolar continuum, say "traditional" to "Anglicized," with an ideal "bicultural" midpoint.

This approach, however, has its faults. For one, designating the unacculturated end of the continuum as "traditional" implies that the parent culture is a static, ahistorical entity; no comparable value-laden assumptions are made for the other extreme. For another, placing biculturalism at the midpoint implies that bicultural individuals are only half-equipped to function at either end of the continuum, instead of describing the ideal Hispanic who functions ably in both worlds. Nonetheless, the promotion of biculturalism in research of the past two decades helped authenticate the Hispanic experience as something other than marginal or aberrant.

But, as Keefe and Padilla point out, the model remains inadequate, primarily because it presumes a unidimensional view of culture; that is, most recent research has sought to determine whether a given Hispanic is "traditional" or "nontraditional." This question is then answered by his or her score on a scale or test that measures acculturation. A more appropriate answer, Keefe and Padilla suggest, would be "it depends."

Whereas earlier methodologies stressed a global measure of acculturation, Keefe and Padilla conclude that ethnic identity is too complex to justify a single measure that will evaluate it. Rather, they seek to map out the diverse manifestations of culture, cognitive as well as behavioral. This approach may be more laborious and less elegant than one that seeks a unified measure of acculturation, but it is also closer to reality. The authors argue that acculturation proceeds at different paces, depending on what is being transformed. Some behaviors are more easily changed than are others. Adapting to new food or music, for example, is easier than changing one's accent or attitudes.

Research on acculturation in the next two decades must also address its complexity. Similarly, academic disciplines that borrow directly from these investigations—for instance, bilingual/bicultural education—will also have to modify their approaches. The methods of the past decades are insufficient, both for the investigator who is left with ambiguous and uncertain findings on acculturation and the teacher who has trouble specifying or justifying a culturally relevant curriculum. In the final analysis, studying the process and implications of acculturation will help enlighten professionals on what the Hispanic culture is and is not.

Although issues in Hispanic mental health are explored at some length in a later section, it is appropriate here to look at the relationship between acculturation and mental health. Padilla and Ruiz (1973) designated the former as a high-stress indicator that may affect the mental health of Latinos. Their argument, which addressed an increasing trend in the 1970s, is even more important today. To some extent, certain advances within the Hispanic community, as well as other breakthroughs, have created another problem; that is, the breaking down of societal barriers that have prevented Hispanics from assimilating into the mainstream culture is not an automatic ticket to assimilation (Keefe & Padilla, 1987). Cognitive strain may result when Hispanics realize that they have paid the price of deserting their native culture without receiving the benefits of assimilation into the new culture. Again, to the extent that acculturation is likely to increase among Hispanics in the next century, its effect on Latino mental health should be a major area of concern in academic as well as practice settings.

Certainly many educators and other advocates of Hispanic culture have for years posited an alternative to acculturation: the bicultural individual. Ideally, bicultural persons can function in traditional and nontraditional contexts with a minimum of conflict. How closely the ideal approximates reality, though, is arguable, especially in environments with a history of prejudice and interethnic strife. Indeed, an early study by Fabrega and Wallace (1968) suggested that Mexican Americans who were neither traditional nor highly acculturated were more likely to appear in a clinical population than in a normal one. Although this finding should not discourage educators and policymakers from promoting biculturalism, it should motivate them to study the phenomenon with an appreciation of the cognitive and emotional difficulties involved. At the very least, future researchers should seek to delineate the parameters of biculturalism. One tack is suggested by Keefe and Padilla's approach: rather than look for bicultural individuals, one should look for individuals who may demonstrate bicultural traits in several, though not all, domains.

Mental Health

Early research on Mexican American mental health indicated that this group was proportionately less likely than other Americans to utilize public health services (Padilla & Aranda, 1974; Padilla & Ruiz, 1973). On that basis, investigators offered two explanations. One line of reasoning (Jaco, 1959) held that Mexican Americans were less likely to suffer from psychopathology because of cultural factors such as a close-knit extended family that provided support for the individual in difficult times. On the surface, this argument sounded like a positive verdict on the virtues of Hispanic culture, but other researchers expressed concern about underlying implications, such as the conclusion that Hispanics do not need mental health services because they "take care of their own." Padilla and Ruiz (1973), for instance, felt that Mexican Americans and other Latinos should have more mental health problems given the high-stress indicators (poverty, prejudice, and so forth) in their lives. They explain the findings from early research as being the result of underutilization of services, not lower incidences of pathology in the population. In turn, the reasons for underutilization can be traced back, in part, to institutional and cultural barriers that discouraged Mexican Americans from seeking appropriate help.

Karno and Edgerton (1969) examined this seeming paradox—disproportionately high-stress factors yet a disproportionately low patient population—and suggested alternative explanations, in addition to institutional discrimination, for this phenomenon. They explored the possibility that cultural expectations may affect group perceptions of mental illness. Thus Mexican Americans may prefer to have a particular mental problem treated by a physician or an indigenous therapist (e.g., *curandera*, or folk healer) rather than a mental health professional. Another implication of their model is that behaviors that are viewed as symptomatic of mental illness in mainstream society may not necessarily be considered problematic among Mexican Americans, at least not to the extent that psychiatric intervention is required.

Karno and Edgerton's thesis has generated valuable research during the past two decades and remains promising (Roberts, 1980; Frerichs, Aneshensel, & Clark, 1981). However, despite their attempt to present a culturally sensitive description of how one Hispanic group defines mental health, several methodological faults have led this line of research into a dead end rather than to new avenues of inquiry. For example, on the basis of responses to vignettes that characterized a number of severe disorders, the authors concluded that Anglos and Mexican Americans did not differ in their perceptions of mental illness. However, the vignettes were textbook cases of severe pathology, and one is less likely to find differences between two Western cultural groups when using extreme examples. It should be expected that Mexican Americans share many assumptions with Anglos; for example, both groups might agree that an individual who hallucinates or who shuns all interpersonal contact is disturbed and requires help. But this does not mean, as Karno and Edgerton suggest, that significant differences between the two groups do not exist. Rather, the perceptual distinctions may be subtle enough that their instrument failed to discriminate among them. Nor does it tell us at which point each group might view an unwillingness to interact as aberrant, a critical distinction if we wish to explore cultural peculiarities.

Karno and Edgerton, along with others (Edgerton, Karno, & Fernandez, 1970; Kiev, 1968), also explored the use of indigenous therapists, including *curanderos* (folk healers). Here too, one must exercise methodological caution. Edgerton et al., for instance, found almost no evidence for the use of *curanderos* in Mexican

American communities (*barrios*), but their results may reflect two crucial factors that possibly affected the findings. The first factor concerns the status of *curanderos* themselves; their work may at times test the limits of practicing medicine without a license, and their clients may be reluctant to disclose their methods, especially when the practice carries the connotation of sorcery (Kiev, 1968). When questions are then asked about the use of folk healers, especially when the interviewers identify themselves with a university affiliation, the answers—limited use—are precisely those that might be expected (Edgerton et al., 1970).

Future research into areas such as these needs to focus special attention on the dynamics of the Hispanic experience. Researchers should not assume that their subjects share the same academic interests or are motivated to disclose their beliefs to those outside the ethnic enclave. A similar caveat can be applied to studies that attempt to catalog the epidemiology of folk illnesses (Rubel, 1964). *Susto* (fright), *mal puesto* (bewitchment), and *envidia* (envy) are culture-bound disorders whose occurrence may be difficult to ascertain through traditional research methods. Many Hispanics learn to be "cultural chameleons," disclosing certain beliefs to others of similar background but not to those who represent the educated, scientific community, which may alter results drastically.

Even when these methodological obstacles can be overcome, even when researchers obtain accurate responses from their sample, the danger of overgeneralizing to the rest of the population still exists. One could argue that much of the research on minorities has sought to accentuate cultural differences; the more esoteric those differences, the better. Although the researchers' motives are usually well-intended, such as determining how certain assumptions in mainstream psychotherapy may have little applicability to the realities of Hispanics, they may have a tendency to exaggerate differences and thus homogenize, romanticize, or stereotype the group. For example, the conclusion that Mexican Americans of a particular class or educational background believe in certain folk illnesses and remedies is overgeneralized to imply that Mexican Americans as a whole subscribe to such beliefs. Culture, at this point, becomes a catch-all explanation, and the group in question becomes unidimensional. We must therefore eschew such simplistic explanations of complex problems.

Future researchers should be similarly warned about the use of therapists from the same background as clients. This concept, similar to the notion that female clients can be best understood and aided by female therapists or that only former addicts can truly help other addicts, has a certain commonsense ring to it.

However, it has not been adequately developed in a way that specifies the context and parameters under which this sort of arrangement might work best. Simply saying that a Hispanic client should be matched with a Hispanic therapist ignores the individual differences that are brought into the therapeutic dyad. For example, it does not take into account the attitude of the Hispanic therapist toward his or her own ethnic identity. A Latino therapist who feels ambivalent about his or her ethnicity is hardly in a position to nurture self-pride or a feeling of being supported in his or her Latino clients. Moreover, a therapist with a Spanish surname may come from a middle-class or acculturated background that sets him or her worlds apart from less acculturated, lower-class clients. Indeed, the therapist may take the attitude that since he or she succeeded in realizing goals, so can "they." The result may be an inability on the part of the therapist to perceive the other's experience with any degree of objectivity. This caveat is not to say that efforts to provide culturally congruent therapy should be abandoned. Rather, future research must go beyond intuitive assumptions and ground premises in empirical work. Perhaps a working compromise might be to accept the issue of ethnic matching in psychotherapy as a necessary, albeit insufficient, condition, then proceed from there.

Finally, researchers and practitioners must confront the question of how findings from the past few decades that do show consistent results and replicability should be applied. For example, early research indicated that Mexican Americans were more likely to use somatic or physiological explanations for psychological complaints as opposed to interpersonal conceptualizations (Karno, Ross, & Caper, 1969); other research showed a similar predilection among Mexicans (Fabrega, Rubel, & Wallace, 1967). Given these findings, what direction should we take in future research and practice? Clearly, such decisions are value-laden; for a population that historically has had the values of a culturally different group imposed upon them, professionals may feel reluctant to make such decisions. However, choices need to be made. Given the above findings, we may choose to educate physicians on the propensity of Mexican Americans to use somatic referents for psychological problems (Karno, Ross, & Caper, 1969). However, another viable approach might be to educate the Hispanic public on how psychological problems tend to be distinct from physical complaints. Here, one takes a more assertive role by deciding that the group's perceptions of mental health fail to address interpersonal issues—a misperception that in turn influences the preferred avenue for treatment (medicine as opposed to psychotherapy).

To use another example, it was suggested earlier that the Hispanic culture may show greater tolerance for idiosyncratic or deviant behavior. Many professionals may argue that this is not necessarily bad, given the mainstream inclination to label even minor maladjustment as pathological. As long as one views the argument in this light, reluctance to label certain misbehaviors as symptomatic is more humane. However, other researchers have concluded that for Hispanics in general (Frerichs, Aneshensel, & Clark, 1981) and Mexican Americans in particular (Roberts, 1980) such conclusions may lead to Hispanics not receiving appropriate treatment for mental problems until it is too late and institutionalization is required. The question then arises: Should such tolerance be encouraged, discouraged, or ignored? Again, research findings suggest that difficult choices must be made and that it is up to investigators and policymakers to apply findings in ways that best suit the Hispanic community, which in itself presumes value judgments.

Postscript: Labels and Related Issues

One finds it difficult to address the issue of labels without taking into account an element of irony. In the past two or three decades, during which Mexican Americans, Puerto Ricans, and other Spanish-speaking minorities have insisted that their ethnic identities be acknowledged as being legitimate, Hispanics have implicitly argued that the melting-pot concept is an inappropriate metaphor for American society—or at least that it is inapplicable to them. The current emphasis on Hispanic homogeneity in some ways resembles, although on a smaller scale, the earlier emphasis on commonalities. In a sense, these diverse groups now find that their struggle to assert their identities has left them stranded under another umbrella: greater numbers provide them with more security while requiring certain concessions, such as deemphasizing regional or culture-specific issues. In the coming years, various Hispanic groups must decide what issues will constitute the Hispanic or Latino agenda.

Such a consensus will not be easy—not because the various Hispanic groups are necessarily opposed to certain undertakings, but simply because these projects may not coincide with their own priorities or historical realities. Thus, being a pluralistic group is problematic. For complex historical and societal reasons, some Hispanic groups, notably Mexican Americans and Puerto Ricans, have experienced considerable discrimination and have had to contend with school dropout rates of epidemic proportions. However, other Hispanics, such as Cuban Americans, are not experiencing an educational crisis, nor is their income level abysmally low. Consequently, the priorities for these groups are quite different. If the federal government targets certain Hispanic issues over others, intergroup tensions may become a problem.

These frictions may intensify in the coming century if some groups perceive—accurately or not—that their agenda on employment and education needs has been relegated to a secondary status, indeed, that their perceived sacrifices may have benefited other Hispanic groups. It should be noted that the designation of "Hispanics" as a social construct is a relatively recent phenomenon. In the 1960s, the struggle for social parity among Spanish-speaking Americans was spearheaded by Mexican American and Puerto Rican activists. In essence, the precursors to the Hispanic struggle were groups who emphasized nationalistic goals and whose socioeconomic plight approximated that of the black community. The decision to subsume these struggles under a common banner for reasons of strategy and strength came at least a decade later. One may legitimately ask, however, to what degree such an alliance will ultimately benefit those groups who initiated the struggle because they were not part of the "American dream."

The most fundamental issue in the coming century is whether these groups will now be ignored in the Hispanic dream as well. The thought may appear implausible, especially for a group the size of the Mexican American community. However, numbers do not assure clout, especially if those numbers include a disproportionate segment of the poor and uneducated.

Obviously, the foregoing paints a worst-case scenario. However, the potential already exists for the perpetuation of stratified subgroups within the Hispanic community. For instance, even a casual observation of Hispanic television at the national level shows that Mexican Americans, by far the largest Hispanic group, are poorly represented at the personnel and programming levels. Although one can point to soap operas and variety shows imported from Mexico, a concerted effort to explore the contemporary Chicano experience is absent (Sykes, 1980). This omission becomes all the more glaring when one compares it with civil-rights issues wherein blacks protested for a more visible and accurate portrayal in the electronic media. The irony is that now, with networks purporting to represent Hispanics more fairly and fully, certain groups (e.g., Mexican Americans, Puerto Ricans) may still end up being ignored.

This is not to place disproportionate emphasis on the media issue. One must put things in their proper perspective, and television programming ranks far below other priorities. But it does suggest that certain Hispanic groups may end up marginalized within their own ranks, their problems ignored or else superficially addressed. At the very least, an alienated community is a disaffected one; the anticipated blossoming of Hispanic cultures in this country may, in fact, be less impressive than expected for this and related reasons.

In this chapter, the problems and future issues facing Hispanics have been presented realistically, not pessimistically. Perhaps the best way of achieving advances for the Hispanic population is to anticipate future problems. The decade of the 1980s was promoted as "the decade of the Hispanic." The near future, however, may see the end of this hypothetical honeymoon, a period when group differences were overlooked in order to promote a cultural marriage. This does not mean that the various Hispanic subgroups will return to their earlier ethnic labels and eschew their common Hispanic heritage with other groups. It does suggest, however, that successful relationships among the various subgroups will require acknowledgment of both differences and similarities as well as the ability to compromise. Should these efforts fail, the various subgroups may return to earlier labels and partnership will continue in name only.

Currently, the academic and research communities are preparing to gradually phase out the Hispanic label. In its place, we are told, Hispanics will be rebaptized as Latinos. How and why these decrees are reached remains something of a mystery, but one cannot doubt the power of a trend. This chapter's title phrase, "Hispanics in the past two decades, Latinos in the next two," is partly a tongue-in-cheek response to the transition, wherein Hispanics enter at one end of the tunnel and Latinos exit at the other end. This new label, however, may in time have subtle, minor consequences for Hispanics/Latinos. One consequence is the group's perception of itself. At an informal level, researchers sometimes argue that the Hispanic label ignores the group's indigenous identity. This is particularly true for Mexican Americans and other *mestizo* groups, whose roots are as much Indian as Hispanic. Similar arguments can be made for other Americans of Latin American ancestry. Designating these groups as Latinos would eliminate the Eurocentric bias in the label.

Although this argument may be valid, it fails to take into account a major reason for the relative popularity of the Hispanic label. Many Spanish-surnamed Americans who balked at being categorized as hyphenated Americans, to say nothing of more radical labels such as Chicano or Boricua, were surprisingly receptive to the Hispanic label. The label's emphasis on the European part of the *mestizo* heritage, along with its implicit ignoring of the indigenous factor, may have appealed to many people who were uncomfortable with their ethnic heritage. Many people may be reluctant to replace the Hispanic label with the more ambiguous Latino label, and non-Latinos may be loathe to embrace it as well. Finally, it is likely that the change to Latino may lose momentum with a reaffirmation of Spanish ties within the Hispanic community during the quintecentennial commemoration of Columbus's voyage to the New World.

This chapter began with an element of uncertainty, which is unavoidable whenever one gazes into the future. In speculating on the relationship between the future and the past, perhaps it is instructive to conclude on a note of irony. Whereas those who advocate use of the Latino label see themselves as part of the cultural vanguard, it should be noted that the term "Latin" was the label of choice for "yesterday's" Hispanics, especially in the 1940s and 1950s. Akin to the "Negro" label, it was also the accepted form of ethnic classification used by Anglos in the first half of this century. Thus it appears that the more things change, the more they stay the same. On a less ironic note, let us hope and work for changes that will bring social and political opportunities for Hispanics/Latinos, regardless of the label in vogue.

References

Acuna, R. (1988). *Occupied America: A history of Chicanos* (3rd ed.). New York: Harper & Row.

Aronson, E. (1977). *The social animal* (2nd ed.). San Francisco: W. H. Freeman.

Buriel, R. (1984). Integration with traditional Mexican-American culture and sociocultural adjustment. In J. L. Martinez, Jr., & R. H. Mendoza (Eds.), *Chicano psychology* (2nd ed.). New York: Academic Press.

Edgerton, R. B., Karno, M., & Fernandez, I. (1970). *Curanderismo* in the metropolis: The diminishing role of folk-psychiatry among Los Angeles Mexican-Americans. *American Journal of Psychotherapy, 24*(1), 124–134.

Fabrega, H., Rubel, A. J., & Wallace, C. A. (1967). Working-class Mexican psychiatric outpatients. *Archives of General Psychiatry, 16*, 704–712.

Fabrega, H., & Wallace, C. A. (1968). Value identification and psychiatric disability: An analysis involving Americans of Mexican descent. *Behavioral Science, 13*, 362–371.

Frerichs, R. R., Aneshensel, C. S., & Clark, V. A. (1981). Prevalence of depression in Los Angeles County. *American Journal of Epidemiology, 113*, 691–699.

Gann, L. H., & Duigan, P. J. (1986). *The Hispanics in the United States*. Boulder, CO: Westview Press.

Jaco, E. G. (1959). Mental health of the Spanish American in Texas. In M. K. Opler (Ed.), *Culture and mental health: Cross-cultural studies*. New York: Macmillan.

Karno, M., & Edgerton, R. B. (1969). Perception of mental illness in a Mexican-American community. *Archives of General Psychiatry, 20*(2), 233–238.

Karno, M., Ross, R. N., & Caper, R. S. (1969). Mental health roles of physicians in a Mexican-American community. *Community Mental Health Journal, 5*(1), 62–69.

Keefe, S. E., & Padilla, A. M. (1987). *Chicano ethnicity.* Albuquerque, NM: University of New Mexico Press.

Kiev, A. (1968). *Curanderismo: Mexican-American folk psychiatry.* New York: Free Press.

Padilla, A. M., & Aranda, P. (1974). *Latino mental health: Bibliography and abstracts.* Rockville, MD: Alcohol, Drug Abuse and Mental Health Administration.

Padilla, A. M., & Ruiz, R. A. (1973). *Latino mental health: A review of mental health.* Rockville, MD: National Institute of Mental Health.

Padilla, A. M., & Ruiz, R. A. (1976). Prejudice and discrimination. In C. A. Hernandez, M. A. Haug, & N. N. Wagner (Eds.), *Chicanos: Social and psychological perspectives* (2nd ed.). St. Louis: C. V. Mosby.

Portes, A., & Bach, R. L. (1985). *Latin journey: Cuban and Mexican immigrants in the United States.* Los Angeles: University of California Press.

Poston, D. L., & Alvirez, D. (1973). On the cost of being a Mexican-American worker. *Social Science Quarterly, 54,* 697–709.

Ramirez, A. (1977). Chicano power and interracial group relations. In J. L. Martinez (Ed.), *Chicano psychology.* New York: Academic Press.

Roberts, R. E. (1980). Prevalence of depressive symptoms among Mexican-Americans. *Journal of Health and Social Behavior, 21,* 134–145.

Rubel, A. J. (1964). The epidemiology of a folk illness: *Susto* in Hispanic America. *Ethnology, 3*(3), 268–283.

Sherif, M. (1966). *In common predicament: Social psychology of intergroup conflict and cooperation.* Boston: Houghton Mifflin.

Sykes, W. R. (1980). *Study of Hispanic television programming in selected markets.* Mount Pleasant, MI: Central Michigan University.

2

The Changing Demographic Face Of Hispanics in the United States

Alejandro García

According to the United States Bureau of the Census, the Hispanic population in the United States has surpassed the 20 million mark (Barringer, 1989). In addition, media reports about the continued growth of the Hispanic population in the United States have discussed the implications of this demographic shift for politics, employment, public education, and other national issues and institutions.

The increasing interest in the growing number of Hispanics in the United States has not been altogether positive. For example, a nativist group known as U.S. English is currently promoting English as the official language of the United States and arguing against bilingual education (Bricker, 1989). Although this type of movement is not new—President Roosevelt promoted a similar proposal and nativist movements of all sorts have proliferated throughout U.S. history—it appears that such attention is focused primarily on Spanish-speaking populations. The Hispanic population is considered the most threatening group, perhaps because it is the largest of the foreign-language-speaking minority groups. In addition, Congress recently debated the issue of including undocumented persons in the 1990 decennial census. Most of these aliens, who are estimated to number between 1.7 and 2.9 million persons (Barringer, 1989), are thought to be from Latin American countries. The implications of this decision are impor-

			Percent change
	March 1988	1980	1980–1988
	civilian non-	civilian non-	civilian non-
	institutional	institutional	institutional
Origin	population	population	population
Total population	241,155	222,461	8.4
Hispanic origin	19,431	14,458	34.4
Mexican	12,110	8,654	39.9
Puerto Rican	2,471	1,983	24.6
Cuban	1,035	799	29.5
Central and South American	2,242	NA	NA
Other Hispanic	1,573	3,022	26.2
Not of Hispanic origin	221,724	208,003	6.6

TABLE 1.
Change in the total and Hispanic populations in the U.S. by type of origin: April 1980 to March 1988 (numbers in thousands).

Note: In the 1980 census, the "Other Spanish" category included persons from Spain, the Spanish-speaking countries of Central and South America, and Hispanic persons who identified themselves generally as Latino, Spanish American, Spanish, etc. In the Current Population Survey, the category "Central and South American" is listed as a separate origin.

Adapted from U.S. Department of Commerce, Bureau of the Census. (1989, August). *The Hispanic population in the United States: March 1988.* Series P-20, No. 438.

tant in that the decennial census is used to determine congressional apportionment. It appears that as the Hispanic population increases and appears more powerful, policymakers have become increasingly concerned about the potential "threat" from this group. Just as the 19th-century influx of Chinese to this country was perceived as a "yellow peril," the growth in the Hispanic population may be considered a "brown peril" by the non-Hispanic majority.

The purpose of this chapter is to examine the changing demography of Hispanics in the United States and to discuss the implications of this phenomenon for future social policy. Specific variables will be examined: population growth, education, employment,

TABLE 2.
Hispanic population for selected states: March 1988
(in thousands).

State	Hispanic population	Percent of total Hispanic population
United States	19,431	100.0
California	6,589	33.9
Texas	4,134	21.3
New York	2,122	10.9
Florida	1,473	7.6
Illinois	801	4.1
Arizona	648	3.3
New Jersey	646	3.3
New Mexico	543	2.8
Colorado	368	1.9

Adapted from U.S. Department of Commerce, Bureau of the Census. (1989, August). *The Hispanic population in the United States: March 1988.* Series P-20, No. 438.

family status, and poverty among Hispanics in general and among the largest Hispanic subgroups (persons of Mexican origin, Puerto Ricans, Cubans, and other Central and South Americans) in particular. Attention will be focused on whether Hispanics in the United States have improved their socioeconomic status and whether available data allow us to predict the future status of this group.

Growth in Hispanic Population

A major finding of the March 1988 census report on the Hispanic population in the United States indicated that the Hispanic civilian noninstitutional population (persons not in institutions—either mental health or correctional) increased by 34% between the years 1980 and 1988, almost five times as fast as the non-Hispanic population increased. Hispanics now represent 8.2% of the total population of the United States (U.S. Department of Commerce, 1989). As noted in Table 1, the two largest Hispanic groups—Puerto Ricans and Mexican Americans—grew the fastest during that period: the Puerto Rican population increased by 39.9% and the Mexican-origin population by 34.4%. There was also considerable growth among Cubans (24.6%) and Central and

	Four years or more high school		Four years or more college	
Source	Hispanic (%)	Non-Hispanic (%)	Hispanic (%)	Non-Hispanic (%)
1988 CPS	51	78	10	21
1980 Census	44	68	8	17
1970 Census	32	53	5	11

TABLE 3.
Years of school completed by persons 25 years old and older: March 1988 CPS, and 1970 and 1980 census.

Adapted from U.S. Department of Commerce, Bureau of the Census. (1989, August). *The Hispanic population in the United States: March 1988.* Series P-20, No. 438.

South Americans (29.5%). It is assumed that the high rate of growth for Puerto Ricans was due to a high fertility rate, whereas the high rate for the Mexican-origin group was due to both high fertility and immigration.

As noted in Table 2, most Hispanics are concentrated in five Southwestern states (California, Texas, Arizona, Colorado, and New Mexico). California and Texas alone have 55.2% of all Hispanics. However, New York has 10.9% and Florida, with its concentration of Cuban Americans, has 7.6% of all Hispanics. The other non-Southwestern states with notable concentrations of Hispanics are Illinois with 4.1% and New Jersey with 3.3%.

Education

Education has always been an important indicator of success in American society; past studies indicate that Hispanics have not attained a high enough educational level to assist them in competing more aggressively in the labor market. The 1988 Current Population Survey notes that the percent of Hispanics ages 25 and older with four years of high school or more rose from 32% in 1970 to 44% in 1980 and 51% in 1988 (U.S. Department of Commerce, 1989). For non-Hispanics in the same age group, the percent of those with four years of high school or more rose from 53% in 1970 to 78% in 1988. While the percent of Hispanics ages 25 and older with four or more years of college doubled from 5% to 10% between 1970 and 1988, the same doubling phenomenon occurred among non-Hispanics, with the percent of those with

TABLE 4.
**Educational attainment for persons of Hispanic origin
by type of origin.**

Education	Mexican origin	Puerto Rican	Cuban	Central/South American
Less than five years (%)	15.9	9.6	5.5	6.7
Four years or more high school (%)	44.6	50.7	60.5	63.8
Four years or more college (%)	7.1	9.6	17.2	16.5
Median school years completed	10.8	12	12.4	12.4

Adapted from U.S. Department of Commerce, Bureau of the Census. (1989, August). *The Hispanic population in the United States: March 1988.* Series P-20, No. 438.

four or more years of education increasing from 11% to 21% (U.S. Department of Commerce, 1989). As indicated in Table 3, despite educational advances of Hispanics, they remain far behind non-Hispanics. Although the proportion of Hispanics with at least a high school education increased from one out of every three in 1970 to one out of every two (51%) in 1988, that improvement is insufficient to make an appreciable difference in terms of employment opportunities and the capacity to participate fully in all aspects of American society.

In the educational arena, it is assumed that all Hispanics perform similarly. However, it is important to note that differences exist (Table 4). For example, for Hispanics 25 years and older, 50.7% of Puerto Ricans had four years of high school or more and 9.6% had fewer than five years of schooling. For persons of Cuban origin in the same age group, 60.5% had four years of high school or more and only 5.5% had fewer than five years of schooling. The percent of persons of Mexican origin in the same age group with four years of high school or more was lowest (44.6%). This group also had the highest rate of persons with fewer than five years of schooling (15.9%). For this age group, Mexican-origin persons had the lowest median school years completed (10.8%), compared with 12% for Puerto Ricans and 12.4% for Cubans. The lower educational-attainment levels for Mexican Americans may be a function of the continuing influx of immigrants with little education and the lower attainments of older Mexican Americans, who may have suffered from the widespread discrimination in education that existed in the United States in their youth (see Rangel & Alcala, 1972).

Although Hispanics are expected to continue to improve their educational attainment level, the school dropout rate for Hispanics ages 18 to 21 years old, which in 1986 was twice that of non-Hispanics, is cause for concern. The Current Population Report points out that the proportion of Hispanics 18 to 21 years old who were not enrolled in school and were not high school graduates in October 1986 was almost three times that of non-Hispanics (31% vs. 12%) (U.S. Department of Commerce, 1989). This report further states that only 59% of Hispanics in the 18-to-21 age group were high school graduates in October 1986, compared with 82% of non-Hispanics in the same age group. These figures do not address the extent to which Hispanics are monolingual or bilingual; it is important to note that a substantial number of the 50% who have not completed four years of education may be fluent only in Spanish and thus unable to obtain suitable employment or social services due to language limitations.

Employment

The percentage of Hispanic women (ages 16 and older) in the labor force has increased from 48% in 1982 to 52% in 1988. This figure contradicts the assumption that Hispanic women continue to occupy traditional roles of housewife and mother. The number of non-Hispanic women in the work force also increased from 52.3% to 56.2% during the same period. It appears that Hispanic women are increasingly behaving as do non-Hispanic women in terms of labor-force participation (U.S. Department of Commerce, 1989). To the extent that the number of Hispanic women in the work force continues to increase, the availability of services for care of dependent children and elderly relatives needs to be examined.

Nearly 63% of employed Hispanic women, compared with 71% of non-Hispanic women, were working in technical, sales, and administrative support and service occupations. An additional 16.6% of Hispanic women and 8.3% of non-Hispanic women were working as operators, fabricators, and laborers. Only 1.5% of Hispanic women were working in farming, forestry, and fishing. These figures challenge the popular view of Hispanics as being primarily farm workers. Median earnings for Hispanic women in the work force rose from $6,597 in 1982 to $8,554 in 1988, while the median earnings for non-Hispanic women rose from $7,264 to $10,745 during the same period. Salary differentials reflect occupational differences due in part to differences in educational attainment level between the two groups. It should be noted that Hispanic women in managerial and professional specialty areas increased from 12.4% in 1982 to 15.7% in 1988. Concomitantly, members of this group working as operators, fabricators, and laborers decreased from 18.2% to 16.6% in the same period (U.S. Department of Commerce, 1989).

Among men in the general population ages 16 and older, the rate of unemployment dropped from a high of 16.3% in 1983 to a low of 7% in 1989, while the rate for non-Hispanic males dropped from 9.3% to 5.4% in the same period (U.S. Department of Commerce, 1989).

In 1988, Hispanic men were more likely to be employed in precision production, craft, and repair (20.5%) and as operators, fabricators, and laborers (28.1%), whereas non-Hispanic males were more likely to be working in managerial and professional positions (27.3%); technical, sales, and administrative support (20.3%); precision production, craft, and repair (19.4%); and operators, fabricators, and laborers (20.3%). A substantially higher percentage of Hispanic males (8.2%) worked in farming, forestry, and fishing than did non-Hispanic males (3.7%). The differentials in median earnings for Hispanics and non-Hispanics reflect the occupations of these two groups. Median earnings of Hispanic males have risen from $10,850 in 1982 to $12,527, while median earnings for non-Hispanic males have risen from $15,359 to $19,588 in the same period. As with women's salaries, differences between Hispanic and non-Hispanic men's earnings can be explained in terms of limitations in occupational choices due to lower educational-attainment levels. However, it is important to note that Hispanic families with a householder age 25 or older had a poverty rate of 36.4%, whereas non-Hispanics in the same category had a poverty rate of 18.6% in 1987 (U.S. Department of Commerce, 1989).

A surprising finding for Hispanic males is that the rate of unemployment has dropped markedly between 1982, when it was 13.6%, and 1988, when it dropped to 7%. During the same period unemployment rates for non-Hispanics also dropped, though not radically, from 8.7% to 5.4% (U.S. Department of Commerce, 1989).

Poverty Rates

Despite the fact that unemployment dropped substantially for Hispanic males, a proportionate drop in the poverty rate did not occur between 1982 and 1988. In 1982, the poverty rate for Hispanic families was 23.5%, increasing to 25.8% in 1988. On the other hand, the poverty rate for non-Hispanic families was 10.5% in 1982, dropping to 9.7% in 1988 (U.S. Department of Commerce, 1989). Possibly the decrease in unemployment is not connected to a decrease in the poverty rate for Hispanic males because these persons may have lost higher-paying jobs in manufacturing and subsequently taken lower-paying jobs in the service sector.

It is important to note some substantial differences in the poverty rate among various Hispanic groups. Puerto Rican families had the highest poverty rate (37.9%), whereas Mexican-origin persons had a 25.5% rate and Cubans a 13.8% rate in 1987. In analyzing the connection between type of employment and the poverty rate, it was found that 31.7% of Puerto Ricans were in managerial and professional specialty areas and technical, sales, and administrative support, whereas 69.1% of Cuban males and 22.6% of Mexican-origin persons worked in these same areas (U.S. Department of Commerce, 1989).

The poverty rates for Hispanic families in which the householder was 65 years of age and older dropped from 25.2% in 1982 to 21.7% in 1988. The poverty rate for non-Hispanic families in the same category also decreased from 8.6% to 6.7% . The cost-of-living adjustments for Social Security may have been a major factor in this slight reduction in the poverty rate for these groups (U.S. Department of Commerce, 1989).

Hispanic female-headed households with no husband present continue to suffer the highest rate of poverty, with slightly more than half (51.8%) presently living below the poverty level, whereas the rate for non-Hispanic female-headed households is currently 32.3%. It is important to note that Puerto Rican families in this category had the highest poverty rate, with 65.3% living in poverty. The poverty rate for Mexican-origin persons in the same category was 47.1% (U.S. Department of Commerce, 1989).

The Hispanic Family

The percent of Hispanic married families has dropped from 74.1% in 1982 to 69.8% in 1989, while the female-headed family with no husband present has increased from 21.5% to 23.4% in the same period. Interestingly, the percent of Hispanic male-householder families with no wife present has increased substantially—from 4.4% in 1982 to 6.8% in 1988. On the other hand, the percent of married-couple families for non-Hispanics has remained fairly constant: 81.8% in 1982 and 80.6% in 1988. Non-Hispanic female-headed families with no husband present have remained fairly constant during the past six years, increasing slightly from 15% in 1982 to 15.8% in 1988 (U.S. Department of Commerce, 1989).

Hispanic families continue to be larger than non-Hispanic families. Only 25.5% of Hispanic families consist of two members, whereas 42.4% of non-Hispanic families consist of two members. Slightly more than one-fourth of Hispanic families consisted of five or more persons in 1988, whereas only 13% of non-Hispanic families fell within this category. One-half (50.2%) of Hispanic families had four or more family members, whereas only one-third of non-Hispanic families were in the same category. The median number of persons per family is 3.7 for Hispanic families and 3.13 for non-Hispanic families. The relatively larger Hispanic family is reflective of the value Hispanics place upon children, as well as adherence to Roman Catholicism and the consequent high fertility rate. However, the higher poverty rate among Hispanics bears heavily on these larger Hispanic families (U.S. Department of Commerce, 1989).

Illegal Aliens

Although the media have focused much attention on the growth in number of Hispanics in the United States, it is important to note that similar attention has been focused on the undocumented or illegal aliens in this country. Most of these aliens are assumed to be Hispanics; therefore any discussion of demographics of Hispanics in the United States must include this group. However, it is difficult to do so, primarily because these persons cannot easily be located and counted. Most illegal aliens are afraid to contact any agent of the government for fear of deportation. Warren and Passel (1987) estimated that 2.057 million illegal aliens lived in the United States and that 55% of them (1.131 million) came from Mexico. They note that of the Mexican-born undocumented population, 54.9% are male and young (approximately 70% in the 15–44 age group and only 5.2% older than 45). As always, it is difficult to determine the number of undocumented persons in the United States. In 1986, 1.6 million undocumented persons were arrested by the border patrol along the U.S.–Mexico border (Rigoni, 1987).

Reasons for Migration

What brings Hispanics to the United States? The major reasons are economic and political. Persons may either seek refuge from a battered economy, as in many Latin American countries, or they seek refuge from ongoing wars in Central America. Rigoni (1987) suggests other reasons that transcend the obvious ones stated above, hypothesizing that

> emigration is the fruit of a cultural process, in virtue of which the models of development and behavior are conceived, planned and carried out. . . . By cultural process here in Mexico, I mean a whole series of economic, social, consumer and prestige evaluations that are patterned after the American society and culture, in its more degrading features (p. 14).

Rigoni notes that in commercials on two television channels in Mexico, most products were presented by blond-haired people; blonds were featured on various other television programs as well. The effect is to brainwash people through "hidden persuasion" and to unleash "psychological and sociological mechanisms that often lead to emigration as a means to realize those aspirations that have almost become necessities of life" (Rigoni, 1987, p. 24). As a result, "there is disdain for everything that is Mexican, especially in the field of industry but in that of agriculture, as well. What is American or European is good. Whatever is made in Mexico doesn't count" (p. 25). Mexicans have a term—*malinchista*—that describes persons who prefer things foreign to things Mexican. The derivation of the term is La Malinche, the legendary mistress of Hernando Cortez, who preferred a European to her own people and ended up betraying her people in helping Cortez conquer Mexico.

Needs of New Refugee Groups

Hispanics in the United States continue to suffer high rates of poverty, unemployment and underemployment, discrimination, and so forth. Moreover, some of the new Hispanic immigrant groups are bringing new problems with them that American society will have to address. It is estimated that approximately 800,000 exiled refugees and others from Central America now live in the United States (Molesky, 1986). In addition to consideration of their legal and economic status, the psychological state of these refugees and policy implications for their American hosts need to be confronted and resolved. Molesky suggests that many of these refugees have "psychological wounds" and are "haunted by recurrent recollections of the traumatic event, become numb to and detached from the external world, or often experience a hyperalertness, exaggerated startle response or sleep disturbance" (p. 19).

There are approximately a half million Salvadorans in the United States: 150,000 in Houston, 80,000 to 150,000 in San Francisco, and more than 250,000 in Los Angeles (Molesky, 1986). Of these, it is estimated that nearly 300,000 Salvadorans are living illegally in the United States. Approximately 25,000 have applied for asylum (Fazlollah, 1984). Rodriguez (1987) estimates that more than 100,000 illegal Central Americans live in Houston, primarily Salvadorans, Guatemalans, and Hondurans. Although it might be expected that extensive competition for lower-paying jobs would take place between Hispanic immigrants and native Hispanic Americans, one study has found that a complementary relationship exists between the two groups (King, Lowell, & Bean, 1986).

The large number of refugees from Central America may support extensive mental health problems among this group.

> In the new country, be it the United States, Mexico, wherever, the refugee lives in two worlds. The refugee's perception of time, space, and his identity is split. He lives again the old time and space, yet in a new time and space. There has been a break in his known way of life. In this dissonant separation, he idealizes his past and sees the present as terrible. He avoids living in the present. It's a survival strategy. Psychic energy is spent on divorcing from what hurts. In this detachment, you don't confront. It can evidence itself in drinking, self-destructive streaks, but always avoiding the storm. However, it is in the development of this state that one prevents a catastrophic breakdown. This psychic phenomenon is the pathology of exile (Molesky, 1986, p. 21).

It has been suggested by the director of a mental health services agency in San Francisco that "most—if not all—Central American refugees" need mental health services and are suffering from symptoms similar to those of post-traumatic stress disorder, which include "reexperiencing the traumatic event; a numbing of responsiveness to, or reduced involvement with, the external world; and a variety of autonomic, dysphoric, or cognitive symptoms" (Molesky, 1986, p. 22). If this is the case, then culturally and linguistically sensitive outreach efforts and mental health services are needed in the metropolitan areas identified above and probably elsewhere.

The Future

A census report projecting the Hispanic population in the year 2080 anticipates that the Hispanic population may double in the next 30 years and perhaps triple in the next 60 years. It was also projected that most of the growth of the Spanish-origin popu-

TABLE 5.
Average annual percent change in population, by race and Spanish origin: 1982–2080.

Period (July 1–July 1)	Total	Spanish origin	White non-Hispanic	Black	Other races
1982–1985	0.9	3.0	0.6	1.6	3.2
1985–1990	0.9	2.8	0.6	1.6	2.9
1990–1995	0.8	2.5	0.4	1.4	2.6
1995–2000	0.6	2.2	0.3	1.2	2.3
2000–2010	0.6	2.0	0.2	1.1	2.0
2010–2020	0.5	1.7	0.1	1.0	1.6
2020–2030	0.3	1.4	-0.1	0.7	1.3
2030–2040	0.1	1.1	-0.3	0.6	1.0
2040–2050	0.0	0.8	-0.3	0.4	0.9
2050–2060	0.0	0.7	-0.3	0.3	0.8
2060–2070	0.0	0.5	-0.3	0.2	0.7
2070–2080	0.0	0.4	-0.2	0.1	0.7

Note: Includes Armed Forces overseas. Data taken from the middle series.

Adapted from U.S. Department of Commerce, Bureau of the Census. (1986, November). *Projections of the Hispanic population, 1983–2080*. Current Population Reports, Series P-25, No. 995.

lation would occur among those aged 35 and older and that the Spanish-origin population aged 65 and older may quadruple by the year 2015 and be seven times its present size in 2030. Even without international migration, the Spanish-origin population may grow more quickly than will most other major population groups with immigration. The white non-Hispanic population may peak in size by 2020, then steadily decrease; in proportion to the total population it is likely to decline in the future (U.S. Department of Commerce, 1986). Table 5 shows the annual percentage change expected between 1982 and 2080.

A study of the future racial composition of the U.S. finds that

> the absolute number of Hispanics and Blacks will be 9 to 10 million higher in 2080 than in 1980 (62% and 38% respectively), while the White non-Hispanic population will fall by 30

TABLE 6.
Total population by race and Spanish origin: 1982–2080.

Year	Total	Spanish origin	White non-Hispanic	Black	Other races
1982	232.1	15.8	183.5	27.7	5.9
1990	249.7	19.9	192.0	31.4	7.5
2000	268.0	25.2	198.9	35.8	9.5
2010	283.2	30.8	202.6	40.0	11.7
2020	296.6	36.5	204.5	44.2	13.7
2030	304.8	41.9	202.4	47.6	15.6
2040	308.6	46.7	197.2	50.3	17.3
2050	309.5	50.8	190.8	52.3	18.9
2060	309.7	54.2	184.8	53.7	20.4
2070	310.4	57.2	180.0	54.9	21.9
2080	310.8	59.6	176.0	55.7	23.4

Note: Data as of July 1. Numbers do not sum to total because the Spanish origin may be of any race. Numbers given in millions. Includes Armed Forces overseas. Data taken from the middle series.

Adapted from U.S. Department of Commerce, Bureau of the Census. (1986, November). *Projections of the Hispanic population, 1983–2080.* Current Population Reports, Series P-25, No. 995.

million. Thus the descendents of the members of the existing three minority groups already residents will account for 30% of the resident population in 2080 as opposed to 20% in 1980 (Bouvier & Davis, 1983, p. 315).

As can be seen in Table 6 (U.S. Department of Commerce, 1986), in 1982 Spanish-origin persons in America numbered 15.8 million, whereas blacks accounted for 27.7 million and white non-Hispanics accounted for 183.5 million. By the year 2000, Spanish-origin persons will grow to 25.2 million, blacks will grow to 35.8 million, and whites will increase to 198.9 million. However, by the year 2050, Hispanics will increase to 50.8 million, and blacks to 52.3 million, whereas whites will decrease to 190.8 million. By the year 2080, it is projected that Spanish-origin persons will surpass blacks—59.6 million compared with 55.7 million, respectively.

TABLE 7.
Median age, by race and Spanish origin: 1982–2080.

Year	Total	Spanish origin	White non-Hispanic	Black	Other races
1982	30.6	24.1	32.1	25.5	27.2
1990	33.0	26.3	34.6	27.7	30.4
2000	36.3	28.0	38.5	30.2	33.5
2010	38.5	29.3	41.4	31.4	35.6
2020	39.3	31.2	42.3	33.5	37.5
2030	40.8	33.0	43.9	35.5	38.4
2050	41.6	36.2	44.2	38.1	39.6
2080	42.8	40.9	43.9	40.9	40.8

Note: Data as of July 1. Includes Armed Forces overseas. Data taken from the middle series.

Adapted from U.S. Department of Commerce, Bureau of the Census. (1986, November). *Projections of the Hispanic population, 1983–2080.* Current Population Reports, Series P-25, No. 995.

Non-Hispanics will continue their decline to 176 million (U.S. Department of Commerce, 1986). The two major contributors to this phenomenal growth of Hispanics is the relatively young age of the population as well as continued high birth and immigration rates. Hispanics will continue to evidence a higher crude birth rate and net immigration rate and lower crude death rate than will either white non-Hispanics or blacks from 1982 until the year 2080 (U.S. Department of Commerce, 1986).

As can be seen in Table 7, the Hispanic population will remain relatively youthful until 2080. In 1982, the median age for Hispanics was 24.1 years old, compared with 25.5 for blacks and 32.1 for whites. In the year 2000, the median age will be 28.0 for Hispanics, 30.2 for blacks, and 41.4 for whites. In the year 2050, the median age for Hispanics will be 36.2, but 38.1 for blacks and 44.2 for whites. Finally, in the year 2080, Hispanics will have almost caught up with blacks and whites in terms of median age: Hispanics will have a median age of 40.9 years, blacks 41.8, and white non-Hispanics 43.9.

The changing face of Hispanic elderly in the United States is of special interest. As shown in Table 8, in 1989, Hispanics constituted only 2.9% of those aged 65 and older, whereas blacks

TABLE 8.
Percent distribution of the population,
age 65 and older, race, and Spanish origin: 1982–2080.

Year	Total	Spanish origin	White non-Hispanic	Black	Other races
1982	11.6	4.9	12.8	7.9	5.9
1990	12.7	6.3	14.3	8.2	7.0
2000	13.0	6.8	14.8	8.3	8.6
2010	13.8	8.0	15.8	8.9	10.8
2020	17.3	10.6	19.9	11.6	14.4
2030	21.2	13.3	24.4	15.3	17.2
2050	21.8	15.6	24.7	17.6	19.3
2080	23.5	20.4	25.3	22.0	21.0

Note: Data as of July 1. Includes Armed Forces overseas. Data taken from the middle series.

Adapted from U.S. Department of Commerce, Bureau of the Census. (1986, November). *Projections of the Hispanic population, 1983–2080.* Current Population Reports, Series P-25, No. 995.

accounted for 8.1% and white non-Hispanics 87.8%. However, by the year 2050, Hispanic elderly will constitute 11.7% of those aged 65 and older, blacks will increase to 13.7%, but white non-Hispanics will decrease to 69.9%. The percentage of Hispanic elderly will continue to grow as the Hispanic population ages. By the year 2080, the percentage of Hispanics aged 65 and older will be 16.7, while the percent of blacks will increase to 16.8, and the percentage of whites will continue to decrease to 60.9 of the elderly population (U.S. Department of Commerce, 1986).

Implications

As noted earlier, the above projections are based upon a number of assumptions that may not be totally accurate. However, if we accept them in general, they suggest important implications for the future of Hispanics in the United States. Although some progress can be found in education and employment among Hispanics, little change has occurred in the poverty rate. In addition, substantial differences exist between Hispanics and non-Hispanic persons in terms of these variables. Of particular concern is the increasing rate of single-parent Hispanic families. In addition, the gradual increase in the entry of Hispanic women into the work force may reflect economic need and a gradual cultural change in the perception of Hispanic women as caretakers of children and the elderly.

The growing numbers of Hispanics have yet to be appreciated as a powerful force in terms of the consumer market. Bouvier and Davis (1983) point out that the presidential campaign of 1988 was the first time in which the Hispanic vote was "openly courted" (p. 12). They further suggest that approximately one-third of Hispanics (36%) are registered to vote, in contrast with 65% of blacks and non-Hispanic whites. One of the major reasons for the low registration of Hispanics is that one-third of them are ineligible to vote because of lack of citizenship. Regardless, of Hispanics eligible to vote, "only 54% were registered in 1986" (p. 12). Efforts to increase voting participation among Hispanics will need to include citizenship classes, registration drives, and voter education.

What happens to Hispanic immigrants over time? In one study of Hispanic immigration to the Northeast, it was found that "overall, Hispanic immigrants in the northeastern United States follow the classic immigration pattern of positive selection at origin, initial downward mobility after immigration, upward mobility over time, increased income and intermarriage, and English language acquisition in the second generation" (Gurak & Kritz, 1985, p. 6). However, Puerto Ricans, who counted for 60% of the Hispanics in New York City, were found to have the lowest household income of any of the Hispanic groups as well as a lower outmarriage rate (Gurak & Kritz, 1985). Fitzpatrick and Parker (1981) concur not only with the fact that Puerto Ricans and Dominicans tend to be in a lower socioeconomic group than are Cubans and other Central and South Americans, but that second and third generations show upward mobility and assimilation. The above data reflect the need to move away from placing all Hispanics under one label and focusing on each of the Hispanic subgroups. Puerto Ricans, as a group, continue to do poorly in comparison with Cuban and Mexican Americans. It will be interesting to see whether Cubans will continue to do better socioeconomically than Mexican Americans or Puerto Ricans as the American-born Cubans come of age.

Conclusion

As noted above, projections indicate that Hispanics will increase as a percent of the total population of the United States over the next century. As this population grows, it is critical that they become an integral part of all aspects of society. Increasingly, the well-being of American society will depend on the well-being of this minority group. For example, Hispanics and blacks will make up the majority of Social Security contributors in the next century. Should they continue to occupy low-paying jobs, they will not be able to sustain the growing number of benefit recipients.

Educational attainment levels will continue to have a direct impact on employment. To the extent that Hispanics fail to graduate from high school, they will not be able to compete in our technologically oriented society. Moreover, inability to compete for higher-paying jobs will cause Hispanics to be disproportionately represented in poverty statistics. Such problems call for major reassessment of current educational approaches on behalf of Hispanic children. The current debate over the value of bilingual/bicultural education and the English-only movement reflects an ethnocentric bias that may have a negative effect on the education of Hispanic and other children whose primary language is other than English.

The continuing influx of legal and illegal immigrants from Mexico and from Central and South America suggests that we need to develop extensive bilingual and bicultural social services. The unique characteristics of refugees from war-torn countries demand that mental health and other support services be made available to address their problems.

Undoubtedly, the growing numbers of Hispanics in the United States will affect every aspect of American life: language, politics, values, cuisine, architecture, art, music, and human relations. The responsiveness of social programs to the needs of this group will be a major determinant in the future well-being of Hispanics *and* the United States.

References

Barringer, F. (1989, October 12). Hispanic population passes 20 million, U.S. says. *New York Times*, p. A12.

Bouvier, L. F., & Davis, C. B. (1983). The future racial composition in the United States. *Mankind Quarterly, 23,* 299–327.

Bricker, K. S. (1989, October 10). Regents' bilingual plan won't work. *Syracuse Post-Standard.*

Fazlollah, M. (1984). Fleeing Salvadorans: The painful journey north. *Migration Today, 12*(2): 22–23.

Fitzpatrick, J. P., & Parker, L. T. (1981, March). Hispanic-Americans in the eastern United States. *Annals of the American Academy of Political and Social Science, 454,* 98–110.

Gurak, D. T., & Kritz, M. M. (1985). Hispanic immigration to the northeast in the

1970s. *Migration Today, 13*(2), 6–12.

King, A. G., Lowell, B. L., & Bean, F. D. (1986). The effects of Hispanic immigrants on the earnings of native Hispanic Americans. *Social Science Quarterly, 67,* 673–689.

Molesky, J. (1986). Pathology of Central American refugees. *Migration World,* 14(4): 19–23.

Rangel, J. C., & Alcala, C. M. (1972). Project report: De jure segregation of Chicanos in Texas Schools. *Harvard Civil Rights-Civil Liberties Review, 7*(3).

Rigoni, F. (1987). Tijuana: The borders on the move. *Migration World, 15*(2), 24–29.

Rodriguez, Nestor P. (1987). Undocumented Central Americans in Houston: Diverse populations. *International Migration Review, 21*(1), 4–26.

U.S. Department of Commerce, Bureau of the Census. (1986). *Projections of the Hispanic population, 1983–2080.* Current Population Reports, Series P-25, No. 995.

U.S. Department of Commerce, Bureau of the Census. (1989, August). *The Hispanic population in the United States: March 1988,* Series P-20, No. 438.

Warren, R., & Passel, J. (1987). A count of the uncountable: Estimates of undocumented aliens counted in the above 1980 United States Census. *Demography,* 24, 375–393.

3

Patterns and Consequences of Illegal Drug Use among Hispanics

Mario De La Rosa

Despite the attention focused on illicit drug use in recent years (National Institute on Drug Abuse, 1989a), little information exists on the extent and nature of the illegal drug problem among U.S. Hispanics (De La Rosa, Rouse, & Kalsa, in press). Hispanics (Mexican Americans, Cuban Americans, and immigrants from Puerto Rico and South and Central America) are expected to become the largest minority group in the United States by the year 2000 (McKay, 1987). Given the seriousness of the drug problem among Hispanics reported by the U.S. Department of Health and Human Services (1985), more information on this topic is needed.

This chapter presents information on the extent of illegal drug use among U.S. Hispanics.[1] The impact that illegal drug use has upon the well-being of Hispanics is also discussed as well as information on Hispanics' utilization of drug-treatment facilities. Recommendations for future epidemiologic research on this topic are made.[2]

Trends in Illegal Drug Use among Hispanics

Results of two National Household Survey on Drug Abuse (NHSDA) studies on the prevalence of illegal drug use among Hispanics living in the mainland United States indicated that white non-Hispanics and black non-Hispanics were more likely than

TABLE 1.
Percentage of lifetime of any illicit drug use by age, sex, and race/ethnicity.

	White		Black		Hispanic	
	1985	1988	1985	1988	1985	1988
Age (years)						
12–17	30.7	26.0	24.4	18.7	27.6	24.3
18–25	69.1	62.5	55.1	47.0	48.1	47.6
26–34	65.9	67.4	56.3	58.0	39.2	50.9
35 and older	20.3	22.8	25.2	27.8	16.3	17.1
Gender						
Male	42.4	39.4	44.5	43.6	37.7	37.8
Female	33.6	34.8	31.0	29.6	21.3	26.9
Total	**37.8**	**37.0**	**37.2**	**35.9**	**29.3**	**32.3**

Adapted from National Institute on Drug Abuse. (1987). *1985 National Household Survey on Drug Abuse: Population estimates.* DHHS Pub. No. (ADM) 87-1539. Washington, DC: U.S. Government Printing Office; National Institute on Drug Abuse. (1989). *1988 National Household Survey on Drug Abuse: Population estimates.* DHHS Pub. No. (ADM) 89-1639. Washington, DC: U.S. Government Printing Office.

were Hispanics to have ever used any illegal drug (i.e., marijuana, cocaine, inhalants, hallucinogens, PCP, nonmedical sedatives, tranquilizers, and analgesics) (National Institute on Drug Abuse, 1987a, 1989b) (Table 1). However, these results also suggest that lifetime use (use of an illicit drug at least once in a lifetime) of any illegal drug increased slightly among Hispanics from 29.3% in the 1985 survey to 32.3% in the 1988 survey. On the other hand, lifetime use of any illicit drug among white non-Hispanics decreased from 37.8% in 1985 to 37.0% in 1988; and for black non-Hispanics, from 37.2% in 1985 to 35.9% in 1988. Other findings from the 1985 and 1988 NHSDA surveys suggested that Hispanic males of all ages use all types of illegal drugs more frequently than do Hispanic females, although lifetime illicit drug use among Hispanic females increased from 21.3% in 1985 to 26.9% in 1988.

In addition, results from these surveys, as shown in Table 2, indicated changes in the lifetime use of cocaine among Hispanics during the past three years. Although data from the 1985 NSHDA

TABLE 2.
Percentage of lifetime cocaine use by age, sex, and race/ethnicity.

	White		Black		Hispanic	
	1985	1988	1985	1988	1985	1988
Age (years)						
12–17	5.5	3.6	2.9	2.1	6.7	4.6
18–25	28.3	21.2	13.5	10.4	14.9	18.7
26–34	26.9	28.6	17.6	19.8	9.8	21.5
35 and older	4.0	3.7	7.3	6.4	2.8	3.4
Gender						
Male	16.1	12.9	14.8	13.8	10.1	13.9
Female	9.0	8.9	5.7	5.9	4.7	8.1
Total	**12.4**	**10.8**	**9.9**	**9.3**	**7.3**	**11.0**

Adapted from National Institute on Drug Abuse. (1987). *1985 National Household Survey on Drug Abuse: Population estimates.* DHHS Pub. No. (ADM) 87-1539. Washington, DC: U.S. Government Printing Office; National Institute on Drug Abuse (1989). *1988 National Household Survey on Drug Abuse: Population estimates.* DHHS Pub. No. (ADM) 89-1639. Washington, DC: U.S. Government Printing Office.

survey indicated that white non-Hispanics were more likely than were black non-Hispanics and Hispanics to have ever tried cocaine, the results from the 1988 NSHDA survey suggested that the lifetime rate of cocaine use was higher among Hispanics than among white non-Hispanics and/or black non-Hispanics (National Institute on Drug Abuse, 1987a, 1989b). Further, the lifetime use of cocaine was higher for Hispanics 12–17 years of age than it was among white and black non-Hispanics in the same age group. The results from both surveys, as shown in Table 2, also indicated a significant increase from 1985 to 1988 in the percentage of Hispanics between the ages of 26 and 34 who had ever used cocaine (9.8% compared with 21.5%). Similarly, the surveys showed that lifetime cocaine use among Hispanic females had increased from 4.7% to 8.1%.

Data from the 1985 NHSDA survey, as shown in Table 3, also seemed to indicate that the percentage of past-month use for most types of illegal drug use was higher among white non-Hispanics than it was among black non-Hispanics and/or Hispanics

TABLE 3.
Percentage of past-month illicit drug use
by type of drug and race/ethnicity.

Drug	White		Black		Hispanic	
	1985	1988	1985	1988	1985	1988
Inhalants	1.0	0.7	*	*	1.1	0.4
Marijuana	9.1	5.6	13.1	6.3	7.4	6.0
Hallucinogens	0.6	0.5	*	*	*	0.3
Tranquilizers	1.2	0.6	0.5	*	0.6	0.6
Sedatives	0.9	0.4	0.8	*	0.6	0.5
Analgesics	1.0	0.5	1.7	0.7	1.7	1.2
Cocaine	3.0	1.3	3.2	2.0	2.4	2.6

*Less than 0.5%; no population estimates made.

Adapted from National Institute on Drug Abuse. (1987). *1985 National Household Survey on Drug Abuse: Population estimates*. DHHS Pub. No. (ADM) 87-1539. Washington, DC: U.S. Government Printing Office; National Institute on Drug Abuse (1989). *1988 National Household Survey on Drug Abuse: Population estimates*. DHHS Pub. No. (ADM) 89-1639. Washington, DC: U.S. Government Printing Office.

(National Institute on Drug Abuse, 1987a). However, results from the 1988 survey, also shown in Table 3, suggested that some slight changes have occurred in the percentage of past-month drug use of most illegal drugs by race/ethnicity groups in the past three years. According to the 1988 survey results, Hispanics were more likely than were white and black non-Hispanics to have used cocaine and analgesics during the past month (National Institute on Drug Abuse, 1989b). It should be noted that past-month use is more indicative than is lifetime use of serious illegal drug use.

Information on the prevalence of illegal drug use among Hispanics was also collected by the 1985 Hispanic Health and Nutrition Examination Survey (HHANES) (National Institute on Drug Abuse, 1987b). The results suggested that the use of illegal drugs varied widely among and within the three major Hispanic groups: Mexican Americans, Cubans, and Puerto Ricans (Figure 1). The findings indicated that Puerto Ricans were twice as likely to have ever used cocaine as were Mexican Americans and Cubans. Both Puerto Ricans and Mexican Americans were twice as likely as were Cubans to have ever used marijuana. On the other hand, Mexican Americans were more likely to have used inhalants than were Puerto Ricans. Data on

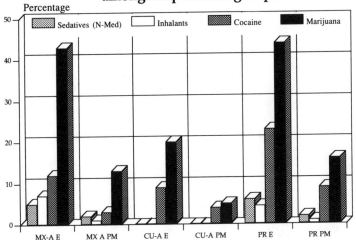

FIGURE 1.
Nonmedical use of licit and illicit drugs among Hispanic subgroups.

Note: MX-A E = Mexican Americans, ever; MX-A PM = Mexican American, past month; CU-A E = Cuban Americans, ever; CU-A PM = Cuban Americans, past month; PR E = Puerto Ricans, ever; PR PM = Puerto Ricans, past month; N-Med = nonmedical use of drugs.

Adapted from National Institute on Drug Abuse. (1987). *Hispanic Health, Nutrition and Examination Survey: Use of selected drugs among Hispanics* (Contract No. 271-84-7308). Washington, DC: U.S. Government Printing Office.

the use of sedatives and inhalants from the HHANES were not available for Cubans (National Institute on Drug Abuse, 1987b).

The results from the 1985 survey also showed that marked differences in the use of cocaine and marijuana existed within the Mexican American and Puerto Rican populations. Data in Table 4 indicate that the use of cocaine and marijuana is highest among Mexican Americans and Puerto Ricans 18–24 years old. Further, Puerto Rican and Mexican American single males between the ages of 18 and 24, whose primary language was English, had the highest prevalence of illegal drug use, whereas Cuban females older than 35 years, who were married and spoke Spanish as their primary language, were the least likely to use illegal drugs. Also, Mexican Americans, Cubans, and Puerto Ricans with incomes above the poverty level were more likely to utilize marijuana and cocaine than were those who lived in poverty (National Institute on Drug Abuse, 1987b).

Several local studies conducted on the use of illicit drugs among Mexican Americans and Puerto Ricans seemed to support

TABLE 4.
Percent of persons using types of illicit drugs
for specified Hispanic groups by age.

Hispanic group	Marijuana		Cocaine		Inhalant		Sedative	
	Ever used	Past month	Ever used	Past month	Ever used	Past month	Ever used	Past month
Mexican Americans								
12–17 years	30.7	10.3	4.2	0.7	4.8	0.7	*	*
18–24 years	56.6	20.7	18.2	4.9	10.2	0.9	4.0	0.7
25–34 years	45.8	11.5	13.1	2.2	5.2	*	5.9	0.6
35–44 years	26.8	4.5	6.7	1.5	*	*	*	*
Puerto Ricans								
12–17 years	25.4	9.4	7.0	2.4	1.9	*	*	*
18–24 years	64.4	25.1	37.2	17.5	8.1	*	3.3	*
25–34 years	56.1	19.9	32.8	12.7	4.9	*	8.4	0.2
35–44 years	25.1	6.2	*	*	*	*	*	*
Cuban Americans								
12–24	20.5	7.3	12.1	*	*	*	*	*
25–44	19.0	4.0	7.4	*	*	*	*	*

* Less than 0.5%; no population estimates made.

Adapted from National Institute on Drug Abuse. (1987). *Hispanic Health, Nutrition and Examination Survey: Use of selected drugs among Hispanics.* (Contract No. 271–84–7308). Washington, DC: U.S. Government Printing Office.

some of the results obtained in these surveys. For example, a study conducted by Padilla, Padilla, Morales, and Olmedo (1979) reported that Mexican American youth aged 12 to 17 were more likely than were their white non-Hispanic counterparts to have ever used inhalants and twice as likely to have used marijuana. Preliminary findings from a 1987 survey by the Hispanic Research Center at Fordham University (Figure 2) indicate that, except for marijuana use, Puerto Rican youngsters living in New York City were more likely than were white non-Hispanic individuals of the same age to use cocaine, hallucinogens, and nonmedically prescribed tranquilizers (O. Rodriguez, personal communication, July 1988).

Consequences of Drug Use for Hispanics

Illegal drug use has been associated with an array of illnesses and injuries that have adversely affected the health status of Hispanics. These negative health-related consequences include fatal and nonfatal drug overdoses, accident injuries, adverse birth outcomes (such as low birth weight and birth defects), suicides, psy-

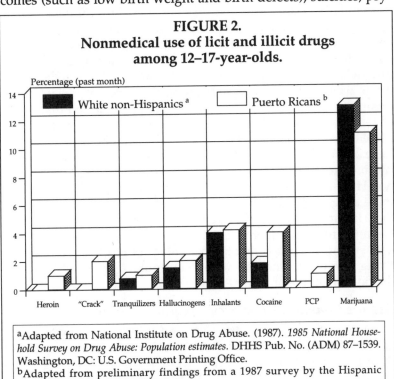

FIGURE 2.
Nonmedical use of licit and illicit drugs among 12–17-year-olds.

Percentage (past month)

White non-Hispanics [a]   Puerto Ricans [b]

Heroin   "Crack"   Tranquilizers   Hallucinogens   Inhalants   Cocaine   PCP   Marijuana

[a]Adapted from National Institute on Drug Abuse. (1987). *1985 National Household Survey on Drug Abuse: Population estimates.* DHHS Pub. No. (ADM) 87–1539. Washington, DC: U.S. Government Printing Office.
[b]Adapted from preliminary findings from a 1987 survey by the Hispanic Research Center, Fordham University.

chiatric problems, and school failure. The following summarizes results from studies that have analyzed the relationship between various negative consequences and drug abuse among Hispanics.

Drug-Related Emergency Room Episodes and Deaths

Results from the National Institute on Drug Abuse (NIDA) 1987 Drug Abuse Warning Network (DAWN) indicated that Hispanics comprised 9.6% of the drug-related emergency room episodes; black non-Hispanics, 37.1%; and white non-Hispanics, 44% (National Institute on Drug Abuse, 1988). The 1987 DAWN data system also reported that although blacks and non-Hispanics comprised a smaller percentage of drug-related emergency room admissions than did white non-Hispanics, a disproportionate percentage of Hispanic and black drug-related admissions were the result of dangerous drugs, that is, drugs that are more capable of causing serious health consequences and/or death. For example, Hispanics accounted for 12.7% of the DAWN emergency episodes due to heroin/morphine, and black non-Hispanics comprised 49.9% of heroin/morphine episodes (Table 5).

Similarly, results from the 1984 and 1987 DAWN data system on drug-related deaths among white non-Hispanics, black non-Hispanics, and Hispanics indicated that cocaine and heroin are the most often mentioned drugs by medical examiners involved in drug-related deaths. However, the frequency with which these two drugs were mentioned varied among the different racial/ethnic groups. The 1984 DAWN data system results indicated that 42.4% of Hispanic drug-related deaths were due to heroin, whereas the percentages of white non-Hispanic and black non-Hispanic deaths were 26.4% and 46.3%, respectively. The percentage of drug-related cocaine deaths in 1987 was 41.5% for Hispanics, 25.2% for white non-Hispanics, and 56.0% for black non-Hispanics. For Hispanics, these drug-related death rates are extremely high if one considers that Hispanics comprise 8.2% of the U.S. mainland population (U.S. Department of Commerce, 1988). Other findings from the DAWN data system suggested that the percentage of Hispanics and blacks dying due to cocaine use more than doubled from 1984 to 1987 (National Institute on Drug Abuse, 1988).

Acquired Immune Deficiency Syndrome (AIDS)

A report released by the Centers for Disease Control (1988) indicated that, as of August 1988, 29.1% of all intravenous (IV) drug users who contracted AIDS were of Hispanic heritage. Furthermore, most of the Hispanic AIDS cases related to IV drug use are concentrated in the New York City–New Jersey greater

TABLE 5.
A comparison of the race/ethnicity distribution for total DAWN emergency room (ER) episodes with the race/ethnicity distribution for selected drugs.

	Race/ethnicity		
	Black	Hispanic	White
Percent of Total DAWN ER episodes	37.1	9.6	44.0
Percent of ER drug mentions for			
Heroin/morphine	49.9	12.7	31.1
Methadone	26.0	17.0	47.4
PCP/PCP combinations	60.4	11.3	22.5
Cocaine	55.1	9.0	28.1
Marijuana/hashish	45.8	7.3	39.8

Adapted from National Institute on Drug Abuse. (1988). *Data from the drug abuse warning network (DAWN)—Annual data 1987*. Statistical Series, Report 1:7, DHHS Pub. No. (ADM) 88-1584. Washington, DC: U.S. Government Printing Office.

metropolitan area. This disproportionately high rate may be related to the high prevalence of heroin use among Hispanics (Mata & Jorquez, 1988). According to the National Coalition of Hispanic Health and Human Service Organizations, if current trends continue, AIDS is likely to claim a larger segment of the Hispanic population, given the expected increase in AIDS cases among IV drug users (COSSMHO, 1987).

Crime and Drugs

Illegal drug use has also been inextricably linked by many Hispanic community leaders and law-enforcement organizations to the high rate of criminal activity found in many Hispanic communities (Moore, 1978; Reed & May, 1984; Moore & Mata, 1981). However, it has only been since the mid-1980s that research has focused on exploring the relationship between illegal drug use and criminal behavior among Hispanics.

In 1981, data from the Crime Analysis Unit of the New York City Police Department indicated that 34.2% of all homicide victims in the city were Hispanic. In 1982, the unit reported that 41.8% of all homicide victims were Hispanic (New York City Police Department, 1982). Furthermore, the findings from a recently completed study on the criminal activities of 285 active female and male adult narcotic addicts living in New York City suggested that Hispanic and black addicts were more likely to be arrested for and/or to report committing certain types of crime more often than were white non-Hispanic addicts (Goldstein, 1988). Hispanic addicts were more likely to report involvement in drug dealing and to be arrested for prostitution than were black or white non-Hispanic drug addicts. Black drug addicts were more likely to be arrested for aggravated assault than were white non-Hispanic or Hispanic addicts and equally as likely as Hispanic addicts to report involvement in drug dealing.

A second study investigated the criminal career of 250 male narcotic addicts in New York City and Baltimore, Maryland, comparing their criminal activities according to racial/ethnic group of origin (Nurco, Shaffer, Ball, Kinlock, & Lengrod, 1986). Results indicated that Hispanic, black, and white non-Hispanic addicts committed more crimes during periods of narcotic addiction than during periods of nonnarcotic addiction. During periods of narcotic addiction, the criminal activities of black and Hispanic addicts did not differ significantly from that of whites. During periods of nonnarcotic addiction, however, blacks were more likely than were Hispanics and white non-Hispanic addicts to commit criminal acts.

The NIDA funded a study that explored the drug-use behavior of Chicano gang members living in east Los Angeles (Moore, 1985). Results indicated that the gang subculture provided both economic and emotional support for young Mexican American adult males who were addicted to or marketed heroin or who go to juvenile and adult correctional facilities. However, socialization into the gang subculture by Mexican American youth often leads many of these youngsters to exposure to drug-dealing activities and drug use and behaviors (Moore, 1985).

Preliminary findings from a study investigating the use of various forms of cocaine among 391 male and female juvenile delinquents from the Miami–Dade County area found some racial/ethnic differences (Inciardi, 1989). Hispanics were more likely to be regular users of cocaine and crack than were black or white non-Hispanics. Hispanic male and black female juvenile delinquents were more likely to have tried cocaine hydrochloride, coca paste, and crack than were black or white non-Hispanics. No data were available on Hispanic females.

Finally, results from a study that sought to analyze the patterns of drug use of 581 Mexican American and white non-Hispanic male narcotic addicts admitted to the California Civil Addict Program (CAP) in 1964–66 found several differences in the drug-use patterns of Mexican American and white non-Hispanic addicts (Anglin, Ryan, Booth, & Hser, 1988). A greater proportion of white non-Hispanics than Mexicans had used hallucinogens, amphetamines, cocaine, and opiates other than heroin or street methadone. Mexicans were younger when they first used inhalants, marijuana, and heroin than were their white non-Hispanic counterparts. Mexican American addicts also used heroin more frequently than did white non-Hispanic addicts.

Drug Abuse and Dropouts

Bruno and Doscher (1979) and Chavez, Edwards, and Oetting (in press) conducted the only studies analyzing the relationship between drug use and school failure among Hispanics. Bruno and Doscher reported that the use of marijuana was higher among Hispanic youngsters who had dropped out of school or who were at risk of dropping out than it was among those who stayed in school. Preliminary findings from the Chavez study revealed that youngsters who identified themselves as school dropouts or students identified as potential school dropouts had a higher rate of illicit drug use than did youth who were still enrolled in school. For example, for males, 33.2% of those who dropped out of school had tried cocaine, compared with 32.3% of the "at-risk" group and 18.3% of the other students. Nine percent of the male dropouts had used cocaine one or two times in the past month, whereas only 8% of the "at-risk" group and 3.3% of the other students had done so. Finally, the rates of being drunk before or during school during the past month for male dropouts and students identified as potential dropouts were almost double that of low-risk students (65% and 54% vs. 38%).

The females in the study, 42% of the dropouts, indicated that they had tried cocaine, compared with 36% for the at-risk group and 13% for the low-risk students. Past-month cocaine use was also higher among the female dropouts and at-risk students than it was among the low-risk students (17% and 12% vs. 0%).

Utilization of Drug-treatment Programs by Hispanics

Admissions to Drug-treatment Programs

Although little information is available on the percentage or characteristics of Hispanics admitted to drug-treatment programs, several national surveys sponsored by NIDA provide some information on this topic. Data from the 1983 National Drug and Alcoholism Treatment Utilization Survey (NDATUS), which collects information on all known private and publicly funded drug-treatment programs and their clients in the United States, indicate that the rate of Hispanic clients in drug- and combined-treatment units per 100,000 persons was similar to that of black non-Hispanics and much higher than that of white non-Hispanics (National Institute on Drug Abuse, 1986a) (Table 6).

Results from the 1983 Client Oriented Data Acquisition Process (CODAP) survey provided additional information on the percentage of Hispanics admitted to drug-treatment facilities by type of illegal drug use and age (National Institute on Drug Abuse, 1986b). The findings (see Table 7) indicated that Hispanic clients were more likely to report a primary problem with heroin and PCP than were either white non-Hispanics, black non-Hispanics, or native Americans. These results are important in that heroin and PCP have been labeled by many health care providers as two of the most dangerous illicit drugs, capable of causing serious health problems and/or death (National Institute on Drug Abuse, 1989a). Other results from the 1983 CODAP survey indicated that Hispanic clients tended to be the youngest for heroin-use admission; 21% of Hispanic clients younger than 25 were admitted as heroin clients compared with 16.1% for white non-Hispanics, 8.2% for black non-Hispanics, and 17.1% for native Americans. Similarly, the percentage of Hispanics younger than 25 admitted to treatment facilities because of a PCP problem was higher than that of their black non-Hispanic, white non-Hispanic, and native American counterparts (73.4%, 47.4%, 63.3%, and 69.8%, respectively). It must be noted that the CO-DAP and NDATUS surveys were done before the outbreak of the cocaine epidemic; thus the reported results may not be representative of the current drug-treatment situation among Hispanics or the other racial/ethnic groups.

The results of the CODAP survey on Hispanic admissions to drug-treatment programs because of heroin problems are corroborated by a number of local surveys. For example, a survey that analyzed the drug-use problem among Mexican Americans living in four border counties

TABLE 6.
Drug-abuse clients in drug- and combined-treatment units per 100,000 population by race/ethnicity.

Race	Rate
Black	203
Hispanic	200
White	68
Total	**93**

Adapted from National Institute on Drug Abuse. (1986). *Data from the National Drug and Alcoholism Treatment Utilization Survey (NDATUS): Main findings for drug abuse treatment units.* Statistical Series, Report F:10, DHHS Pub. No. (ADM) 83-1284. Washington, DC: U.S. Government Printing Office.

TABLE 7.
Percent distribution of clients by primary drug according to race/ethnicity CODAP, 1983.

Primary Drug	White	Black	Hispanic	Native American
Heroin	43.8	60.3	70.6	44.8
Other opiates	8.5	3.4	1.0	2.3
Marijuana	19.1	12.0	13.0	27.4
Barbiturates	2.0	1.2	0.5	1.0
Amphetamines	9.0	2.9	1.2	5.6
Cocaine	8.3	9.7	2.8	5.0
PCP	2.2	7.1	7.8	5.0
Other hallucinogens	1.5	0.3	0.3	1.5
Tranquilizers	2.0	0.7	0.3	1.0
Other sedatives	2.2	0.5	0.3	1.2
Other	1.5	1.9	2.1	5.2
Total	98,504	40,538	40,625	862

Note: Based on 23 states, Washington, DC, and territories. California represented 46% of treatment admissions.

Adapted from National Institute on Drug Abuse. (1986). *Demographic characteristics and patterns of drug use of clients admitted to drug abuse treatment facilities in selected states: Annual data 1983.* DHHS Pub. No. (ADM) 271-84-7308. Washington, DC: U.S. Government Printing Office.

in Texas suggested that Mexican American admissions to drug-treatment programs as a result of a heroin problem were higher than those of white non-Hispanics (43.1% vs. 33.7%, respectively) (Adams, 1986). Another survey conducted by the State of New York on the number of Hispanics admitted to drug-treatment facilities in New York City reported similar results. For the first part of 1987, 46% of admissions for treatment of heroin were Hispanics, a much higher percentage than the estimated percentage of Hispanics living in New York City (Frank, Hopkins, & Lipton, 1988).

Despite the information now available on Hispanic admissions into drug-treatment programs, researchers continue to argue that treatment programs are inaccessible to Hispanics (Moore & Mata, 1981). They attribute this inaccessibility to the fact that drug-treatment services are oriented toward meeting the needs of the white non-Hispanic and, to a lesser extent, black non-Hispanic populations. This lack of sensitivity to the needs of Hispanics may be the cause of low retention rates for Hispanics who enter drug-treatment programs. Obeso and Bordatto (1979), De La Rosa (1987), and Delgado (1980) suggested that for drug-treatment programs to be more accessible and effective in treating the drug-use problems of Hispanic clients, health care professionals should recognize the importance of the family and cultural values such as *respeto* (respect), *dignidad* (dignity), and *orgullo* (pride) when providing drug-treatment services to Hispanics. Involving the family in the counseling process may have a positive influence on the treatment outcome of Hispanic clients undergoing drug treatment (Delgado & Humm-Delgado, 1982). Similarly, integrating some of the traditional values of Hispanics into the different phases of the counseling process (assessment, engagement, intervention, termination, and follow-up) can result in more effective delivery of drug-treatment services to Hispanic clients.

Moore and Mata's assertions that drug-treatment services are inaccessible to Hispanics are supported by a recent study that explored the drug-use behavior and criminal activities of serious juvenile delinquents living in Miami, Florida (Inciardi, 1989). The findings suggested that although all the youth in the sample (Hispanics, white non-Hispanics, and black non-Hispanics) were seriously involved in drug and alcohol use, Hispanic youth were less likely to seek treatment for their substance-abuse problem than were either their white or black non-Hispanic counterparts.

Summary and Recommendations

Changes have occurred in the prevalence of illegal drug use among Hispanics in the past three years. Although lifetime drug-use rates remain lower for Hispanics than for white non-Hispanics and black non-Hispanics, rates for Hispanics in the use of a specific illicit drug—cocaine—have increased significantly. The 1988 NHSDA results suggested that Hispanics have a higher lifetime rate of cocaine use than do white non-Hispanics and black non-Hispanics. Other results from the survey indicate that significant changes have occurred in the lifetime use of cocaine among Hispanics between the ages of 26 and 34 and among Hispanic females. Moreover, the 1985 HHANES and a number of local epidemiological studies suggest that the use of illegal drugs varies widely among Hispanics according to the type of drug, level of use, specific Hispanic subgroup, age, gender, and even degree of acculturation into American society. Puerto Rican and Mexican American male adolescents born in the United States, whose primary language is English, were found to be the most vulnerable to using illegal drugs. This result is significant when one considers that approximately 75% of the mainland U.S. Puerto Rican population and 60% of all Mexican Americans are younger than 30 (McKay, 1982).

Studies on the patterns of drug use among Hispanics suggest that cocaine, heroin, PCP, and inhalants are the drugs most often used by Hispanics, which is distressing given the fact that research suggests that these drugs cause physical harm and are closely associated with violent behavior (Moore & Mata, 1981; Goldstein, 1985). The drug-use pattern of Hispanics may partly explain the high admission rates of Hispanics into drug-treatment facilities, with heroin, cocaine, PCP, and/or inhalants reported as the primary drug. Moreover, the high incidence of AIDS cases and crime among Hispanics can be blamed in part on their use of illegal drugs.

When analyzing the drug use of Hispanics, one must exercise caution. The surveys and local studies mentioned in this chapter have limitations. For example, because of sample weakness, the findings of the 1985 HHANES were limited in scope and usefulness. Failure to include Hispanics living in the Midwest, lack of subjects in many of the survey cells, and exclusion of Hispanics older than 45 from the illegal drug use section of the survey limit the ability of the survey to determine accurately the extent of the problem.

Other, less empirically based information needs to be used when analyzing the drug-use problem of Hispanics. For example, the relationship between the low socioeconomic and educational status of Hispanics and their drug-use behavior remains largely unexplored. Further, the impact of racial discrimination, acculturation-related stress, and the disintegration of the Hispanic extended-family system upon drug-use behavior has received little attention in the literature (De La Rosa, 1987).

Little information is available regarding the effectiveness of drug-prevention and treatment models designed to address the drug problem of the Hispanic population. Preliminary results from evaluations conducted on various community-based drug-use prevention, education, and outpatient treatment programs funded by the U.S. Department of Health and Human Services, Office of Substance Abuse Prevention, are beginning to provide information on "what works" with Hispanics. Programs that involve the extended-family system and other natural support systems and that recognize the adverse environmental conditions faced by Hispanic youth and their families (racism, acculturation-related stress, poverty) are more likely to provide effective services to this population (Office of Substance Abuse Prevention, 1989). For example, results of a study of an outreach, prevention, and drug-treatment program designed to serve Hispanic youth who were at risk of using drugs and/or in the earliest stages of drug use suggested that involvement of the family and other significant members of the community in program activities (e.g., recreation programs, church activities) was critical to the success of the program. Youth who had family support were more likely to improve their self-esteem and thus become less vulnerable to drug use than were those who received little or no support from their families (Office of Substance Abuse Prevention, 1989). Similarly, a five-year study conducted under the auspices of the National Institute for Mental Health suggested that Hispanic children who have behavior problems and who may be at risk of becoming substance abusers evidenced better treatment outcomes when a family-oriented as opposed to individual-treatment approach was used (Szapocznik, Santisteban, Rio, Perez-Vidal, & Kurtines, 1989).

We need accurate and reliable information on the nature and extent of drug problems among Hispanics. The following types of studies and surveys should be initiated:

◆ Cross-sectional surveys and/or longitudinal studies to determine (1) the extent of the nonmedical use of licit and illicit drugs and related social and health problems among and within the various Hispanic subgroups according to type of drug use, age, gender, and socioeconomic status and (2) whether the drug-use behavior of Hispanic females is changing and, if it is changing, what are the factors affecting this change.

◆ Ethnographic and longitudinal studies to investigate (1) the role of cultural values and factors such as *machismo* (manliness), *fatalism* (fatalism), *respeto* (respect), *verguenza* (shame), *orgullo* (pride), *confianza* (trustworthiness), religious orientation, and general attitudes in the drug-use behavior of Hispanic subgroups; (2) the role of acculturation-related stress; (3) the cultural and historical differences among Mexican Americans, Puerto Ricans, Cubans, and South and Central Americans and whether these differences are related to the drug-use behavior patterns that have been reported for the Hispanic subgroups; and (4) the role of social support systems (family, religious institutions, and indigenous institutions such as the *compadrazco* [godparenting] system).

◆ Cross-sectional surveys and/or longitudinal studies to determine the accessibility and availability of drug-treatment services for Hispanic subgroups, reasons for their admission to treatment facilities, and effectiveness of cultural-specific prevention and drug-treatment programs.

◆ Cross-sectional surveys or ethnographic studies to investigate (1) the relationship between gang membership and drug use, including the process through which Hispanic youngsters become involved in gangs, and (2) the relationship between crime and drugs among Hispanics and whether it differs from that among blacks and whites.

The U.S. Hispanic population is rapidly growing, and its presence in the social, economic, and political life of the United States will become increasingly prominent. If society fails to address the drug-use problem among Hispanics, the results could be disastrous for Hispanics and non-Hispanics alike.

Notes

1. For the purpose of discussion, in this chapter U.S. Hispanics include Mexican Americans, Cubans, Puerto Ricans, and South and Central Americans living in the mainland United States. Because little or no information exists about the illicit drug-use behavior of South and Central Americans residing in the United States, this review concentrates on analyzing the drug-use behavior of the first three Hispanic subgroups, which comprise approximately 85% of the Hispanic population living in the mainland United States (U.S. Department of Commerce, 1985). Mexican Americans and Cubans, in particular those who arrived in the United States after 1980, and Puerto Ricans share some common immigrant experiences and socioeconomic problems, which may help to explain their drug-use behavior. Puerto Ricans living in Puerto Rico were excluded from this review because either little or no epidemiological data on their drug-use behavior exist, they are not included in most of the major U.S. epidemiological drug-use surveys, and because their special political, economic, and social ties to the United States are considered by many to indicate a population group that needs to be studied separately (Ford Foundation, 1984).

2. Opinions expressed in this manuscript are those of the authors and do not necessarily reflect the opinions or official policy of the National Institute on Drug Abuse or any other part of the U.S. Department of Health and Human Services.

References

Adams, E. H. (1986, April). *An overview of drug use in the United States and along the U.S. Mexico border*. Paper presented at the U.S. Mexico Border Public Health Association Meeting, Monterey, Mexico.

Anglin, M. D., Ryan, M. T., Booth, M. V., & Hser, Y. (1988). Ethnic differences in narcotic addiction: Part I, characteristics of Chicano and Anglo methadone maintenance clients. *International Journal of Addictions, 23*(2), 125–149.

Bruno, J., & Doscher, L. (1979). Patterns of drug use among Mexican-American potential dropouts. *Journal of Drug Education, 9*(1), 1–10.

Centers for Disease Control. (1988, September 5). *Weekly surveillance report, United States programs*. Atlanta: Author.

Chavez, E., Edwards, R., & Oetting, E. R. (in press). *Preliminary findings from a report on drug use among Mexican-American dropouts*. Submitted to the National Institute on Drug Abuse, Rockville, MD.

COSSMHO. (1987, December). COSSMHO AIDS program advances. *The COSS-MHO Reporter*, p. 6.

De La Rosa, M. (1987, June). *Toward the development of better counseling approaches for Puerto Ricans*. Paper presented at the 1987 Annual Conference on Minority Issues of the National Association of Social Workers. Washington, DC.

De La Rosa, M., Rouse, B., & Kalsa, J. (in press). Illicit drug use among Hispanics: A review of recent findings. *International Journal of Addictions*.

Delgado, M. (1980). Consultation to a Puerto Rican drug abuse program. *American Journal of Drug and Alcohol Abuse, 7*(1), 63–72.

Delgado, M., & Humm-Delgado, D. (1982). Natural support systems: Source of strength in Hispanic communities. *Social Work, 27*, 83–89.

Ford Foundation. (1984). *Hispanics: Challenges and opportunities, a working paper*. New York: Author.

Frank, B., Hopkins, W., & Lipton, D. (1988). *Current drug trends in New York City*. New York Division of Substance Abuse, Albany, NY.

Goldstein, P. J. (1985). The drugs/violence nexus: A tripartite conceptual framework. *Journal of Drug Issues, 15*(4), 493–506.

Goldstein, P. J. (1988). *Drug related involvement in violent episodes*. Unpublished report, Narcotic and Drug Research, Inc., New York.

Inciardi, J. A. (1989). *Drug use and serious delinquency*. Unpublished manuscript, Preliminary National Institute on Drug Abuse grant report.

Mata, A., & Jorquez, J. (1988). Mexican American intravenous drug users: Implications for AIDS prevention. In R. Battjes & R. Pickens (Eds.), *Needle sharing among intravenous drug users: National and international perspective* (pp. 40–58). Monograph 80, DHHS Pub. No. (ADM) 88-1567. Washington, DC: U.S. Government Printing Office.

McKay, E. (1982). *A compendium of data on Hispanic-Americans*. Washington, DC: National Council of La Raza.

McKay, E. (1987). *The changing demographics of the Hispanic family*. Washington, DC: National Council of La Raza.

Moore, J. (1978). *Homeboys*. Philadelphia: Temple University Press.

Moore, J. (1985). Isolation and stigmatization in the development of an underclass: The case of Chicano gangs in East Los Angeles. *Social Problems, 33*, 1–12.

Moore, J., & Mata, A. (1981). Women and heroin in Chicano communities. Unpublished manuscript.

National Institute on Drug Abuse. (1986a). *Data from the National Drug and Alcoholism Treatment Utilization Survey (NDATUS): Main findings for drug abuse treatment units*. Statistical Series, Report F:10, DHHS Pub. No. (ADM) 83-1284. Washington, DC: U.S. Government Printing Office.

National Institute on Drug Abuse. (1986b). *Demographic characteristics and patterns of drug use of clients admitted to drug abuse treatment facilities in selected states: Annual data 1983*. DHHS Pub. No. (ADM) 271-84-7308. Washington, DC: U.S. Government Printing Office.

National Institute on Drug Abuse. (1987a). *1985 National Household Survey on Drug Abuse: Population estimates*. DHHS Pub. No. (ADM) 87-1539. Washington, DC: U.S. Government Printing Office.

National Institute on Drug Abuse. (1987b). *Hispanic Health, Nutrition and Examination Survey: Use of selected drugs among Hispanics* (Contract No. 271-84-7308). Washington, DC: U.S. Government Printing Office.

National Institute on Drug Abuse. (1988). *Data from the Drug Abuse Warning Network (DAWN)—Annual data 1987*. Statistical Series, Report 1:7, DHHS Pub. No. (ADM) 88-1584. Washington, DC: U.S. Government Printing Office.

National Institute on Drug Abuse. (1989a). *Drug abuse among race/ethnic minorities.* Unpublished report, National Institute on Drug Abuse, Rockville, MD.

National Institute on Drug Abuse. (1989b). *1988 National Household Survey on Drug Abuse: Population estimates.* DHHS Pub. No. (ADM) 89-1639. Washington, DC: U.S. Government Printing Office.

New York City Police Department. (1982). *Homicide analysis.* Crime Analysis Unit, New York.

Nurco, D. N., Shaffer, J. W., Ball, J. C., Kinlock, T. W., & Langrod, E. (1986). A comparison by ethnic group and city of the criminal activities of narcotic addicts. *Journal of Nervous Disorders and Mental Health, 174*(2), 112–117.

Obeso, P., & Bordatto, O. (1979). Cultural implications in treating Puerto Rican females. *American Journal of Drug and Alcohol Abuse, 6*(3), 337–344.

Office of Substance Abuse Prevention. (1989). *Report from work group meeting on Hispanic high risk youth.* Rockville, MD: Author.

Padilla, E. R., Padilla, A. M., Morales, A., & Olmedo, E. L. (1979). Inhalant, marijuana, and alcohol abuse among barrio children and adolescents. *International Journal of Addictions, 14*(7), 943–964.

Reed, B. J., & May, P. A. (1984). Inhalant abuse and juvenile delinquency: A control study in Albuquerque, New Mexico. *International Journal of Addictions, 19*(7), 789–803.

Szapocznik, J., Santisteban, D., Rio, A., Perez-Vidal, D., & Kurtines, W. (1989). Family effectiveness training: An intervention to prevent drug abuse and problem behaviors in Hispanic youth. *Hispanic Journal of Behavioral Sciences, 6,* 317–344.

U.S. Department of Commerce, Bureau of the Census. (1985). *Persons of Spanish origin in the United States* (Series P-20, No. 403). Washington, DC: U.S. Government Printing Office.

U.S. Department of Commerce, Bureau of the Census. (1988). *The Hispanic population in the United States: Current population reports* (Series P-20, No. 431. Washington, DC: U.S. Government Printing Office.

U.S. Department of Health and Human Services. (1985). *Report of the secretary's task force on black and minority health.* DHHS Pub. No. 85-487. Washington, DC: U.S. Government Printing Office.

4

AIDS: A Challenge to Hispanics and Their Families

Fernando I. Soriano

Hispanics are a diverse population, ethnically, culturally, and in terms of their geographic origin. However, although diverse, all Hispanics have one thing in common: as a population they are currently disproportionately being affected by AIDS and human immunodeficiency virus (HIV).

The virus is responsible for the development of AIDS. It is passed on only through the exchange of blood, semen, or vaginal fluids. It is not transmitted through tears, sweat, urine, feces, or saliva. Infection with HIV occurs through any of the following methods: (1) sharing needles and syringes with an infected person, common among intravenous (IV) drug users, (2) unprotected sexual activity with infected individuals, wherein blood, semen, or vaginal fluids are exchanged, (3) transmission to children from infected mothers during pregnancy, childbirth, or breast feeding, or (4) through transfusions of infected blood (COSSMHO, 1989).

The proportion of Hispanic AIDS cases is nearly twice that of their representation in the U.S. population. Hispanics make up 8.2% of the U.S. population, yet they currently represent 15.6% of all AIDS cases. Furthermore, Hispanic women, men, and children with AIDS are likewise overrepresented within their respective gender and age categories (Amaro, 1987). Forty-one percent of Hispanics with AIDS contracted the disease through homosexual contact, but an ever-increasing number—currently 46%—contract it from heterosexual contact (Centers for Disease Control, 1990b). These staggering statistics indicate that AIDS is a serious problem for Hispanics of all ages and of both genders. Hence, for Hispanics, AIDS is not just an individual problem, but a family problem as well.

This chapter provides an overview of AIDS among Hispanics. An attempt is made to point out the effects of AIDS on Hispanic families and to suggest ways that society, the family, and culture can be called upon to address this health problem.

AIDS and the Family

Altogether, there were 24,545 Hispanic AIDS cases in the United States as of October 1990 (Centers for Disease Control, 1990a). This number represents a 46% increase from February 1989, when only 13,300 Hispanic cases were reported (Fimbres & McKay, 1989). Statistics make it clear that AIDS is not a problem of individuals, but of entire families. One reason for this is that Hispanics are more likely to rely on families for assistance and support in times of crisis (Sabogal, Marin, Otero-Sabogal, Marin, & Perez-Stable, 1987). Thus, AIDS cases weigh heavily on Hispanic families—emotionally, financially, and otherwise. However, AIDS is also a family concern because it affects all family members—fathers, mothers, and, in ever-increasing numbers, children.

Males and AIDS

Even with the increase in the number of females with AIDS, males are still more likely to contract AIDS than are females. Eighty-seven percent of adult Hispanics with AIDS are males and 13% are female. As of September 1990, among Hispanic male adults with AIDS, 46% contracted AIDS through homosexual or bisexual contact, compared with 80% of whites with AIDS. However, a large and growing number of Hispanics are becoming infected through intravenous injections, usually when taking drugs. In this regard, as an ethnic group, Hispanics stand in contrast with non-Hispanic whites. Approximately 46% of Hispanics contracted AIDS through IV drug use, compared with only 13% of whites. In contrast with Hispanic women, Hispanic males at present rarely contract HIV through heterosexual contact. Heterosexual contact with other HIV-infected persons accounted for only 1% of Hispanic males with AIDS, whereas the comparable percent for Hispanic females infected through sex with males was 37% (Centers for Disease Control, 1990b).

Females and AIDS

The increased number of women with AIDS has drawn greater attention to the effect of this disease on females. This increased attention to women has led to several concerns. One of the more important concerns is our lack of medical understanding of the disease's impact on women. Several of the typical symptoms associated with HIV infection and AIDS in men are somewhat different from those of women. For example, it is common for HIV-positive women to experience chronic vaginitis, such as yeast infections, as well as symptoms associated with pelvic inflammatory disease such as inflammation of the uterus, fallopian tubes, and ovaries. These symptoms call for specialized medical care, and health care providers need to recognize that these symptoms may indicate HIV infection. According to Denenberg (1990), the lack of adequate understanding of AIDS symptoms experienced by women has led health care professionals to a misdiagnosis or late diagnosis of the disease. This, in turn, is believed to be responsible for women with AIDS dying twice as quickly as do men with AIDS.

Clearly, more funding is needed for research on the medical condition of women with HIV infection and AIDS so that medical care can be improved for this group. Such research is important because the symptoms associated with AIDS in women have implications for the way AIDS is officially defined, which, in turn, affects our count of women with AIDS. Furthermore, the health care and social service benefits available to women with AIDS are adversely affected, because individuals need to fit the current definition of AIDS to be eligible for many medical and social service benefits (including Social Security benefits).

These problems pose a particular challenge to Hispanic women, who are proportionately more likely to be affected by AIDS than are white women. Among all Hispanic AIDS cases, 12.5% are women, compared with 4.6% among whites with AIDS. As of September 1990, contracting AIDS through IV drug use accounted for approximately half (51%) of Hispanic females with AIDS, compared with 40% of white females with AIDS. Having sex with infected IV drug users accounted for an additional 30% among Hispanic women with AIDS, compared with only 15% of white females. Together, IV-related AIDS cases comprised about two-thirds of all AIDS cases among Hispanic females, compared with slightly more than half for white females (55%).

Children and AIDS

Although the total number of Hispanics with AIDS has significantly increased, children with AIDS (younger than 13 years old) and women showed the greatest increases over the past year. For example, from December 1989 to October 1990, the number of Hispanic children with AIDS increased by 42%. This compares with 29% for white and African American children over this same period.

Overall, Hispanic children comprise 26% of all pediatric AIDS cases, although they make up less than 11% of the total population of children that age. Of all non-Hispanic whites with AIDS, less than 1% are children. Hispanic children, however, make up 2.8% of all Hispanic AIDS cases (Centers for Disease Control, 1990a).

Drug use is heavily implicated in the spread of AIDS among Hispanic children and youth. Contraction through mothers using infected needles for drugs accounted for the majority of Hispanic pediatric AIDS cases (44%) and another 27% resulted from mothers having sex with IV drug users. In all, drug use was implicated in 71% of all Hispanic pediatric AIDS cases (Centers for Disease Control, 1990a).

Adolescents and AIDS

One study revealed that Hispanic teens knew less about AIDS transmission and prevention than did other groups (DiClemente, Boyer, & Morales, 1988). Yet adolescent sexual experimentation and behavior place them at risk for exposure to HIV infection (Nader, Wexler, Patterson, McKusick, & Coates, 1989). Currently, only 1% of people with AIDS are younger than 20 years of age, but seropositivity in adolescents is likely to be higher. Because 21% of current AIDS cases are persons between the ages of 20 and 29 and HIV has a long incubation period (an average of five years), many of the current young adult AIDS cases in this age range were adolescents at the time of infection.

Nader et al. (1989) reported the findings of three recent surveys that showed adolescents (11–14 years old) are becoming more knowledgeable about AIDS. They indicated that 51% learned about AIDS and HIV infection from TV and radio, whereas 16% became informed through magazines or newspapers. However, these studies still showed several knowledge gaps. In a 1986 phone survey not specific to Hispanic youth, only 15% of sexually active adolescents claimed to have changed their behavior due to educational campaigns, and only 10% said they use condoms. These findings cannot be generalized to Hispanic adolescents. Clearly, more research is needed on the attitudes, beliefs, and practices of Hispanic adolescents.

In general, these figures on gender and children show that AIDS is indeed affecting all members of Hispanic families and to a greater extent than among whites. It is also clear that for Hispanics, AIDS affects heterosexuals to about the same extent as it does homosexuals, which stands in contrast with the white population. These statistics show that the problem of the spread of AIDS among Hispanics needs to be treated separately. Several factors influencing the spread of this disease among Hispanics need to be considered. One of the most important factors is the spread of AIDS through IV drug use.

Considerations in the Spread of AIDS

Spread of AIDS through IV Use

As the preceding data suggest, the sharing of IV needles is responsible for many of the AIDS cases among Hispanics. However, it is important to note that the spread of AIDS through sharing of IV needles is not due only to illicit drug use. Hispanics share IV needles for reasons other than for illegitimate drug abuse. For example, some Hispanics in the U.S. use needles and syringes for ear piercing and for injecting vitamins and medications (Compagnet, 1987). This practice is particularly common among new arrivals to the United States. One reason for the common use of IV needles is that injectable prescription and over-the-counter medicines are commonly available in Latin American countries. A study in San Francisco found that 13% of Hispanic respondents occasionally injected medicine and vitamins in the home (Fairbank, Bregman, & Maullin, Inc., 1987), and some evidence suggests that family vitamin injection has spread HIV (Koenig, Gantier, & Levy, 1986). Furthermore, a survey of San Francisco Hispanics found that most did not identify injection of vitamins and medicines in the home as a possible method of HIV transmission (Marin & Marin, 1989).

Although the use and sharing of needles for legitimate purposes is a concern, the sharing of needles for drug abuse is a greater concern. Drug abuse among Hispanics tends to be greater in communities with fewer opportunities to make money. Hispanic drug users appear to be infected with HIV at higher rates than are non-Hispanic white drug users (Chaisson, Moss, & Onishi, 1987). This is thought to be due to the economic difficulties of obtaining clean syringes as well as substance-use patterns of Hispanics, who favor drugs requiring IV administration, such as heroin (B. Marin, 1989).

Knowledge

A statewide survey of California adults revealed that Hispanics had less information about AIDS than did any other group (study cited in B. Marin, 1989). Marin and Marin (1989) found that Hispanics in San Francisco were aware that HIV could be transmitted sexually and through needle sharing, but often believed that the virus could be transmitted casually as well. Many respondents in the survey were unaware that a person could look healthy and have AIDS. In general, they found that Hispanics have more misconceptions about AIDS than do other population groups.

Acculturation

The concept of acculturation has been used to show how Hispanics differ among themselves (Padilla, 1980). *Acculturation* refers to the functional adoption of mainstream values, while keeping some traditional cultural values. Marin and Marin (1989) found that the less acculturated tend to speak Spanish and have more Hispanic friends than do the more acculturated. Acculturation has been shown to be closely associated with health behavior and education (B. Marin, 1989). For example, highly acculturated Hispanics more commonly use drugs (Smith-Peterson, 1983). Acculturation levels also bear on children. Children of immigrants, being more acculturated than their parents, are more likely to be involved with drug use than are immigrants (Santisteban & Szapocznik, 1982). Moreover, acculturation bears on all Hispanic subgroups and has implications for the spread of AIDS. For instance, the majority of Puerto Ricans with AIDS who were born in Puerto Rico contracted the disease through IV drug use and heterosexual contact (Selik, Castro, Pappaioanou, & Buehler, 1989).

In a telephone survey done in San Francisco, acculturation was strongly associated with knowledge about AIDS—with the less acculturated generally having many more erroneous beliefs about "casual" transmission and being less aware that someone can be affected without looking ill (Marin, 1990; Marin & Marin, 1990). Acculturation differences persisted even after controlling for education. In this same study, the more acculturated Hispanics had more accurate information about AIDS and HIV transmission. Another study by Marin and Marin (1989) had similar findings. In the later study, the researchers found that the less-acculturated individuals in San Francisco had less accurate information about HIV transmission than did the more highly acculturated. B. Marin (1989) concluded that campaigns seeking to educate the Hispanic community about AIDS should target messages to less-acculturated Hispanics (i.e., those who speak Spanish). Moreover, it was recommended that schools teach about the nature of the virus and emphasize ways in which the virus is not transmitted.

Homophobia

Homophobia refers to the strong attitudinal and emotional rejection of individuals preferring intimate relations and commitments with persons of the same sex. According to Carrier (1976, 1985), Hispanic culture includes a powerful homophobic component. One indication of this is that Spanish has no nonpejorative equivalent to the word "gay." In an unpublished study conducted in Chicago, Hispanics were found to be more homophobic than were non-Hispanic whites but less homophobic than African Americans (reported in Carrier, 1976). Commonly, Hispanic men who have sex with other men continue to consider themselves heterosexual, not homosexual (Carrier, 1985; Ronquillo, 1987). This has important implications for informational campaigns that are directed specifically to homosexuals, or "gays," because they may be ignored by Hispanic males engaging in sex with other men.

Risky Behavior

Fairbank et al. (1987) found that substantial numbers of Hispanics in San Francisco reported anal sex with either male or female partners within the past month. Of those who indicated having sex with only one partner, only 5% used a condom. Among those with one or more partners, only 11% used condoms. This study suggested that the rate of anal sex may be high in this community because of the importance placed on sexual pleasure by males and because of the contraceptive nature of anal sex.

Condom Use

Promotion of condoms is likely to be difficult among Hispanic men, who associate condoms with prostitutes. A study in Bogota, Colombia, found that men used condoms more often for sexual activities outside marriage than for marital sex (Daily, Lopez-Escovar, & Estrada, 1973). Studies show Hispanics in the United States also have a pattern of infrequent condom use. In 1982, the National Survey of Family Growth showed that a much lower proportion of Hispanics reported ever using condoms (39.5%) than did non-Hispanics (52.8%) (National Council for Health Statistics, 1986).

Some problems that occur in promoting the use of condoms by Hispanics are their association not only with prostitution, but with perceived physical discomfort, diminished sensation, and inconvenience (Marin & Marin, 1989). The reluctance of Hispanics to use condoms is not necessarily related to a reluctance to practice birth control, because even among Catholics, Hispanics are as likely to practice birth control as are non-Hispanics—despite the

Catholic Church's official prohibition against it (National Council for Health Statistics, 1986). A study by B. Marin (1989) found that among married Hispanic women, 14% used condoms for birth control, compared with 25% of non-Hispanic women. Even so, Sabagh (1980) suggested that campaigns to promote condom use may be impeded by many Hispanics' desires for large families. Efforts to promote the use of condoms by Hispanics will need to be directed at changing the associative connotations of condoms and stressing their importance in abating the spread of AIDS and other sexually transmitted diseases.

Health Care Issues

Testing for the Virus

Early diagnosis is critical to more effective treatment of HIV infection and AIDS. Inadequate information about testing is one factor responsible for the late diagnosis of the disease and the shorter life span of persons with HIV. Unfortunately, at-risk Hispanics are less likely than are non-Hispanics to get tested for the presence of HIV. Information is lacking about specific reasons Hispanics do not get tested at earlier stages of the disease. However, several reasons are likely. One is the geographic inaccessibility of testing sites to Hispanics. Most current testing sites are located either in hospitals or in health clinics, which typically are inaccessible geographically to Hispanic communities.

Another barrier to testing is language. The U.S. Bureau of the Census (1983) reported that from 30% to 60% of Hispanics speak or prefer to speak only in Spanish. Yet many of the testing clinics lack Spanish-speaking staff. The language problem becomes even more serious when counseling seropositive Hispanics who are monolingual Spanish speakers. But perhaps the most important reason Hispanics do not seek AIDS testing is lack of information and education about AIDS and about those behaviors that put them at risk of contracting the disease.

Medical Coverage

Even before the AIDS crisis, Hispanics experienced problems with availability of and access to adequate health care (U.S. Department of Health and Human Services, 1986). The increasing number of Hispanics with AIDS is exacerbating an already critical health care problem. For example, Hispanics continue to be less likely than any other minority group to have medical insurance (U.S. Department of Health and Human Services, 1986). Approximately one-third of Hispanics lack either private health insurance or coverage through a governmental health program such as Medicare or Medicaid, compared with 11% of the general population (Anderson, Lewis, & Giachello, 1981).

The poor health coverage of Hispanics is due to several factors. One factor is the occupational status of Hispanics. Hispanics are more likely to hold jobs that pay less and are more marginal than those of non-Hispanics. Currently, 46% of employed male Hispanics and 42% of female Hispanics work as operators, fabricators, and laborers or in service-related occupations, compared with 29.3% and 25.4% of non-Hispanics, respectively. Only 12.1% of Hispanics are employed in professional or managerial occupations, which usually offer health insurance (U.S. Bureau of the Census, 1990). Moreover, many Hispanics are unemployed and are overrepresented in part-time positions, which are also associated with limited or no insurance coverage (U.S. Department of Health and Human Services, 1986).

Other Barriers to Health Care

Other factors limit Hispanics' access to health care, including awareness/information, physical distance, language barriers, and cultural insensitivity among health care providers. In the report *Black and Minority Health*, by the U.S. Department of Health and Human Services (1986), it was suggested that an important factor in the limited use of health care facilities by Hispanics is a basic lack of awareness of the services available and the benefits of good health practices. However, this same report suggested that community health centers are not adequately prepared to interact effectively with Hispanics. Community health centers need bilingual and bicultural staff so that health information is targeted to Hispanics. Other suggestions in this comprehensive report included developing health care promotion messages and health care services for Hispanics that are delivered within a social and people-centered frame of reference. Moreover, the report suggested that Hispanics prefer to receive medical treatment by a general practitioner rather than from a multitude of specialists.

Combined, all of these barriers hinder Hispanics in seeking health care, particularly those affected by AIDS. Minority health advocates have called attention to the difficulty of obtaining drug treatments experienced by ethnic minority persons with AIDS or HIV. Few medical treatments are available for persons with AIDS or HIV, and many of the promising drug treatments are still in the experimental or testing stage. These treatments represent AIDS patients' only hope, but opportunities to receive new medications are limited to those participating in studies through clinical trials.

Clinical Trials

In general, treatment costs and few opportunities to participate in clinical trials are largely responsible for the lack of adequate medical treatment for Hispanics with AIDS. Several experimental drugs, such as Dideoxynosine or Dideoxycytidine, have been shown to slow down the degenerative process among HIV-infected persons. However, many of them are available only through clinical trials. Until now, both ethnic minorities and women have been largely excluded from clinical trials either because research hospitals are inaccessible to them and/or because researchers prefer white male subjects.

Women are also commonly excluded because of ethical and legal questions concerning risks to their reproductive functions (Public Health Services, 1988). The government's official technical definition of an AIDS patient also excludes women from participating in clinical trials. The current definition is based on the symptoms common to male AIDS patients. However, many of women's early physical symptoms of AIDS are specifically gynecological, such as pelvic inflammatory disease (Denenberg, 1990).

The availability of only a few therapeutic drugs for AIDS makes it imperative that Hispanics and women with AIDS have fair access to experimental vaccines and therapeutic agents.

Intervention Efforts: Focus on Family and Culture

Prevention

Although Hispanics are heterogeneous, social scientists have pointed to a number of cultural values that are shared by most Hispanics, regardless of country of origin. According to G. Marin (1989), Hispanic cultural values, such as familism, need to be taken into consideration in developing effective AIDS-prevention programs for Hispanics. Selection of wording and channels of communication need to be considered. Clearly, many Hispanics lack information about the protection against HIV infection offered by condoms. A study found that slightly more than half of the respondents mentioned the use of condoms as a possible means of protection from HIV infection (Fairbank et al., 1987).

Familism

Familism is one of the most salient and strongest cultural values among Hispanics. Familism refers to the strong identification with and attachment of individuals to their nuclear and extended families; it involves strong feelings of loyalty, reciprocity, and solidarity among family members (Triandis, Marin, Betancourt, Lisanski, & Chang, 1982). According to social scientists, the family is the most important institution for Chicanos (Alvirez & Bean, 1976), Puerto Ricans (Glazer & Moynihan, 1963), Cuban Americans (Szapocznik & Kurtines, 1980), and Central and South Americans (Cohen, 1979).

In addressing AIDS issues among Hispanics, familism can be both a hindrance and an asset to stopping the disease. For example, loyalty to the family is a strong value for the majority of Hispanics, and personal issues and problems are considered private family matters (Brown, Oliver, & de Alva, 1985).

In a study of the differences between 218 Hispanics and 201 non-Hispanics concerning talking to a relative at risk for HIV infection, Marin, Marin, and Juarez (1990) found that Hispanics were more willing than were non-Hispanics to talk to a relative about methods of preventing HIV transmission. Hispanics also indicated that the most appropriate person to initiate contact would be an older person and family member. The authors of this study concluded that the family could become a useful source of AIDS prevention information in the Hispanic community.

According to B. Marin (1989), the familistic orientation of Hispanic culture creates a number of obligations but is also a source of support in times of trouble. Hispanics feel a need to consult with other family members before making important decisions. They have a sense of obligation to help others in the family, both economically and emotionally, and a strong sense of love and nurturing toward children (Sabagh, 1980).

Family ties can be used as a motivator to change high-risk or detrimental behavior. For example, regarding drug abuse, it has been suggested that familism can be used to help Hispanics stop using drugs. Messages about drugs might portray the bad example that drug use gives to one's children or siblings or the failure of the drug-using father to protect or provide for the family (Marin, 1990). The same type of message can be used in AIDS-prevention efforts, similarly emphasizing the effects of AIDS on the family and children.

Loyalty of family members to one another and the need for the family to present a good image to the outside world dictate that problems, such as drug abuse, will be hidden by the family (Smith-Peterson, 1983). Similarly, the risk of contracting AIDS through unprotected sex or other high-risk behavior may also be hidden or ignored in order to preserve a positive image of the family.

The importance of children to Hispanics also has implications for Hispanics faced with AIDS. For example, the importance placed on children may increase the willingness of HIV-positive women to carry a pregnancy to term (Gross, 1987). Although familism may create special problems for AIDS prevention, it may also be used to motivate a change in high-risk behavior among Hispanics (B. Marin, 1989). Hispanics may also be motivated to talk to family members about prevention (B. Marin, 1989).

In a study by the National Council for Health Statistics (1989), almost half of all Hispanic adults reported having discussed AIDS with their children aged 10–17 years, and another 60% stated that their children in that age range had received instruction about AIDS in school. Hispanic men were less likely than Hispanic women to have discussed AIDS with their children (39% versus 56%). Persons of Mexican ancestry were less likely to discuss AIDS with children than were other Hispanics (42% and 57%, respectively). Hispanic persons were less likely to have discussed AIDS with their children than were non-Hispanics (48% and 62%, respectively).

According to some researchers, *collectivism* is another important cultural value of Hispanics (B. Marin, 1989). Collectivism places great emphasis on the concerns and needs of others (Hofstede, 1980; Marin & Triandis, 1985). It is expressed in Hispanic culture as a strong orientation toward the family (Sabogal et al., 1987), including the extended family and extended kin. It places great importance on respect in social relationships. *Simpatia*, or being nice to others, is another manifestation of collectivism. *Simpatia* has important implications for health intervention methods, in that confrontation and assertiveness are incompatible with being *simpatico* (Marin, 1990). These cultural values are important in that they influence and shape health attitudes of Hispanics (B. Marin, 1989).

Conclusions

Clearly, more information is needed regarding the impact of AIDS on Hispanics as well as ways to address the problem. Researchers state that education is the major and preferred method for preventing untimely mortality and the spread of HIV among Hispanics (Nader et al., 1989). Bracho de Carpio, Carpio-Cedraro, & Anderson (1990) suggest that Hispanic families need to understand the reality of the threat of AIDS. Families need to receive appropriate information that takes into consideration the language, literacy level, socioeconomic status, culture, and social values of Hispanics. After receiving this information, Hispanics should be given the opportunity to demonstrate their understanding of it. Audiovisual methods should be used to facilitate understanding. Adults must feel comfortable talking about AIDS to children. Parents need to participate in the creation of educational materials that will be used by their children. Family members need to actually do something that can help them avoid the infection (Bracho de Carpio et al., 1990).

For most Hispanics, the family system extends beyond the immediate family to include friends, neighbors, and co-workers. This extended network is valuable as a support system in the treatment setting when other resources are scare, particularly among those at lower socioeconomic levels (Minuchin & Montalvo, 1977). The unique cultural characteristics of Hispanics can also be considered a source of strength in caring for AIDS-challenged members. For instance, Hispanics with AIDS can benefit from a typical Hispanic family environment in which fathers place emphasis on "respect," mothers on "love," children on "being loved," and grandparents on providing "wisdom" (Ruiz, 1982).

Hopkins (1987) stated that sensitivity or embarrassment surrounding AIDS should not prevent serious and urgent efforts to discuss drug abuse or sexual promiscuity in ethnic communities. People who are or who may be at risk should be urged to undergo testing voluntarily. It is likewise important to remember that AIDS is not the only important health problem confronting Hispanics; they are disproportionately confronted with other serious causes of death or illness, such as diabetes and cancer. Thus, it may make sense to combine or coordinate AIDS-related efforts with other health prevention and intervention efforts. Besides being cost effective, coordinated efforts would diminish the risk of negative and false images of Hispanics being the primary carriers of HIV infection.

Although some educational materials printed in Spanish are available for Hispanics, most of the literature is simple translations of the existing literature in English. There is a need for culturally appropriate printed materials in both Spanish and English. The Spanish language *Guide to Quit Smoking* (Sabogal, Marin, Otero-Sabogal, & Perez-Stable, 1988) is a fine example of a successful health-promotion booklet that incorporates Hispanic cultural values. The booklet was carefully pretested to increase its efficacy and users' comprehension of it. It incorporates testimonials from the community, graphic pictures of the effects of smoking, and appropriate reasons for quitting. The four-color photographs were costly but made the booklet less likely to be discarded. A recent survey indicated that 25% of the Hispanic community in San Francisco still had a copy of the guide 19 months after receiving it.

Although public attention to the problem of AIDS and HIV infection in the Hispanic population is urgently needed, efforts to draw such attention must not promote a negative and false image of Hispanics as being more likely than are non-Hispanics to be promiscuous, homosexual, or drug abusers. Historically, the strong family orientation of Hispanics has helped this population cope with many physical, environmental, and social challenges. This characteristic needs to be appreciated, nurtured, and utilized in efforts to address AIDS and HIV infection in the Hispanic community. Clearly, more medical resources need to be devoted to Hispanics with AIDS. These resources include the provision of additional health care services, AIDS testing, counseling services, increased access and funding for medications, community awareness programs, and prevention programs targeted at Hispanic communities.

Hispanic men and women need to be better represented in clinical trials of medications. The existing definition of AIDS cases needs to be modified to be more sensitive to symptoms associated with seropositive women. Moreover, increased funding is needed for research on the social, psychological, and medical issues surrounding AIDS and HIV infection among Hispanics. Hispanic researchers need to take the lead here. Funding bodies need to consider Hispanic investigators with research experience but who lack a funding track record and the traditional "mentoring" experience available to white non-Hispanics. Funders should also be more open to "nontraditional" studies, which often gain better information on Hispanics (e.g., ethnographies, case studies, etc.).

Note

I appreciate the assistance of Ms. Felicia Fernandez in gathering the information contained in this chapter. This chapter is dedicated to my family—Sandy, Fernando A., and Anthony Soriano.

References

Alvirez, D., & Bean, F. D. (1976). The Mexican American family. In C. H. Mindel & R. N. Haberstein (Eds.), *Ethnic families in America*. New York: Elsevier.

Amaro, H. (1987). *Hispanic women and AIDS: Considerations for prevention and research*. Paper presented at the NIMH/NIDA Research Workshop on Women and AIDS: Promoting Healthy Behaviors, Boston, MA.

Anderson, R., Lewis, S., & Giachello, A. L. (1981). Access to medical care among the Hispanic population of the southwestern United States. *Journal of Health and Social Behavior, 22*(1) 78–89.

Bracho de Carpio, A., Carpio-Cedraro, F. F., & Anderson, L. (1990). Hispanic families learning and teaching about AIDS: A participatory approach at the community level. *Hispanic Journal of Behavioral Sciences, 12*(2), 165–176.

Brown, L., Oliver, J., & de Alva, K. (Eds.). (1985). *Sociocultural and service issues in working with Hispanic American clients*. New York: Rockefeller College.

Carrier, J. M. (1976). Family attitudes and Mexican male homosexuality. *Urban Life, 5*, 359–375.

Carrier, J. M. (1985). Mexican male bisexuality. In F. Flein & T. J. Wolf (Eds.), *Bisexualities: Theory and research.* New York: Haworth Press.

Centers for Disease Control. (1990a, November). *HIV/AIDS surveillance report.* Atlanta, GA: U.S. Department of Health and Human Services.

Centers for Disease Control. (1990b, October). *HIV/AIDS surveillance report.* Atlanta, GA: U.S. Department of Health and Human Services.

Chaisson, R. E., Moss, A. R., & Onishi, R. (1987). Human immunodeficiency virus infection in heterosexual intravenous drug users in San Francisco. *American Journal of Public Health, 77*, 169–172.

Cohen, L. (1979). *Culture, disease and stress among Latino immigrants.* Washington, DC: Smithsonian Institution.

Compagnet, A. (1987, December 28). Hispanic culture redefines AIDS fight. *Washington Post,* p. A1.

COSSMHO. (1989). *AIDS: A guide for Hispanic leadership.* Washington, DC: National Coalition of Hispanic Health and Human Services Organizations.

Dailey, J., Lopez-Escovar, G., & Estrada, A. (1973). Colombian view of the condom. *Studies in Family Planning, 4*(3), 60–64.

Denenberg, R. (1990, October). Women and HIV-related conditions. *Treatment and Research Forum,* 3–5.

DiClemente, R. J., Boyer, B. C., & Morales, E. S. (1988). Minorities and AIDS: Knowledge, attitudes, and misconceptions among black and Latino adolescents. *American Journal of Public Health, 78*, 55–57.

Fairbank, Bregman, & Maullin, Inc. (1987). *Report on a baseline survey of AIDS risk behaviors and attitudes in San Francisco's Latino communities.* San Francisco: Author.

Fimbres, M. F., & McKay, E. G. (1989). *Getting started: Becoming part of the AIDS solution. A guide for Hispanic community-based organizations.* Washington, DC: National Council of La Raza.

Glazer, N., & Moynihan, D. P. (1963). *Beyond the melting pot.* Cambridge, MA: Harvard-MIT Press.

Gross, J. (1987, August 27). Bleak lives: Women carrying AIDS. *New York Times,* p. 1.

Hofstede, G. (1980). *Culture's consequences.* Beverly Hills, CA: Sage Publications.

Hopkins, D. R. (1987). AIDS in minority populations in the United States. *Public Health Report, 102*(6), 677.

Koenig, R. E., Gautier, T., & Levy, J. (1986). Intrafamilial transmission of human immunodeficiency virus. *Lancet, 2*(8507), 627.

Marin, B. V. (1989). Hispanic culture: Implications for AIDS prevention. In J. Boswell, R. Hexter, & J. Reinisch (Eds.), *Sexuality and disease: Metaphors, perceptions and behavior in the AIDS era.* New York: Oxford University Press.

Marin, B. V. (1990). Drug abuse treatment for Hispanics: A culturally appropriate, community-oriented approach. In R. R. Watson (Ed.), *Prevention and treatment of drug and alcohol abuse.* Clifton, NJ: Humana Press.

Marin, B. V., & Marin, G. (1989). *Information about human immunodeficiency virus in Hispanics in San Francisco.* San Francisco: University of California, Center for AIDS Prevention Studies.

Marin, B. V., & Marin, G. (1990). Effects of acculturation on knowledge of AIDS and HIV among Hispanics. *Hispanic Journal of Behavioral Sciences, 12*(2) 110–121.

Marin, B. V., Marin, G., & Juarez, R. (1990). Differences between Hispanics and non-Hispanics in willingness to provide AIDS prevention advice. *Hispanic Journal of Behavioral Science, 12*(2), 153–164.

Marin, G. (1989). AIDS prevention among Hispanics: Needs, risk behaviors, and cultural values. *Public Health Reports, 104*, 411–415.

Marin, G., & Triandis, H. C. (1985). Allocentrism as a cultural characteristic of Hispanics and Latin Americans. In R. Diaz-Guerrero (Ed.), *Cross-cultural and national studies in social psychology.* Amsterdam, The Netherlands: Elsevier.

Minuchin, S., & Montalvo, B. (1977). *Families of the slums.* New York: Basic Books.

Nader, P. R., Wexler, D. B., Patterson, T. J., McKusick, L., & Coates, T. (1989). Comparison of beliefs about AIDS among urban, suburban, incarcerated, and gay adolescents. *Journal of Adolescent Health Care, 19*, 413–418.

National Council for Health Statistics. (1986). *Contraceptive use. United States, 1982.* Data from the National Survey of Family Growth, Series 23, No. 12 (DHHS Publication No. (PHS) 86-1988). Washington, DC: U.S. Government Printing Office.

National Council for Health Statistics. (1989). *AIDS knowledge and attitudes of Hispanic Americans: Provisional data from the National Health Interview Survey* (DHHS Publication No. (PHS) 89-1250). Hyattsville, MD: U.S. Department of Health and Human Services.

Padilla, A. M. (1980). *Acculturation.* Boulder, CO: Westview Press.

Public Health Service. (1988). Cross-cutting issues: Women and AIDS. *Journal of the U.S. Public Health Service, 103*(1), 88–90.

Ronquillo, Y. (1987, November 4–7). *Prevention in the Latino community.* Paper presented at the National AIDS Conference, San Francisco.

Ruiz, P. (1982). The Hispanic patient: Sociocultural perspectives. In R. M. Becerra, M. Karno, & J. I. Escobar (Eds.), *Mental health and Hispanic Americans: Clinical perspectives.* New York: Grune and Stratton.

Sabagh, G. (1980). Fertility planning status of Chicano couples in Los Angeles. *American Journal of Public Health, 70*, 56–61.

Sabogal, F., Marin, G., Otero-Sabogal, R., Marin, B. V., & Perez-Stable, E. J. (1987). Hispanic familism and acculturation: What changes and what doesn't. *Hispanic Journal of Behavioral Sciences, 9*(4), 397–412.

Sabogal, F., Marin, B., Otero-Sabogal, R., & Perez-Stable, E. (1988). *Guia para dejar de fumar. Quit smoking guide.* Washington, DC: U.S. Government Printing Office.

Santisteban, D., & Szapocznik, J. (1982). *The Hispanic substance abuser: The search for prevention strategies.* New York: Grune and Stratton.

Selik, R. M., Castro, K. G., Pappaioanou, M., & Buehler, J. W. (1989). Birthplace and the risk of AIDS among Hispanics in the United States. *American Journal of Public Health, 79*, 836–839.

Smith-Peterson, C. (1983). Substance abuse treatment and cultural diversity. In G. Bennet, C. Vourakis, & D. Woolf (Eds.), *Substance abuse: Pharmacologic, developmental and clinical perspectives.* New York: John Wiley.

Szapocznik, J., & Kurtines, W. (1980). Acculturation, biculturalism and adjustment among Cuban Americans. In A. Padilla (Ed.), *Acculturation.* Boulder, CO: Westview Press.

Triandis, H. C., Marin, G., Betancourt, H., Lisanski, J., & Chang, B. (1982). *Dimensions of familism among Hispanic and mainstream Navy recruits.* Technical Report No. 14, Department of Psychology, University of Illinois, Champaign, IL.

U.S. Bureau of the Census. (1983). *1980 census of U.S. population and housing.* Washington, DC: U.S. Government Printing Office.

U.S. Bureau of the Census. (1990). *The Hispanic population in the United States: March 1989.* (Series P-20, No. 444). Washington, DC: U.S. Government Printing Office.

U.S. Department of Health and Human Services. (1986). *Black and minority health—Volume VIII: Hispanic health issues* (DHHS Report). Washington, DC: U.S. Government Printing Office.

5

Strengthening Family and School Bonds in Promoting Hispanic Children's School Performance

Herman Curiel

The educational reform movement of the 1980s has rightfully espoused the cause of educational equity. It has, in general, raised the expectations citizens have for their schools. Perhaps most important, it has kept the subject of education in the forefront of national attention by making a pragmatic and important case: Our country's economic role in the world will surely decline unless we improve American education (Cheney, 1987). The 1990s will test public schools as the proportion of minority students increases and demands intensify for a better-educated work force. Statistics from the U.S. Department of Education (Baker & Ogle, 1989) indicate that Hispanics are increasingly becoming a larger portion of the public school population and continue to experience low achievement levels, low levels of college preparatory coursework, and high dropout rates. Hispanics have one of the lowest levels of educational attainment in the country. Hispanic students fail grades early on and are held back and placed in remedial courses. Many never catch up. According to census data (U.S. Department of Commerce, 1987), 28% of Hispanic children in grades one through four are enrolled below the normal grade level compared with 20% of non-Hispanic white children. Between the fifth and eighth grades, the numbers climb to the point where nearly 40% of all Hispanic children are behind their grade level compared with 25% of their non-Hispanic white peers. By the ninth and tenth grades, 43% are behind. The proportion drops to 35% in the 11th and 12th grades, but mostly because many students have dropped out (Fields, 1988). The National Council of La Raza (1989) reports that in 1987 only 51% of Hispanics 25 years old and older completed four or more years of high school, compared with 78% of non-Hispanics; almost three-fourths of Hispanic students are enrolled in non–college-bound curriculum tracks; in 1988 only 10% of Hispanics 25 years and older completed four or more years of college, compared with 21% of non-Hispanics. As the United States continues to develop into a highly technological society, new skills and knowledge will be required to perform the jobs that become available. Lacking the education to acquire such skills, Hispanics will find it difficult to obtain gainful employment in the computerized society of the future (Brown & Swanson, 1985).

Dunn's (1987) monograph, *Bilingual Hispanic Children in the U.S. Mainland: A Review of Research on Their Cognitive, Linguistic, and Scholastic Development*, has been the subject of heated debate among Hispanic professional-interest groups. It is discussed here to highlight some of the concerns that have been expressed elsewhere as well as to familiarize social workers with the issues surrounding the question of how to strengthen schools' holding power over Hispanic children from low-income families. Most of the criticism directed at Dunn has been in regard to his assertion that the poor performance of impoverished Hispanic children "may be due, in part, to genetic factors" (p. 64). In hindsight, Dunn admits that he did not give sufficient consideration to environmental factors. His revised position is that most of the poor performance of impoverished Mexican American and Puerto Rican children can be explained by environmental factors such as low socioeconomic status, uneducated parents, poor health and nutrition, poor living conditions, lack of cultural opportunities, and so forth (Dunn, 1988).

Other sources of debate and controversy include Dunn's negative position on bilingual education. He believes that the research on bilingual education for impoverished Mexican Americans and Puerto Ricans living in the mainland United States has not demonstrated that this approach has been successful in helping these children progress in school. Furthermore, he argues, bilingual programs are detrimental because they remove children from their mainstream peers, who can help Hispanic children adapt to mainstream values and coping styles. This argument suggests that Dunn subscribes to a "melting pot" ideology. Historically, this ideology has shaped the foundations of the American way of life. It provided the early settlers of this country with a rationale for mutual acceptance and cooperation. Of course, history reveals that certain groups such as blacks, Hispanics, native Americans, and Asians suffered discrimination and were not encouraged to become part of the mainstream. Even in the 1800s civic leaders subscribed to the "melting pot" ideology and also were advocates for cultural pluralism. For example, William Torrey Harris, superintendent of St. Louis schools in the 1870s and later U.S. Commissioner of Education, believed that the mission of the schools was to "Americanize" language-minority children. At the same time, he argued for cultural tolerance, arguing that "national memories and aspirations, family traditions, customs and habits, moral and religious observances cannot be suddenly removed or changed without disastrously weakening the personality" (Crawford, 1989, p. 21). Germain (1988) provides further support for the psychological importance of acknowledging cultural differences:

> From birth to death, levels of self-esteem and the sense of having a socially valued personal and cultural identity depend on the perceptions and evaluations by others of oneself and one's family and cultural group and on the self-evaluation of one's relatedness, competence and self-direction (p. 264).

Dunn's position on pupil integration is well-meaning. He is known as "the father of mainstreaming" in the context of special education. He believes that generally it is in the best interest of children to be integrated with a cross section of pupils of all colors, creeds, and ability levels.

Dunn charges that Hispanic professionals are doing a disservice to Hispanic children by explaining away low academic achievement and intelligence test scores and not spreading the blame among the Hispanic community. He argues that the lagging proficiency of poor Hispanic youth is likely to divide and cripple the nation and that a substantial part of the blame must be borne by the Hispanic community.

Dunn has succeeded in stimulating discussion and raising valid questions that merit consideration by Hispanic as well as non-Hispanic civic leaders and professionals from education and allied disciplines such as social work, psychology, nursing, and guidance counseling. The problems are so complex that solutions require expertise and teamwork from multiple professions. A united effort is required to address the complex educational barriers that Hispanic children encounter. Without change, Dunn (1988) warns that education for poor Hispanic children will continue to be largely a sham, unless people of all colors, creeds, and beliefs immerse themselves vigorously in fostering a total comprehensive thrust upward for these children.

A Social Work Perspective

What can social workers do to promote the educational progress of Hispanic youth? Social workers practice in public and private social agencies where they come in contact with school children and families who are consumers of education. Through these contacts, social workers have opportunities to interact with school system representatives who need the valuable inputs that a professional social worker can offer. Social workers possess knowledge of systems and organizational theory and human development as well as expertise in assessing the impact of environmental stressors such as poverty on individuals and family functioning. Social workers have access to the network of social services outside the school system and possess interpersonal skills useful in dealing with individuals, family groups, and communities. School social workers who possess similar skills are in a better position to share with their colleagues in education a social work perspective in assessing the multiple needs of limited English proficient (LEP) children and their families. Given the wealth of knowledge and skills that social workers possess in dealing with environmental issues, the profession has a unique opportunity to make a contribution to enhance educational outcomes for Hispanic youth.

Change can begin with individual contacts with educators, students, and parents as well as meetings with school board members, civic leaders, and public officials. Contacts can also be indirect, such as writing or calling influential leaders to express appreciation or to advocate for a particular policy position that supports effective education for Hispanic youth. Change can be introduced through inclusion of courses in the training of teachers and school social workers that includes an ecological perspective for examining school, family, and community dynamics. Training should also include exposure to humanistic psychology that stresses appreciation and respect for cultural differences, professional ethics, and strategies for empowering both care providers and recipients in teacher–pupil interactions. It is important that the content be considered in terms of its implications for meeting the needs of ethnic-minority children and in particular LEP students. Pennekamp (1986) notes that future teachers and social workers are rarely presented with opportunities to explore complementary roles. Costin

(1983) urges social workers to work with their educator colleagues to explore creative strategies to enable more children and youth to utilize the public schools in ways that develop competence and skills essential in a rapidly changing world.

At the macro level, social workers can organize parent groups to serve on advisory panels, to speak on issues of concern to parents, or to collect data to document specific needs. Social workers can help organize Hispanic parents to help them learn about the school's decision-making structure and process and make changes or petition for the development of new programs (e.g., adult or bilingual education). As citizens, workers can have an impact on school policies by participating as advocates for change in their roles as parents, members of advisory or school boards, or other community leadership roles in which they have opportunities to share their expertise and knowledge with educators and public policymakers.

Format

The goal of this chapter is to familiarize school social workers with the problems that Hispanic children from low-income families encounter in their interactions with the school. Evidence is mounting that when parents are involved in their children's education, the children perform better in school (Walberg, 1984). Since the beginning of school social work, working with family members has been considered essential for assisting troubled students to resolve school-related problems and for helping parents maintain a home environment with more resources and fewer threats to learning (Kurtz & Barth, 1989). This chapter will examine barriers to school participation by Hispanic parents and explore strategies for increasing levels of interaction between the family and the school. Demographic data are included to familiarize the reader with the growth and changing characteristics of the Hispanic population in the United States.

A brief review of the history and experience of bilingual education in the United States is presented to familiarize readers with the federal legislation that prescribes program alternatives and goals of Title VII bilingual education programs. The author's rationale for inclusion of this subject is that a school's bilingual education program in high-density Hispanic schools is evidence of administrative sensitivity to the special needs of LEP students and serves as an internal resource for the school social worker in meeting the needs of LEP students. To answer concerns that have been raised by critics such as Dunn (1988), both critical and supportive student outcome research on the effectiveness of bilingual programs are cited.

A major thrust of the "English only" movement is to do away with bilingual education. Thus it is important to include a brief history of language-policy changes in the United States. The final section of the chapter attempts to apply the concepts described by Germain (1988) in her monograph *School as a Living Environment within the Community* to work with LEP Hispanic children and their families.

Demographics

The school problems experienced by Hispanic youth may soon become a national priority simply because of demographics. The overall number of young people in the country is shrinking while the number of Hispanic children is growing. The United States desperately needs young people for its labor force; therefore, it can no longer afford indifference to the plight of Hispanics and others in similar straits (Levine, 1988).

The Hispanic population in the United States includes a number of subgroups—Mexican Americans or Chicanos, Cubans, Puerto Ricans, and a growing number of Central and South American groups. From 1961 to 1980, approximately 2.3 million legal immigrants from Latin America and Mexico entered the United States. Some chose to return to their native countries, but the majority are now permanent residents in the United States (Bean, Cullen, Stephen, & Swicegood, 1984). These subgroups differ in what Solomon (1987) describes as the three subjective characteristics of ethnic groups: a shared history, self-identification, and a heightened sense of separateness when in contact with other groups. As with other immigrant groups, Solomon observes, it is not the common language or even the shared discrimination by the majority society that most significantly influences the course of human development; it is more likely to be the shared values that have roots in their traditional cultures.

Because of the magnitude of Hispanic immigration, Spanish is the most frequently spoken non-English language in the United States. According to the U.S. Department of Commerce (1981), 5% of all people older than five years speak Spanish. This represents more than 12 million individuals—an increase of more than 2 million since 1970 (Estrada, 1987). Two-thirds of those who speak Spanish report that they are proficient in English, too.

School-related issues of race, social class, and gender have received major attention from educators and social scientists over the past two decades. The common aim has been to understand how education can be constructed and provided so that it does not discriminate against major social groups (Grant & Sleeter, 1986). Horace Mann, referred to as the father of American education, recognized that the school is but one of several educative institutions, and thus is limited in power. The child is molded by his or her family, church, community, and state before the child comes to school, and these multiple sources of influence continue throughout the child's school years (Cremin, 1964).

Bilingual Education

Bilingual education, commonly referred to as the use of two languages as media of instruction, is an educational approach that builds on the knowledge that a LEP child brings to the school. From a social work perspective this approach makes sense. Implicitly, it sends a message to the child and family that the school values and respects cultural differences, which include the knowledge and language skills that the parents have provided their child through the home language. Cummins (1980, 1981) proposed a sound theoretical basis for bilingual education. He suggested that the literacy-related aspects of a bilingual child's proficiency in both first and second languages are common and interdependent across languages. Such a linguistic interdependence assumes that instruction in the first (native) language is effective in promoting proficiency in the second language and that transfer of this proficiency to the second language will occur provided the child is adequately exposed to and motivated to learn the native language. Cummins would thus posit that well-implemented bilingual programs should have a reasonable degree of success in developing English academic skills by promoting initial proficiency in the child's native language.

The enactment of the Bilingual Education Act of 1968, referred to as Title VII of the Elementary and Secondary Education Act of 1965, initiated the federal government's direct involvment with bilingual education. The Bilingual Education Act was reauthorized in 1974, 1978, 1984, and 1988. Its legislation provides educational services primarily for school-age "limited English proficient" students to help them learn sufficient English to enable them to function in a regular classroom where instruction is in English.

In the Bilingual Education Act, a "limited English proficient" pupil is defined as a child who comes from a home environment in which a language other than English is predominantly relied upon for communication and who has sufficient difficulty in understanding, speaking, reading, and writing English to deny the individual the opportunity to learn successfully in all English classes (Gainer, 1987). Estimates of the number of LEP students vary widely. The Department of Education estimates that there are 1.2 to 1.7 million LEP school-age children (ages 5–17). This estimate is based on the number of children who (1) score at or below the 20th percentile on a national English proficiency examination and (2) demonstrate a dependence on their native language (Gainer, 1987). The Twelfth Annual Report of the National Advisory and Coordinating Council on Bilingual Education (U.S. Department of Education, 1988) indicates that 12.5% of the student population nationwide are from language-minority groups. The general rate of limited English proficiency in the non-English language population, which includes more than 100 unique language groups, falls in the range of 40% to 53%; approximately 75% of Hispanics are considered LEP when they start school.

Several years after the federal government enacted the Bilingual Education Act of 1968, a number of states enacted similar legislation or established state education agency policies that prescribe special instruction for LEP students. Massachusetts was the first in 1971, followed by Oregon, Alaska, and the Virgin Islands. Twenty-six states had passed legislation by 1985, and several others issued state education agency policies. Among the 26 states, 13 have laws that include specific mandates for the institution of bilingual programs under certain circumstances. A few others have policies that mandate these programs. For example, most states have provisions by which the presence of specific numbers of same-language LEP students in a given school or school district necessitates the creation of a bilingual education or English as a second language (ESL) program. English as a second language is a methodology developed in the 1930s to meet the needs of foreign diplomats and international students (Crawford, 1989).

The original legislation restricted program funding to those school districts that had a high concentration of children whose families were considered indigent. The revisions in the law include similar language that gives priority to LEP children coming from homes with incomes below the national poverty guidelines.

The 1988 amendments to the Bilingual Education Act (Hawkins & Stafford, 1988) provide funds for three types of programs. The "transitional bilingual education" program model represents the major portion of programs funded by the Office of Bilingual Education and Minority Languages Affairs (OBEMLA). In fiscal year 1986, 519 awards served 173,903 students. In fiscal year 1987, 578 awards served 204,572 students. Local and state agencies fund additional programs that are not reflected in the above figures. The National Advisory and Coordinating Council on Bilingual Education (U.S. Department of Education, 1988) Annual Report indicates that approximately 5,000 local education agencies and community and volunteer organizations are currently operating bilingual education programs.

The revised legislation (Hawkins & Stafford, 1988) places emphasis on "structured English language instruction" and "to the extent necessary, instruction in the child's language." This revision provides support to what seems to be common practice in the operationalization of bilingual programs, the use of English as the primary language to teach LEP students. McLaughlin (1984) comments on this practice, concluding that the transitional bilingual programs in the United States rarely use the first language of the LEP child, which is the means for developing early cognitive skills. In fact, she says, in many so-called bilingual classrooms the child's first language is viewed as a necessary evil and is avoided to the extent possible. Other surveys support McLaughlin's observations. Development Associates, Inc., and Research Triangle Institute (1984) surveyed services provided to a nationally representative sample of LEP students in 397 schools and found that instruction was predominantly in English. O'Malley (1982) also found little difference in the amount of English-language instruction received by students in a bilingual program and by students in an English-instructed classroom.

The Hawkins and Stafford (1988) amendments include language that for the first time limits the enrollment time of LEP students in bilingual programs to three years, with a maximum of five years for exceptional cases based on a formal determination. This legislative language reflects the concern of policymakers who believe LEP students should be integrated into the regular school program as soon as possible. It also satisfies critics who argue that continued enrollment in bilingual programs retards the learning of English. Although the intent is well meant, it has had the effect of encouraging practices that push children out of programs before they are sufficiently proficient in the second language to progress in the regular classroom.

To facilitate integration of LEP students with non-LEP students and to promote bilingual literacy in both sets of children, the revised act permits the enrollment of children who are English-proficient and who come from homes in which English is the dominant or only language spoken. The "developmental bilingual education" might be considered an experimental model that has low funding priority because its emphasis is not remedial. For example the Office of Bilingual Education in 1986 and 1987 awarded only two grants in this category for each year (Bennett, 1988).

A third category of compensatory programs for LEP students is included in the Hawkins and Stafford (1988) amendments. This category is designated as the "Special Alternative Program" to meet the needs of school programs that have experienced past or current barriers to implementing a bilingual program because of staff limitations or insufficient LEP students with a common language.

The 1988 amendments also include a new requirement, the "Special Information Rule," which mandates that parents of children who are candidates for bilingual instruction be given reasons for recommended placement and alternatives when they elect not to accept the placement recommendation. Alternatives may include instructional approaches that do not emphasize language instruction. The best known is English as a second language—a required component of all bilingual programs in the United States. This approach assumes that the learner has achieved a high level of literacy in the first language and it has been very effective in teaching English to foreign students seeking admission to U.S. institutions of higher learning. Other approaches that deemphasize native-language instruction include *structured immersion* and *sheltered English*. In structured-immersion programs, children are taught subject matter in the second language with an emphasis on contextual clues and with lessons geared to the students' level of competence. This approach is distinguished from submersion, which characterized the traditional "sink or swim" instructional approaches used with LEP children. In sheltered English, also known as alternate immersion, children receive second-language instruction that is "sheltered" from input beyond their comprehension, first in subjects that are less language-intensive, such as mathematics, and later in those that are more so, such as social studies (Crawford, 1989).

Research Evidence

Before the early 1960s, most research comparing bilingual and monolingual subjects documented negative effects for bilinguals in the form of mental confusion, linguistic handicaps, and emotional instability (Darcy, 1963). Frequently, the subjects studied were children of immigrant or guest workers. More recent research suggests that the earlier studies probably described what is now considered a normal phase of confusion as the children tried to make sense of what they knew (native language) and how the second language was similar or different. Peal and Lambert (1962) were among the first to document the cognitive advantages for bilinguals based on their comparative study of bilinguals in Canadian English and French with both English and French monolinguals. In the past 20 years, numerous studies have reported results supporting the educational value of native-language literacy instruction (Leyba, 1978; Powers & Rossman, 1984; Sancho, 1980; Fulton-Scott & Calvin, 1983; Saldate, Mishra, & Medina, 1985; Willig, 1985; Curiel, Rosenthal, & Richek, 1986; De la Garza & Medina, 1985).

Despite the apparent validity of bilingual instruction for LEP children, a number of investigations have reported conflicting results that support critics of legislation that mandates these programs. Studies frequently cited include the widely publicized study conducted by the American Institutes of Research (AIR) (Danoff, Coles, McLaughlin, & Reynolds, 1977a, 1977b, 1978a, 1978b) and the Baker and de Kanter (1981) study. A number of other researchers have challenged these findings (Cardenas, 1977; Gray, 1977; Arias & Navarro, 1981). As suggested earlier, evaluating outcomes in bilingual education is complicated by the variability in program interpretation. McLaughlin (1982) suggests that it is correct to say that there are as many bilingual programs as there are bilingual classrooms in the United States. Furthermore, her observation, which is supported by others, that the child's native language is rarely used as a means of developing cognitive skills raises questions about the intent of the programs and undermines the basic principles of bilingual education. Willig (1988) observes that a major problem with general survey data is the assumption that all programs with the label bilingual are actually bilingual programs and that the quality of the programs is uniform. In actuality, the label alone carries little meaning because the term "bilingual program" has been defined in various ways. To view the first language simply as an interim carrier of subject matter until the second language can take over is to fail to appreciate the possibility that the first language can be used as a means through which conceptual and communicative proficiency can be developed (McLaughlin, 1982). Part of the problem is ineffective preparation of bilingual teachers. In many cases, teachers themselves have not mastered the child's native language and therefore teach what they know best—English. Bilingual education represents an attempt to correct educational approaches that failed to consider the long-term consequences of having LEP children begin their formal education with the challenge of having to learn to speak, read, and write a foreign language while implicitly discounting what the children learned at home from their non–English-speaking parents.

The English-Only Movement

A major thrust of the English-only movement involves a vigorous attack on Title VII programs. Most Americans are surprised to learn that the constitution does not provide for an "official" language. Although the English-only movement, with its focus on the introduction and enactment of legislation to mandate English as the official national language, is relatively new as an organized effort, the history of U.S. language policy is long. Linguistic minorities have been viewed and treated in a variety of ways, and public policy regarding language has been inconsistent (Edwards & Curiel, 1989). Trueba (1988) provides a historical account of efforts to mandate English as the official language in the United States from 1890 to 1927:

> In 1890, the states of Connecticut, Massachusetts, Rhode Island, New York, Wisconsin and other states made English their mandatory school language. California, Texas, Pennsylvania and Georgia prohibited the use of languages other than English to conduct public affairs. Nebraska even went so far as to forbid the teaching of any foreign language in public schools. In 1923, the U.S. Supreme court in *Meyer v. Nebraska* invalidated that legislation. In 1922, Oregon enacted laws of compulsory attendance for all children 8 to 15 in public schools where only English was used. In 1923, 34 states passed legislation requiring English to be the only language of instruction, while Vermont, Connecticut, New Hampshire and Massachusetts adopted laws restricting the use of French, and Ohio the use of German. In Hawaii, attempts to prevent Japanese, Chinese, Korean and Hawaiian children from using their mother tongues were repealed by the Supreme Court in 1927 (p. 259).

Because the English-only movement is focused on bilingual education, school social workers should be informed about the issues surrounding the controversy and the potential effects of the movement. If supporters of the English-only movement are successful in getting their legislative agenda enacted, the impact on schools and society will be significant (Edwards & Curiel, 1989).

Role of Social Work

To be effective in schools, professionals must be able to respond to the "felt needs" of administrators, teachers, support personnel, children, and families (Levine, Allen-Meares, & Easton,

1987). Roskin (1979) describes the social worker's mandate in the school as "promotion of normal adjustment and prevention of those conditions deemed detrimental or potentially detrimental to learning." The National Association of Social Workers' (NASW) (1978) Standards for Social Work Services in Schools prescribes three levels of social work services: (1) remedial, (2) crisis resolution, and (3) developmental. Given the problems encountered by LEP children and their families, school social work requires bold new approaches. Allen-Meares (1977), in a survey of school social work tasks, found that efforts to prevent school failure in target groups of pupils or to change adverse conditions or policies in the school and community were rarely identified. This suggests that school social workers tend to view their roles primarily in terms of meeting individual and family needs in the context of educational concerns.

Two tasks identified in the NASW (1978) standards support outreach or advocacy roles that social workers may undertake in providing services to LEP students and their families. One task involves preventive services:

> 1. Aid in identification of child or target group of children needing preventive social services (p. 21).

Brown (1981) argues that a school social worker should become involved with minority families not only when a problem has occurred but also as part of a preventive effort based on recognition of the experiences of such families in a racist society. Moore (1976) stated that little doubt exists that Mexican American parents want their children to have formal education, including education after high school. The task of the school social worker is to assist the parents so that their aspirations for their children can be fulfilled (Brown, 1981).

The other identified task prescribed in the NASW standards is pertinent to providing services to LEP students:

> 2. Collaborate with school personnel to develop avenues for pupil pursuit of life goals, equality of the sexes, and respect for cultural differences (p. 21).

This social work task is presented in the form of a challenge. What can school social workers do to promote respect for cultural differences? Cummins (1986) suggests that students from "dominated" social groups are "empowered" or "disabled" as a direct result of their interactions with educators in the schools. These interactions are mediated by the implicit or explicit role definitions that educators assume in relation to four institutional characteristics. Two areas for consideration in the context of the present discussion include:

the extent to which minority students' language and culture are incorporated into the school program; and the extent to which professionals involved in assessment become advocates for minority students rather than legitimizing the location of the "problem" in the students (p. 21).

Cummins suggests that the major reason previous attempts at educational reform have been unsuccessful is that the relationship between teachers and students and between schools and communities have remained essentially unchanged. The required changes involve personal redefinitions of the way classroom teachers interact with the children and communities they serve. In the literature of school social work, Brown (1981) notes that the literature has increasingly addressed the need for school workers to gain a broader practice perspective, to go beyond the traditional approaches of providing counseling services to children and their families.

> The burden of change must be removed from minority families and placed on institutions. Too many minority children are adversely affected when the school fails in its mission. School social workers have too often viewed themselves as instruments of the school—as agents of social control instead of social change (Brown, 1981, p. 25).

Implications for Practice

Many Hispanic parents feel powerless to make a difference in their children's education because they feel unable to participate effectively. Orum (1988) indicates that some studies suggest that approximately 56% of Hispanic adults are functionally illiterate in English. Many of these parents themselves had previous unsuccessful experiences in the educational system, and thus often lack the skills to help their children succeed in school.

Germain (1988) views the school as a living environment within the community. It contains both a social and physical environment that shapes the quality of teaching, learning, and life for children and staff. Students are affected by properties of the school social environment such as size of student body and staff. Large schools may offer students more in terms of curriculum options and faculty but may also present barriers for students who are excluded from leadership roles because of their lack of personal and family resources. Small schools, on the other hand, are more likely to have fewer concrete educational resources but may provide students with more individualized attention and opportunities for development of leadership skills.

Another property of the school social environment is the bureaucratic structure that shapes and provides opportunities for participation in the decision-making process. Again, the size of the school affects interactions between staff and students and their families. Large schools are more likely to inhibit the participation of low-income Hispanic parents, who may feel uncomfortable with the English language as well as unfamiliar with the bureaucratic process, the school curriculum, teaching methods, and appropriate roles for parent participation.

Attitudes of the school staff also shape the social environment of the school. Germain (1988) states that the attitudes of administrators, teachers, social workers, guidance counselors, nurses, maintenance personnel, cafeteria workers, and bus drivers affect the students and their families. Negative attitudes toward Hispanic children and their parents on the part of staff may be based on language barriers, cultural differences, different educational expectations as a result of different socioeconomic backgrounds, false assumptions regarding parents' interest in their children's education, and so forth. Pennekamp and Freeman (1988) note that many teachers, due to their American middle-class values, may find it difficult to deal positively with the diversity of backgrounds, histories, and values represented by the students and their families. School staff may not have been exposed to regular communications with culturally diverse families as part of their education and inservice training. Germain (1988) states:

> Nonrespectful attitudes and practices based on a child's ethnicity, gender, socioeconomic status, disability, or family form have a negative impact on learning and the educational and emotional climate of the school, quality of peer interaction, parent involvement, and pupil and staff competence and self-esteem (p. 261).

The physical environment also communicates how teachers, staff, and students are valued. The physical environment, according to Germain (1988), includes spacial arrangements of classrooms, play, and staff areas. The level of repair, maintenance, and security, including physical access for disabled pupils and staff, is also important. In urban schools with large minority student enrollments, it is not uncommon to observe signs of poor building maintenance. To safeguard pupils, staff, and property, extra security measures have been taken in some urban schools, such as bars on windows, locked doors, and security officers who control access to buildings. When schools look like prisons, it should not be surprising that students elect to drop out.

As Germain notes, the overall climate of the school is affected by the attractiveness and functionality of facilities such as bathrooms, water fountains, cafeteria, and gymnasiums. Minority student populations are more likely to feel more comfortable in an environment that incorporates architecture or decor symbols with which they can identify. For example, displays that honor former students or national heros who are members of the students' ethnic group provide role models for students. In schools with multiple ethnic groups, such displays can be rotated to focus on the contributions of various ethnic groups. Art and photographs in staff offices can be used to communicate acceptance of the children's ethnic culture. Directional signs in other languages in addition to English can be used to designate entrances and exits, bathroom facilities, offices, and so forth. Bilingual signs elevate the status of minority languages and convey to non–English-speaking parents that the school respects their native language.

Germain and Gitterman's (1987) environmental concepts are based on the ecological model, which emphasizes the interaction of persons and environmental factors. The model views "people and environment as parts of a unitary system which are constantly shaping and being shaped by each other" (Bloom, 1981, p. 12). Ecological intervention requires restructuring the interaction of significant adults, changing expectations and priorities of individuals and significant others, improving competencies of individuals, and developing support systems (Levine et al., 1987).

The major problem in most schools is the lack of positive, cooperative relationships among students, staff, parents, and administration (Mintzies & Hare, 1985). The ecological model provides a framework for assessing school–community relations and identifying possible points of intervention. The limited parental involvement of Hispanic parents in education is in part due to language barriers, lack of familiarity with structural arrangements of schools, and negative attitudes that are shared by both school authorities and parents. Increased parental involvement can change attitudes of both school staff and parents and have a positive effect on Hispanic children's school performance. Group-work theory (Homans, 1950) posits that the more people get together, the more they interact; the more people interact, the more they like each other; the more people like each other, the more they interact. Negative attitudes of school staff, teachers, pupils, and parents are subject to change when opportunities are provided to increase contact among and within these various groups. Parents need to be educated about the school structure, the decision-making processes, and their opportunities for input.

Increasing Hispanic parents' participation in the school requires an administrative commitment to increased support for social work services. Such support might take the form of increased funding to reduce case loads or acquire additional bilingual staff. Administrative support may require additional funding and negotiations with unions or teacher certification bodies to create positions for paraprofessionals who can help connect families in need with resources. To increase parent participation will require staff teamwork as well as a flexible structure that supports innovative roles for both the providers and consumers of educational services.

The role of the school social worker needs to be expanded to include work with educators, parents, and children at risk. Perlman and Edwards (1982) describe a model, ENABLE, that grew out of the 1960s' War on Poverty. This acronym stands for Education and Neighborhood Action for Better Living Environment. The program was a joint effort of three national organizations: Family Service Association of America (now Family Service America), the National Urban League, and the Child Study Association. The program was operationalized throughout the country in family service agencies. Its primary goals were two: (1) to increase effective parenting skills of low-income families and (2) to empower families by teaching them macro-level problem-solving skills. This approach is consonant with Germain's ecological approach. To implement this model, school social workers need to possess skills in group work and community organization. Given the complexity of problems that schools must address in providing services to LEP Hispanic children and their families, policymakers for schools need to make greater use of the expertise of social workers.

The following illustrates how this model was operationalized in one community. The staff for the model included two master's-level social workers and four indigenous case aides. Professional staff participated in an initial two-week inservice training program that covered conducting parent-education groups, community organization, and data collection as well as training and supervision of case aides. The concentrated training was followed by ongoing supervision and consultation with experts in family life education and community organization.

Going door to door, the case aides recruited parents who expressed an interest in becoming more effective in their parenting role. The aides were responsible for making arrangements for child care and transportation to the meetings, which were usually held in the parents' neighborhood. The aides visited families between sessions. The parent-education groups met once a week for eight weeks; each session lasted 90 minutes, which included time for socializing and refreshments. The discussions were conducted in Spanish with Spanish-speaking groups. The aides administered a pre– and post–parent-education attitude scale in the parents' homes before the initial session and at the end. The groups varied in size from 7 to 14 participants.

During the initial meeting the leader identified the group's areas of interest, which would become the topics of discussion for the remaining sessions. Each topic became the focus of guided discussion by the leader (a social worker), who would encourage maximum participation with pauses to reinforce sound ideas or to probe for additional ideas and to summarize. When community social problems were identified, the leader would solicit interest in forming a second group to do something about the issue. The community group would meet at a different time and frequently was composed of a core group from the parent group plus additional members—often the spouses. In the community groups the task was to identify clearly the dimensions of the community problem, determine how many people were affected by the problem, identify previous joint efforts to resolve problems and the consequences of those efforts, identify change goals desired, examine barriers to resolution, decide on a plan of action, and implement it. Families needing individual attention were identified during the group meetings and in case-aide family contacts between group meetings. Team meetings were used to provide supervision and to identify tasks that needed to be done in helping the identified families.

The project ENABLE model described here is applicable nationwide. A dual approach to addressing family and community problems can be a vehicle for strengthening bonds between the school and the wider community. The time is right for change, and social workers can make a difference in meeting the needs of all children, but in particular children who start school with limited English proficiency.

Other efforts will be required to sensitize staff to the collaborative effort needed to improve the emotional climate of schools for everyone. Such efforts can take the form of inservice training for school personnel at all levels, with the goal of increasing positive interpersonal interactions among students, families, staff, administration, and community.

References

Allen-Meares, P. (1977). Analysis of tasks in school social work. *Social Work, 22,* 196–201.

Arias, M. B., & Navarro, R. (1981). *Title VII, bilingual education: Developing issues of diversity and equity.* Palo Alto, CA: Stanford University Institute for Research on Educational Finance and Governance.

Baker, C. O., & Ogle, L. T. (1989). *The conditions of education 1989, vol. 1, elementary and secondary education.* Washington, DC: U.S. Government Printing Office.

Baker, K. A., & de Kanter, A. A. (1981). *Effectiveness of bilingual education: A review of the literature.* U.S. Department of Education, Office of Planning, Budget and Evaluation.

Bean, F., Cullen, R. M., Stephen, E. H., & Swicegood, C. G. (1984). Generational differences in fertility among Mexican-Americans. *Social Sciences Quarterly, 65,* 573–582.

Bennett, W. J. (1988). *The condition of bilingual education in the nation: 1988—A report to congress and the president.* Washington, DC: U.S. Government Printing Office.

Bloom, M. (1981). *Primary prevention: The possible science.* Englewood, Cliffs, NJ: Prentice-Hall.

Brown, J. A. (1981). Parent education groups for Mexican-Americans. *Social Work in Education, 3,* 22–31

Brown, J. A., & Swanson, J. (1985). Demographic forecasting, Chicanos, and school social work. *Social Work in Education, 7,* 183–191.

Cardenas, J. A. (1977). *The AIR evaluation of the impact of the ESEA Title VII—Spanish/English bilingual education programs and IDA response.* San Antonio, TX: Intercultural Development Research Associates.

Cheney, L. V. (1987). *American memory: A report of the humanities in the nation's public schools.* Washington DC: U.S. Government Printing Office.

Costin, L. (1983). Education reform and school social work (editorial). *Social Work in Education, 6,* 3.

Crawford, J. (1989). *Bilingual education: History, politics, theory, and practice.* Trenton, NJ: Crane Publishing.

Cremin, L. A. (1964). *The transformation of the school: Progressivism in American education, 1876–1957.* New York: Vintage Books.

Cummins, J. (1980). The cross-lingual dimensions of language proficiency: Implications for bilingual education and the optional age issue. *TESOL Quarterly, 4,* 175–187.

Cummins, J. (1981). The role of primary language development in promoting educational success for language minority students. In *Schooling and language minority students: A theoretical framework.* Los Angeles, CA: Evaluation, Dissemination and Assessment Center, California State University.

Cummins, J. (1986). Empowering minority students: A framework for intervention. *Harvard Education Review, 56*(1), 18–36.

Curiel, H., Rosenthal, J. A., & Richek, H. G. (1986). Impacts of bilingual education on secondary school grades, attendance, retentions, and drop-out. *Hispanic Journal of Behavioral Sciences, 8,* 357–367.

Danoff, M. N., Coles, G. J., McLaughlin, D. H., & Reynolds, D. J. (1977a). *Evaluation of the impact of ESEA Title VII Spanish bilingual education programs, vol. 1: Study designs and interim findings.* Palo Alto, CA: American Institutes of Research.

Danoff, M. N., Coles, G. J., McLaughlin, D. H., & Reynolds, D. J. (1977b). *Evaluation of the impact of ESEA Title VII Spanish/English bilingual education programs, vol. 2: Project descriptions.* Palo Alto, CA: American Institutes of Research.

Danoff, M. N., Coles, G. J., McLaughlin, D. H., & Reynolds, D. J. (1978a). *Evaluation of the impact of ESEA Title VII Spanish/English bilingual education programs, vol. 3, Year two impact data, education process, and in-depth analysis.* Palo Alto, CA: American Institutes of Research.

Danoff, M. N., Coles, G. J., McLaughlin, D. H., & Reynolds, D. J. (1978b). *Evaluation of impact of ESEA Title VII Spanish/English bilingual education programs, overview of study and findings.* Palo Alto, CA: American Institutes of Research.

Darcy, N. T. (1963). Bilingualism and the measurement of intelligence: Review of a decade of research. *Journal of Genetic Psychology, 103,* 259–282.

De la Garza, J. V., & Medina, M., Jr. (1985). Academic achievement as influenced by bilingual instruction for Spanish dominant Mexican-American children. *Hispanic Journal of Behavioral Sciences, 7,* 247–259.

Development Associates, Inc., & Research Triangle Institute. (1984). *LEP students: Characteristics and school services.* Arlington, VA: Author.

Dunn, L. M. (1987). *Bilingual Hispanic children on the U.S. mainland: A review of research on their cognitive, linguistic and scholastic development* (a first draft). Honolulu, HI: Dunn Education Services.

Dunn, L. M. (1988). Has Dunn's monograph been shot down in flames—Author reactions to the preceding critiques on it. *Hispanic Journal of Behavioral Sciences, 10,* 301–323.

Edwards, R. L., & Curiel, H. (1989). Effects of the English-only movement on bilingual education. *Social Work in Education, 12,* 53–66.

Estrada, L. F. (1987). Hispanics. In *Encyclopedia of social work* (18th ed.) (pp. 732–739). Silver Spring, MD: National Association of Social Workers.

Fields, C. (1988). The Hispanic pipeline. *Change, 20*(3), 20–27.

Fulton-Scott, M., & Calvin, A. D. (1983). Bilingual-multicultural education vs. integrated and non-integrated ESL instruction. *NABE Journal, 7*(3), 1–12.

Gainer, W. J. (1987). Briefing report to the chairman, committee on labor and human resources, United States Senate. *Bilingual Education: Information on Limited English Proficient Students.* Washington, DC: U.S. General Accounting Office.

Germain, C. (1988). School as a living environment within the community. *Social Work in Education, 10,* 260–276.

Germain, C. B., & Gitterman, A. (1987). Ecological perspective. In *Encyclopedia of Social Work* (18th ed.) (pp. 448–449). Silver Spring, MD: National Association of Social Workers.

Grant, C. A., & Sleeter, C. E. (1986). Race, class and gender in education research: An argument for integrative analysis. *Review of Educational Research, 56*(2), 195–211.

Gray, T. (1977). *Response to AIR study: Evaluation of the impact of ESEA Title VII Spanish/English bilingual education program.* Arlington, VA: Center for Applied Linguistics.

Hawkins, A. F., & Stafford, R. T. (1988). *Elementary and secondary school improvement amendments of 1988,* PL 100-297.

Homans, G. C. (1950). *The human group.* New York: Harcourt Brace Jovanovich.

Kurtz, D. P., & Barth, R. P. (1989). Parent involvement: Cornerstone of school social work practice. *Social Work, 34,* 407–420.

Levine, A. (1988). Rebuilding the dream (editorial). *Change, 20*(3), 4.

Levine, R. S., Allen-Meares, P., & Easton, F. (1987). Primary prevention and the educational preparation of school social workers. *Social Work in Education, 9,* 145–158.

Leyba, C. F. (1978). *Longitudinal study, Title VII bilingual program, Santa Fe public schools, Santa Fe, New Mexico.* Los Angeles, CA: National Dissemination and Assessment Center, California State University.

McLaughlin, B. (1982). Child second language acquisition: State of the art. *Language and Education: Theory and Practice.* Arlington, VA: Center for Applied Linguistics.

McLaughlin, B. (1984). Are immersion programs the answer for bilingual education in the United States? *Bilingual Review, 11*(1), 3–11.

Mintzies, P., & Hare, I. (1985). *The human factor: The key to excellence in education.* Silver Spring, MD: National Association of Social Workers.

Moore, J. W. (1976). *Mexican-Americans.* Englewood Cliffs, NJ: Prentice-Hall.

National Association of Social Workers. (1978). *NASW Standards for social work ser-*

vices in schools. Silver Spring, MD: Author.

National Council of La Raza. (1989). *Reversing the trend of Hispanic undereducation.* Unpublished paper, National Council of La Raza, Washington, DC.

O'Malley, J. M. (1982). *Children's English and services study: Educational and needs assessment with limited English proficiency.* Rosslyn, VA: Inter America Research Associates.

Orum, L. S. (1988). *Making education work for Hispanic Americans: Some promising community-based practices.* Paper presented at American Education Research Association annual meeting, New Orleans.

Peal, E., & Lambert, W. (1962). The relation of bilingualism to intelligence. *Psychological Monographs, 76,* 1–23.

Pearlman, M. H., & Edwards, M. (1982). Enabling in the eighties: The client advocacy group. *Social Casework, 63,* 532–539.

Pennekamp, M. (1986). The relationship of school social workers and educators. *Social Work in Education, 8,* 202–203.

Pennekamp, M., & Freeman, E. M. (1988). Toward a partnership perspective: Schools, families, and school social workers. *Social Work in Education, 10,* 246–259.

Powers, S., & Rossman, M. H. (1984). Evidence of the impact of bilingual education: A meta-analysis. *Journal of Instructional Psychology, 11,* 75–78.

Roskin, M. (1979). School social work and primary prevention: Integration of setting and focus. *School Social Work Quarterly, 1,* 31–44.

Saldate, M., IV., Mishra, S. P., & Medina, M. J. (1985). Bilingual instruction and academic achievement: A longitudinal study. *Journal of Instructional Psychology, 12,* 24–31.

Sancho, A. R. (1980). Bilingual education: A three-year investigation comparing the effects of maintenance and transitional approaches on English language acquisition and academic achievement on young bilingual children. *Dissertation Abstracts International, 41,* 3935A.

Solomon, B. (1987). Human development: Sociocultural perspective. In *Encyclopedia of social work* (18th ed.) (pp. 856–866). Silver Spring, MD: National Association of Social Workers.

Trueba, H. T. (1988). Comments on L. M. Dunn's bilingual children on the U.S. mainland: A review of research on their cognitive, linguistic, and scholastic development. *Hispanic Journal of Behavioral Sciences, 10,* 253–262.

U.S. Department of Commerce, Bureau of the Census. (1981). *General social and economic characteristics: U.S. summary* (P.C. 80-1-cl). Washington, DC: U.S. Government Printing Office.

U.S. Department of Commerce, Bureau of the Census. (1987). *The Hispanic population in the United States: March 1986 and March 1987* (Advance report), Series P-20, No. 6. Washington, DC: U.S. Government Printing Office.

U.S. Department of Education, Office of Bilingual Education and Minority Languages Affairs. (1988). *Twelfth annual report of the national advisory and coordinating council on bilingual education.* Washington, DC: U.S. Government Printing Office.

Walberg, H. J. (1984). Families as partners in educational productivity. *Phi Delta Kappan, 2,* 397–400.

Willig, A. C. (1985). A meta-analysis of selected studies on the effectiveness of bilingual education. *Review of Educational Research, 55,* 269–317.

Willig, A. C. (1988). A case of blaming the victim: The Dunn monograph on bilingual children on the U.S. mainland. *Hispanic Journal of Behavioral Sciences, 10,* 219–236.

6

Phenotyping, Acculturation, and Biracial Assimilation of Mexican Americans

Frank F. Montalvo

The influence of skin color on the lives of Hispanic Americans has been largely overlooked by researchers and human service and mental health practitioners. A recent within-group study on racial phenotypes reported that education and income levels of Chicano subjects increased significantly according to the lightness of their skin color and the extent to which their appearance seemed European (Arce, Murgia, & Frisbie, 1987). On the assumption that the less control Mexican Americans have of their opportunities, the greater psychological distress they experience, Codina and Montalvo (in preparation) are currently studying the effects of phenotypes on mental health and self-esteem.

This chapter examines the concepts of phenotyping, acculturation, and biracial assimilation and their effect on the Latino family's accommodation to the cultural and racial standards for social integration in the United States. This theoretical framework helped design the mental health study discussed in this chapter. The chapter summarizes the results of this research and considers the need to include the Hispanic client's phenotype and his or her racial self-perceptions as additional variables in the assessment of ethnoracial stress.

A review of the available social science literature related to skin color indicated that the Latino's social identity was uniquely shaped by the group's cultural and multiracial experience in colonial Latin America, which continues to influence its patterns of adjustment in contemporary American society (Montalvo, 1987). Ascribing higher social status to those with light skin tone and European appearance was practiced in the Americas, but it did not threaten the darker members' firm cultural identity. In the biracially oriented United States, although all Latinos are expected to acculturate, they are selectively assimilated because they are typically regarded as dark people. Accordingly, the wide variation in skin coloration of Hispanic children causes them to experience differing stress and to develop differing response patterns as they and their families strive to balance sociocultural continuity with accommodation to America's system of racial stratification.

This general proposition is developed below by means of historical records and the current literature. It is illustrated with the childhood memories of Mexican Americans obtained from more than 500 field interviews conducted by social work students. The proposition was tested with a national sample of Mexican Americans living in the southwest and in Chicago.

Theoretical Framework

Phenotypes and Phenotyping

Phenotypes are created from a combination of skin color and physiognomic features, allowing society to identify and classify individuals as being racially similar to or different from other members of a group. Visible racial characteristics in face, hair color and texture, and body build—physiognomy—are essential for identifying phenotypes, although the permanent skin color tends to be the more salient marker. Phenotypes, however, are important only in their consequences.

Phenotyping is a crucial factor in influencing the process of allocating more social and economic opportunities to individuals who most resemble racially the members of the dominant group. Despite its varied racial composition, the United States operates as a biracial society in which light skin color and Caucasian features associated with Europeans are valued more highly than are dark skin and Asian, native American, or African racial features. This concept is one of the social mechanisms that propels racism; it can be used to assess the differential effects of discrimination based on degrees of racial similarity and difference. It is necessary to understand variations in the life chances of people who strongly identify with an ethnic group by sharing a language and culture while differing in phenotype. A unique feature of the Hispanic population is Hispanics' wide variation in racial characteristics, from dark to light skin tone and from African and/or native American to European appearance.

Indeed, a recent study by Arce, Murgia, and Frisbie (1987) clearly indicates that educational and economic opportunities vary according to skin color. This held true for two generations studied, even as the children improved their income levels over their parents. Also, differences existed in quality of life within the community: the darker the skin color, the greater the tendency to report experiencing discrimination as a Mexican American. The study was conducted after Relethford, Stern, Gaskill, and Hazuda (1983) revealed that the Chicano population's skin color became progressively lighter as neighborhoods changed from the low-income barrios to the more affluent suburbs.

Emergence of Phenotypes

The events that led to differences in racial characteristics in Latin Americans were analyzed by Harris (1964) and Morner (1967), in Caribbean Latinos by Denton and Massey (1989), and in Mexicans by Massey and Denton (1990). They were also reviewed by Garcia Saiz (1989), head curator of the Colonial Section of the Museum of the Americas, Madrid, Spain, in her introduction to a remarkable series of 135 family portraits that document the 18th-century caste system in Mexico.

Harris (1964) reported that among the key influences in the emergence of phenotypes was the colonists' need for trustworthy intermediaries to operate plantations and agencies of social control. This need arose because there were too few male colonists with families to enable them to administer and oversee effectively the plantations as well as police the vastly larger native population. Another critical factor was the often disregarded "rule of racial descent." This rule condemned offspring of slaves to slavery. In disregarding the rule, children of female slaves and male colonists were legally free to marry anyone and to inherit the father's name and property. Also, Garcia Saiz (1989) stated that intermarriage was encouraged among all men and women by the Spanish Crown and colonial Spaniards in order to defuse interracial hostilities between natives and settlers in the Americas, due partly to the settlers' mistreatment of native women. Quoting from a historical record of 1503, she noted that it was also done so "the two groups could communicate and learn from each other" (p. 32). Gordon (1949) observed that the quasi open racial attitudes that followed "were reinforced by family ties over the course of time" (p. 386). Political power and status, however, were kept by the colonists.

As a result, Latin America developed multiracially stratified societies structured by the unequal distribution of rights and privileges among the various racial groups. The white colonials who had been born in Spain had the highest prestige and social position and were always portrayed as such in 18th-century paintings; colonials of Spanish or European heritage born in the Americas (*Ladinos* and *criollos*) who could claim white racial purity were next, followed by a large array of intermediate groups with mixed racial heritage. Persons with strong or pure native and/or African lineage never appeared in higher social settings. Morner (1967) reported boundary conflicts and tensions between the higher and the next lower stratum as a result of the former's effort to distinguish itself from the latter. The initial interracial hostility became diffused and contained within a complex caste system, which was later abolished in Mexico along with slavery after its war of independence from Spain in 1821. In time, the two white populations merged, resulting in three major social groups composed of light, intermediate, and dark phenotypes for much of Latin America. However, intergroup tensions continued.

Race Relations in the Americas

Various studies, mainly of Puerto Rican society, have described each population's social and psychological dilemmas. These studies may also be used to explain the ethnoracial dynamics confronting U.S. Hispanic families and their children.

The light group. The light group, *blancos*, which was composed primarily of whites born in Latin America, was never fully certain of its lineage because of its country's multiracial history. Sereno (1946) refers to "cryptomelanism" as the light Puerto Rican's effort to hide the existence of a color problem within the self out of fear of not being "perfectly" white. Light Puerto Ricans tried to reaffirm their racial purity by stressing their symbolic ties to Spain and by connecting the "best" aspects of their culture (meaning from Spain) to light skin and upper-class status (Rogler, 1948). The veneration of Spanish heritage among Mexican Americans led to the notion of the "Spanish myth"—the belief that local customs and the indigenous people were inferior to those from Spain, the taproot and spiritual motherland (Forbes, 1968). Consequently, European immigrants, especially Spaniards, who assured a new source of *sangre pura* (pure blood), had easier access to the upper class. The group's social circle tended to be small and tight, and elaborate procedures were used to admit new members from the indigenous population into its ranks (Fitzpatrick, 1971).

The intermediate group. Those with moderate coloration and racial features tended to experience the most adjustment problems in Latin America. *Mestizos* (mixture), referred to persons with Indian-Iberian roots. They varied from the lighter *trigeños* (the color of wheat) to *mulatos*, which described those with Afro-Iberian heritage. Their various coloration and racial features did not allow easy assessment and acceptance by the white group. In Mexico, 30 castes were formed from approximately 100 white, black, and native racial combinations, with agreement in no more than half of the examples shown in portraits (Garcia Saiz, 1989). In Brazil, there were more than 40 racial categories, each of which held slightly different social standing, but among which it was difficult to classify individuals except those who were white (Harris, 1964).

As a result, in Puerto Rico, persons in the intermediate group frequently felt uncertain about their social status and interpersonal support (Gordon, 1949, 1950). They strove to be regarded as lighter than their dark peers in order to identify with the privileged group. Nevertheless, only the most successful intermediates became candidates for membership in the privileged group. Longres (1974) noted that dark intermediates were treated better as they became educated and achieved wealth, and sometimes "became socially designated as white, acceptable in every way" (p. 70). As if to affirm their newly won status, the upwardly mobile within this group were often perpetrators of antiblack hostility (Sereno, 1946).

The dark group. *Indios* and *Negros* were most socially discriminated against, even though some could be found in the higher-status occupations and in influential positions. Puerto Rican folklore and literature are replete with deprecating references to dark people (Rodriguez de Laguna, 1987). Folklore also noted the duplicity of their middle- and upper-class white countrymen, although resentment was more often focused on the intermediates who attempted to pass by keeping their darker relatives out of sight (Sereno, 1946). Among intermediate and dark members of the lower class, however, there was little or no race distinction because their similar socioeconomic condition tended to neutralize appearance differences and to bar social differentiation along racial lines (Rogler, 1948). Together, they represent the largest segment of the population and give Puerto Rico its characteristic interracial social informality.

Nevertheless, the source of the dark group's dilemma was clear: half of them felt that having light skin was better and almost no one thought it was best to be black (Tumin & Feldman, 1969). As a consequence, they often preferred to have their children marry lighter in order to improve their social standing. The act of racially "passing" from one group to another underlines the existence of prejudice in the Americas, where subterfuge was necessary in order to become socially accepted.

In summary, it would be a mistake to assume that the vestiges of racial stratification, with its consequent tensions, are absent in Latin America today. (See De Cordoba, 1988, for the influence of race on Panamanian politics.) Still, cultural patterns in the Americas provide for more open forms of conviviality, intimacy, and marriage among the races and permit a wider range of phenotypical differences to exist in families while allowing their cultural identity to remain firm. When Latinos emigrate to the United States, they expect to encounter a similar pattern of race relations. They tend to arrive with high hopes for social mobility, given their belief in this country's democratic tenet that economic status and social integration are based on equal opportunity and individual achievement. But "Hispanics in general, and Puerto Ricans in particular, do not understand race as do most people in the United States" (Denton & Massey, 1989, p. 795), nor do they understand how a biracial system will affect the cultural identity and ethnic affiliation of their children.

The Acculturation of Hispanic Children

Acculturation is the process of learning the values, beliefs, and normative behaviors of the dominant culture informally through instruction, modeling, and social interaction at home and in the neighborhood and more formally through its social institutions. The concept is in keeping with Gordon's (1964) cultural and behavioral aspects of assimilation of white, European ethnic groups, although acculturation is viewed as a more complex process for Latinos (Casas & Vasquez, 1988; Padilla, 1980, 1987).

Acculturation is largely a conscious and voluntary act of linguistic and cultural acquisition that is within the minority person's control and is thus sensitive to the individual's motivation. Similar to the child's own ethnic enculturation, it also requires learning the subjective and deep aspects of the dominant culture that are reinforced through interaction with other members of the society. The minority child's first encounter with ethnoracial differences usually occurs in school after his or her ethnic culture has taken hold. The acculturation process is hindered by segregated neighborhoods that limit intergroup contact. It has been observed that housing patterns follow distinct racial lines among Mexican Americans (Relethford et al., 1983; Massey & Denton, 1990) and Caribbean Latinos (Denton & Massey, 1989). In the latter, controls for socioeconomic variables indicated that race, not class, accounted for the patterns of residential segregation.

Children are raised in social class life-styles that also prepare them to enter into the primary groups that are the main sources of intimate relationships, such as friendships, dating, courtship, and mate selection. Acculturation is often associated with attaining middle-class status and values, but these are also attainable within the socially stratified ethnic community. Having the combined cultural and social class experience, which Gordon (1964) referred to as "ethclass," is deemed essential for social integration.

The parents' task becomes especially difficult when society lacks consensus about its national policy toward minority populations. As a result, many families are uncertain whether acculturation improves their children's opportunities, social integration, and psychological adjustment when they encourage them to learn the dominant culture as a replacement for their own or when they encourage them to retain both cultures by adhering to multicultural values that facilitate a bicultural orientation.

Empirical studies of U.S. Hispanic populations provide scant comfort for resolving the acculturation dilemma facing minority families. Contrary to the "melting pot" replacement model, increased anxiety was associated with the stress generated by acculturation (Codina & Roberts, 1987), as were social adjustment problems in the studies reviewed by Griffith (1983). The concept of "acculturative stress" refers to significant but nonpathological responses such as these to the acculturation process. In terms of "cultural pluralism," Griffith (1983) found that Mexican-origin bicultural persons experienced the most psychosocial dysfunction, which he suggested may have been due to their experiencing conflicting pressures in social relations and conflict between their own traditional and the Anglo-American values.[1] This finding varied from earlier studies he cited of bicultural advantage: bicultural Mexican American adolescents were better adjusted than were highly acculturated peers (Dworkin, 1965; Buriel, Calzada, & Vasquez, 1982), and bicultural Cuban American students were better adjusted in school than were those who were more traditionally oriented (Szapocznik & Kurtines, 1980).

This research suggests that biculturality might create a bimodal situation of very well and very poorly functioning individuals, depending on how well individuals deal with the dual-culture experience. An example of one extreme is taken from field interviews.

> A fair-haired young man was burdened with the family's nickname of "golden boy" and was expected to carry the family out of poverty. He experienced intense conflict as the result of his belonging to an Anglo-dominant fraternity where

he found himself defending his ethnic group against asper-
sions and rejecting his exceptional status as a "good Mexican." It contributed to his heavy drinking, leaving school, and
feeling ashamed for disappointing his family.

Lest the parents conclude that acculturation should be avoided altogether, Neff, Hoppe, and Perea (1987) found that escapist
drinking and alcohol-related problems were even more common
among the least acculturated second-generation Mexican American males. Griffith (1983) also found that the least acculturated individuals experienced the greatest anxiety, due possibly to their
disadvantaged socioeconomic standing, even though they had the
fewest problems of psychosocial dysfunction, due in part to a
supportive ethnic network.

Acculturation also includes contending with the stereotypic
attitudes held by the dominant society about minorities, which include associating dark skin with members of the Hispanic community. Erikson (1963, 1968) observed that minority children have
special difficulty integrating positive ego prototypes, multiple social roles, and group memberships when the dominant culture de-
values their objects of identification generally and images of their
parents and ethnic group in particular. He believed that unsuccessful mastery of these tasks could result in extreme sensitivity to
one's difference; internalization of negative stereotypes as self-
stereotypes; denial and distortion; or denigration of one's body
image, skin color, and self-esteem. His conclusions regarding
body image were supported by Hurstfield's (1978) study of
preadolescent Hispanic youths who needed to come to terms with
their ethnicity before they could accept their body image. The following presents a case in point.

> A Mexican American high school honor student in treatment
> denied she knew Spanish, rejected her Hispanic heritage, and
> equated being dark with being Mexican and dirty. She was
> determined to prove her self-worth, always dressed very
> neatly, and kept herself extremely clean as if to compensate
> for her dark skin and Indian appearance. She fantasized, "As
> a young child, I frequently dreamed that I woke up and look-
> ed in the mirror and saw a white face. I was then happy.
> Sometimes I still feel that when I grow up I will be white and
> everything will be all right."

Parental uncertainty as to whether they should replace or retain the ethnic life-style as the preferred survival strategy may result in inconsistent and uneven acculturation of the children. This
may be a major reason for the widely varying degrees of biculturality of Hispanic peoples in the United States. The parents' dilemma is compounded when they are unprepared to help the chil-

dren deal with skin color as an additional factor in the latter's capacity to assimilate in biracial society.

Biracial Assimilation

Assimilation is the process of socially integrating minorities into the dominant society by recruiting them into primary groups and social institutions (Ruiz, 1981). The process is controlled by the dominant group, with the preferred applicants for assimilation being those who are racially as well as socially and culturally similar to its members. "In the United States, the national ideal is English-speaking, Protestant, northern European in descent, and light Caucasoid in physical appearance" (Wagley & Harris, 1958, p. 243). Although no Hispanic American meets all of the criteria, some can approximate these criteria while others cannot.

Social acceptance and economic opportunities are held out as the rewards for assimilation. They create "assimilative pressures" by acting as powerful incentives for acculturation. It is through the intimate social networks of friends and families that one often finds opportunities for gaining entry into society's opportunity structure, just as gaining professional and managerial status increases induction into influential social circles.

Among the selective criteria used for recruitment into primary groups is the person's suitability for marriage and family membership. The probability of intimate contact that leads to dating, courting, and marriage is increased when individuals live in the same neighborhoods and attend the same schools. As mentioned earlier, Hispanic residential patterns follow racial lines and provide clear evidence of who is and who is not capable of assimilation. Massey and Denton's (1990) analysis of census data noted that suburbanization of Chicanos was associated with higher income, having a non-Mexican spouse, and choosing "white" as one's race. "The fact that mestizos are less likely to attain suburban residential location [compared with white Mexican Americans] means that they are less able to achieve contact with Anglos" (p. 29). Neighborhood segregation is even more severe for Latinos of African descent: "No matter how Hispanics view themselves, Anglos perceive anyone of mixed race as black and treat them accordingly" (Denton & Massey, 1989, p. 802).

Residential segregation, then, can serve the gatekeeping function of limiting the number of Hispanics who are unsuitable for interfamily membership. It also places limits on the children's learning through interpersonal contact about the social life-style and the deep aspects of the dominant culture that are necessary to become fully acculturated and assimilated. Moreover, the quality of the interpersonal contact, when it occurs, tends to stress racial difference and commitment to ethnicity. Massey and Denton (1990) learned that Mexican Americans with school-age children were less likely to identify themselves as "white." They conclude, "If we assume that having children [and] attending U.S. schools . . . draws parents more closely into American society and its institutions, then whatever message is transmitted to parents through the schools would appear to reinforce their distinctiveness from the Anglo-American majority and strengthen their commitment to a mestizo identity" (p. 22). The field interviews indicate that the message is very clear and most of the critical incidents that had lasting effect on the Chicanos' ethnic identity occurred in school.

Growing Up Dark and Indian-looking

Most of the darker Mexican Americans interviewed were acutely aware of their skin color and the role it had played in their lives. The attributes of the national ideal become known to Latino families through their personal and collective experience with discrimination in school, housing, and the marketplace. They are confirmed by the prevailing white norm of beauty and attractiveness and by the unfamiliar role models children encounter. The U.S. media produce stereotypes of Latinos as dark-skinned people who fill in the background to provide "local color" (Montalvo, 1987), or share the Mexican national media's protrayal of the Hispanic ideal as light, European, and successful individuals who are served by dark-skinned domestics (Walsh, 1987).

These experiences usually begin in school, and the message that is sent to the parents is often conveyed by the child, which may contribute to the parents' further alienation from the educational system (Montalvo, 1984). Five-year-old Chicano preschool children learn to prefer light-skinned playmates and to avoid coloring face drawings in brown (Cota-Robles de Suarez, 1971). One man learned in grade school to feel ashamed of his brown skin:

> An older Chicano recalled with some bitterness that as a child he could never get the dark skin on the back of his hand "white enough to pass that school teacher's inspection for cleanliness. I used to scrub and scrub, and nothing. It stayed the same and I kept blaming myself for something I couldn't help.

The message sent to parents can also be that their child cannot learn. Covington (1989) stated that research indicates that feelings of shame, lowered expectations, and further poor performance are likely to occur when past failure in school is causally linked in the child's mind to an inherent lack of ability. For minority children, the causal chain begins with low scholastic expectations stemming from an internalization of the ethnic stereotype that they lack the ability to learn. A self-fulfilling prophecy can be set in motion. Cota-Robles de Suarez (1971) cites the case of a bright 13-year-old who doubted her ability to achieve and began a downward spiral of performance as she learned to associate her denigrated ethnicity and phenotype with pessimism and shame:

> To begin with, I am a Mexican. That sentence has a scent of bitterness as it is written. I feel that if weren't for my nationality I would accomplish more. My being Mexican has brought about my lack of initiative. No matter what I attempt to do, my dark skin always makes me feel that I will fail (p. 121).

Most of the darker Mexican Americans interviewed were acutely aware of their skin color and the role it had played in their lives. As parents see the strivings of their dark-skinned children repeatedly frustrated and their hopes attentuated, assimilation in time fails to act as an effective incentive and acculturation is seen as a less viable path toward integration. Some children grow up to reject assimilation as a goal altogether. Some persevere, "biculturate," and achieve success within the social constraints as a way of confirming their personal worth and dignity. Others foreshorten their aspirations and applaud their lighter peers' achievements while harboring resentment over an unjust world. Still others internalize their feelings, blame themselves, and try to accommodate by changing who they are. They avoid suntans and seek ways to lighten their skin, or as in the following case, look for a magical cure.

> As the darkest member of his family, one young man remembered feeling stereotyped as a Mexican when the family moved to a new town, while his light-skinned sister experienced few problems. He dreamed of changing his Spanish surname so his grade school classmates would mistake him for an Anglo.

The darker the Latinos' skin color, the more they reported being expected to speak Spanish regardless of their level of acculturation. The kernal of truth in this stereotype is found in a study connecting skin color to language acquisition and loss, which are measures of acculturation. Codina's (1990) study found that Mexican-born subjects who preferred "Mexican" as an ethnic label were darker and more Spanish- and less English-language proficient than were those who were also born in Mexico but identified themselves as "Mexican American." Expecting darker Latinos to know Spanish conforms to the media image of the Hispanic immigrant, but it also implies believing that dark Latinos retain their mother tongue because they are less able to assimilate and have

fewer opportunities to acculturate. This belief intuitively acknow-
ledges racism as a social reality.

Lewin (1948) noted that people develop a sense of marginal
identity not because they belong to two or more groups, but because they are uncertain about where they belong.

> A deep-olive-skinned woman recalled the pain and punish-
> ment she received in school for not understanding English.
> She blamed her Spanish-speaking, dark-skinned, uneducated
> parents for being a constant source of embarrassment to her
> and for not preparing her better for the "real world." "I want-
> ed to think, feel, and be white because that is how you become
> accepted." She referred to herself as "Spanish," married an
> Anglo professional, lived in an Anglo neighborhood, wore ex-
> pensive clothes, sent her children to exclusive schools, and did
> not teach them Spanish. When she could no longer afford to
> give her time and money to a socially prominent charity orga-
> nization, she lost all the friends she had made. She felt bitter,
> used, and alone. She ended the interview by saying "I don't
> belong to any group. I don't really know who I am!"

Growing Up Light and European-looking

Many light-skinned Mexican Americans reported seldom
having thought about skin color as an issue in their lives or about
the fact that few, if any, of their dates or Hispanic friends were
dark.

Nevertheless, skin-color preference was subtly communicated
to them when they were children. After sensitive probing, some of
them recalled being showered with attention because of their fair
complexion, or having overheard relatives remark "nacio bien
guerita y bonita [o bien prieta]" (was born very white and pretty
[or very dark]). The experience was ego-enhancing and resulted
in their seldom questioning their acceptability. Hurstfield's (1978)
study of preadolescents found that Anglo children with positive
self-concepts seldom reported their race as an important part of
their self-concept; those who did report race as part of their self-
concept were less positive and certain about their identity.

Thus most light Hispanic subjects regarded their skin color as
inconsequential and as a norm in their assumptive world, whereas some felt dismay over the ethnoracial inconsistency it created
for them.

> One interview subject found it a constant struggle and ex-
> tremely frustrating when Anglos acted surprised and some-
> times "let down" to learn that she was Mexican. She felt that
> she was always playing a dual role. "Sometimes I feel that I
> am betraying my Mexican heritage and, on the other hand, I

can experience the advantage of being Anglo and also passing for white at times."

Assimilation pressures often occur in the form of requiring increased association with the dominant group, which constantly
challenges the minority person's sense of group loyalty. As candidates for assimilation, Latino youths of light and moderate skin
tone may minimize contact with darker, more visibly ethnic peers
in an effort to disassociate themselves from the disparaged members. Those who feel less able to assimilate often attribute the shift
in reference group to an effort by their peers to reject them per-
sonally and deny their ethnic origins. Labels such as "Tío Taco"
(Uncle Tom) or "coconut" (brown skin, white sentiments) reflect
the hostility reserved for them regardless of their color.

Some who strive to acculturate believe that their motives are
misunderstood by their ethnic friends and resent their efforts being perceived as acts of ethnic disloyalty. Their sometimes uneven
command of the native language may be taken as a reflection on
their loyalty, rather than seen as a function of monolingual education and pressures to assimilate. Those who did not learn to speak
Spanish well disengage even further from their reference group.

> A light-complected woman recalled that her parents would
> not teach the children Spanish or let them speak the language
> in the home. When she was 13 years old, her darker ethnic
> peers teased her by uttering vulgarities in Spanish. She found
> herself associating more and more with her Anglo friends.
> Then her classmates accused her of trying to "act white." Re-
> cently, when planning a 10-year high school class reunion, a
> Hispanic friend said wryly, "I always knew you would marry
> an Anglo." There was still resentment in the subject's voice as
> she related the incident.

Others remain caught in ethnoracial contradictions as they
strive both to assimilate and accommodate themselves to their
ethnic group. One person was burdened with guilt and hints of
cryptomelanism:

> A young, light-skinned Chicana steadfastly defended her dark-
> er peers against slurs by her Anglo husband's friends while re-
> maining fearful that her unborn child might turn out to have
> unacceptable dark skin.

Another person made a conscious choice to balance the contradictions with a curious charade.

> One Chicano was perceived as light skinned by the inter-
> viewer but identified himself as intermediate because he
> learned while growing up that if he were light his friends
> would think that he was trying to "pass off" as white, and be-

ing dark, he added, suggests that the person may be an "illegal alien."

Not feeling grounded in either group may account partly for the cross-pressures in social relations experienced by many biculturals, which might have been the source of the psychosocial dysfunction reported by Griffith (1983). It resulted in the proposition that although lighter-skinned Hispanics may have better life chances and are in better control of opportunities, a subgroup of persons among them experience intense psychological distress. It was believed to be particularly intense among some intermediates whose ambiguous phenotype created uncertainty in their relations with dominant-group members.

Summary

Societal integration must be understood within the acculturation–assimilation crucible from which the child's ethnoracial identity emerges. Sociocultural differences encountered during acculturation can produce psychological stress, but the critical role played by society's valuation of skin color as a requirement for assimilation compounds the damaging consequences for family functioning, formation of the members' ethnic identity, and the community's social and cultural integrity. No phenotype escapes stereotyping and discrimination. Unlike what occurs in Latin America, in the United States ethnoracial stress is created by the interacting effect of race and ethnicity under the conditions described. It is seen as a key factor in the variation among Mexican Americans in the development of psychosocial problems, response patterns, and accommodations to the dominant society and to their ethnic group.

Phenotype and Mental Health

Method

Two studies of phenotypes (Arce, Murgia, & Frisbie, 1987; Codina & Montalvo, in preparation) used data from the National Chicano Survey conducted by the University of Michigan in 1979. It was based on a probability sample of approximately 1,000 Mexican Americans living in the southwestern states and in the metropolitan area of Chicago. Interviewers used a 5 X 5 phenotype scale to estimate the respondents' light-to-dark skin color and their Indian-to-European appearance. The 25 cells were collapsed into three groups and resulted in 26% being identified as light European, 45% as intermediate, and 28% as dark Indian. The numbers in the collapsed groups accounted for 96% of the sample subjects.

Codina and Montalvo (in preparation) analyzed phenotypes by five major indices of psychological distress derived from the Chicano Survey; symptoms of depression, anxiety and feelings of ill health, and public and private aspects of self-esteem. The indices are described more thoroughly in the work in progress. Briefly, depression was associated with the frequency with which people felt lonely, alone, and sad, rather than with extreme vegetative states. Anxiety consisted of worrying and states of nervousness, and ill health gauged somatic symptoms and their influence on work habits. Private self-esteem was measured by asking subjects negatively worded questions about feelings of low self-worth, incompetence, and pessimism about the future. Public self-esteem focused on social supports, tapping into the subjects' feeling that no one paid attention to them or cared about them, that they could not count on others, and that they were disliked and ignored. This differentiation is similar to Frank and Marolla's (1976) distinction between inner and outer self-esteem, wherein the former refers to personal efficacy and competence and the latter to dealing independently with acceptance and approval by significant others.

An analysis of variance (ANOVA) was conducted. Comparison was made of the mean difference in scores as well as the proportion of members of phenotypes with extreme scores one standard deviation above the mean. The latter were identified as subjects at risk. Differences in subject responses by gender and acculturation levels, as measured by country of birth, were investigated.

Major Findings

The major findings underscored the general thesis that social status and phenotypes are intricately linked and create ethnoracial stress. On the interpersonal level of self-esteem, phenotyping affected the entire sample, regardless of gender and level of acculturation. The more dark and Indian in appearance they were, the more Mexican Americans felt disliked, ignored, and uncared for, which is consistent with darker Chicanos reporting more discrimination (Arce, Murgia, & Frisbie, 1987).

Growing up in the United States was particularly hazardous psychologically for dark Mexican American males, who also had the poorest life chances. Their experience, however, seemed to be a very private one. Their significantly higher score for depression, anxiety, and ill health, compared with other men, was accompanied by the lowest levels of self-worth as measured by private self-esteem. This result is consistent with studies cited by Bhatti, Derezotes, Kim, and Specht (1989), who found that self-esteem was negatively correlated with depression. Dark-Indian males also reported having more anxiety and ill-health than did other men, although the pattern was significant only when compared with intermediates. By contrast, light-European men had the lowest mean score for depression and a better sense of self-worth than did dark Chicanos.

Most Mexican American men with moderate coloration and appearance generally managed quite well, reporting less anxiety and ill health than light Europeans. However, a significantly greater number of native-born intermediates showed extreme scores for depression. This response pattern may point to the predicted subgroup of intermediates whose racial ambiguity may cause them to experience a particular type of stress.

Lastly, women scored significantly worse than did men on all mental health measures except public self-esteem, on which they scored significantly better. Surprisingly, dark-Indian women fared equally as well and, on one important measure, better than did their lighter Chicana cohorts. The Mexican-born, light-European women felt most depressed. This unexpected finding may be explained by Vegas-Willis and Cervantes's (1987) observation that a significant group of women, upon immigrating to the United States, experience the loss of the social status that they enjoyed in Mexico. Under the assumption that high status and privilege are linked to fair skin in Mexico (Walsh, 1987), the phenotype study may have identified a subgroup of light-European women who experienced radical discontinuity in social standing when they arrived in the United States and were treated as a Spanish-speaking minority-group member for the first time.

A significantly higher percentage of light-skinned Chicanas who were born in the United States were also at risk for depression and for experiencing public, rather than private, self-esteem than were their dark-Indian cohorts. Further study of this subgroup might reveal that the sources of their symptoms are a sense of marginality and ambivalent ethnic loyalty.

Discussion: Assessment of Ethnoracial Stress

At the heart of the Hispanic experience in the United States is a form of racism that both binds light and dark Latinos to each other and divides them into separate groups. Race may prove to be a more pernicious element in their lives than are linguistic, cultural, and socioeconomic differences. Skin-color prejudice is not a new discovery in race relations, but knowledge of it is an important addition to our knowledge about the formation of ethnoracial identity in Hispanic Americans.

The mental health research indicated that Hispanic clients should be assessed for ethnoracial stress because the psychological and social consequences of acculturation and biracial assimilation are so pervasive. As such, the concept of phenotyping is extended to include the experience of psychic benefits as well as improved life chances, the more the person racially resembles members of the dominant society.

The influence of skin color in the client's life should be given special attention when his or her problems involve self-acceptance and identity formation. A risk among some dark-Indian Chicanos with low educational and socioeconomic attainment is the potential for their blaming themselves for their situation because of a low sense of self-worth that accompanies their psychological impairment. Phenotyping was seen as an important factor in substance abuse among Puerto Ricans in an early field study in New York City by Berle (1959), who reported that all of the 20 drug addicts encountered were the darkest members of their families.

Self-doubt and ethnic ambivalence are risks among some light-European Mexican Americans, who may question the basis of their achievements and find themselves at odds with darker friends and relatives. Some experience marginality in that they are caught between identifying with the dominant society and their ethnic group. Practitioners should be aware of the plight of some light-European immigrant women, whose first encounter with discrimination was in marked contrast with their previous high status, and of some born in the United States, whose feelings of depression were associated with a lack of interpersonal support. Case studies presented earlier provide some understanding of the ethnoracial dilemmas many of them face. Why light Mexican American males seemed less affected by this dilemma than do women awaits further study.

Racial Self-Perception

Racial self-perception is a complex phenomenon that requires investigation. Comparison of phenotype, as reported by the client and as observed, should be routinely noted in client records along with other important ethnic-specific information, such as country of origin, language use, and acculturation level. The tendency for some individuals to psychologically distort their racial self-perception is largely unreported in clinical practice with Latinos. Berne (1983) reported the case of a severely depressed Latina whose mother and grandmother convinced her that she was much darker than she really was. Comas-Diaz and Minrath (1985) saw attitude toward skin color as a key issue in the psychotherapy with ethnoracial-borderline clients, who often associate good and bad personal attributes with light and dark skin.

Standardized scales are needed in order to have reliable protocols available for consistent assessments of phenotype. Separate scales are needed for the two major Hispanic groups, Chicanos and Puerto Ricans, for whom Indian and African genetic heritage are at issue. Both groups are subject to biracial assimilative pressures and provide insights into the other's response patterns, but their intergroup experiences in the United States are sufficiently unique to caution against overgeneralization.

Some empirical evidence indicates how accommodating to racial attitudes in the United States affects the racial self-perceptions of Latinos. Bilingual interviewers in the National Chicano Survey classified 26% of the subjects as light European, 45% as intermediate, and 28% as dark Indian. By contrast, Denton and Massey's (1989) report indicated that more than twice as many Mexican Americans (55%) called themselves white, 38% selected "Spanish race" (assumed *mestizo*), and less than 1% selected Indian as a self-description. These differences suggest a tendency to report themselves as lighter than they appeared to other Mexican Americans. Massey and Denton (1990) also noted that choosing "white" was positively related to socioeconomic status.

Yet, the pioneering studies by Rodriguez (1980, 1989) found a stronger trend among many Puerto Ricans toward "browning," wherein the subjects saw themselves as darker than they were seen by others, although some saw themselves as lighter than they were. Rodriguez proposed that the patterns were in response to prevailing racial attitudes in the community. Many intermediate (nonwhite and nonblack) Caribbeans shared neighborhoods with white Latinos, but their level of segregation from Anglos was nearly as high as that of black Caribbeans (Denton & Massey, 1989). It is possible that "browning" may have occurred mostly among Caribbean intermediates who were sensitive to being viewed as black Hispanics by the Anglo community, whereas lighter self-perceptions may have occurred among moderates whose primary comparative reference group was white Latino neighbors.

Impressions from student field interviews with Mexican Americans also indicated that skin color may be perceived as light when most peers are darker, and dark when they are lighter. At times, this phenomenon can account for the sudden discovery or disappearance of race as a salient issue when the person moves to where the ethnic density of the neighborhood and school are different. The case example of a dark-skinned boy who wished to change his Spanish name in a new school was presented above. Further study might reveal that the propensity to see oneself as darker is more common among the depressed Chicano intermediates in our study, who may have been unsure of their racial identity in a predominantly white environment. To add to the complexity, Massey and Denton (1990) found that there was a greater tendency among Mexican Americans to choose "white" as a racial classification when high ethnic density was coupled with high residential segregation. They suggest that these community variables lead to an acute perception of discrimination in the environment by the deprecated minorities and a desire to identify with the advantaged group. This may account partially for the large discrepancy between the observed and self-reported phenotypes discussed above.

Finally, although a child's phenotype is largely unchangeable, parents should be helped to evaluate the disparate values that are placed on skin color by society; how they are subtly communicated to the children; and how assimilative pressures can influence family relationships, raising children, and children's acculturation into American society. Phenotyping has an impact on children throughout their school years and it may play a role in some children becoming discouraged and dropping out of school. Nevertheless, the ambiguous racial nature of critical incidents requires careful sorting of behaviors that are inaccurately attributed to prejudice but are so interpreted because of the heightened sensitivity created in the minority child. In this connection, Rodriguez (1980) reported intrafamily comparisons when the darkest children in the families perceived their pigmentation as darker than their actual color.

Field interviews confirm that parents play a critical role in mitigating the painful assaults on the ethnic child's self-image and self-esteem by dealing with the subject openly, preventing internalization of negative stereotypes and affirming cultural roots and that "brown is beautiful." There are few better examples of how parents can help their children deal with the pain and confusion than the following:

> A father found his young daughter running home crying because her classmates had made fun of her brown skin. She was bewildered because she thought her skin was white like that of the other children. He told his little girl that she was brown like him and that she should be proud of it because she came from a "wonderful culture made up of beautiful people."

Epilogue

A major purpose of my initial treatment of this subject was to understand why there was a dearth of empirical research and public interest in race as an influence in the Latino's life chances in the United States (Montalvo, 1987). My conclusion, albeit speculative, points to the subtle and insidious power of racism to narrow our construct of social reality.

Mexican Americans' initial experience with racial discrimination by Anglo settlers in the Southwest made them fear that they would be racial outcasts. They argued that the differences between them and the dominant group that prevented their entry into the opportunity structure were not race but language and culture. (The early legal arguments against school segregation, for example, were based on the Mexican Americans not being racially different from whites.) This focus allowed some Mexican Americans to be assimilated after their acculturation overcame the cultural differences. One author referred to obscuring race as an issue in the United States as "a conspiracy of silence" between Mexican Americans and Anglo-Americans. The argument fits well with their Latin American experience, in which cultural identity superseded racial differences. Emphasizing culture also served further to disguise race as a potential source of internal division in family and community and stressed that race was a taboo and repugnant subject for public discussion.

The argument was persuasive. In exchange for the silence, Anglo-Americans were relieved from being blamed for subjugating Mexican Americans on the basis of race by placing the burden of assimilation at the door of the ethnic group. The collective wisdom proposed that "it was up to them to assimilate." Lack of assimilation was due to their inability or lack of motivation to manage the cultural transition, rather than to racial discrimination. Underachievement in school and in the economy, and the attendant psychosocial problems, can be attributed to the family's cultural deprivation and difference in life-style from middle-class Anglos. The victim was blamed. Structural barriers to opportunities did not have to be addressed seriously because the arrangement maintained intact the American belief that social and economic parity is gained through perseverance. The evidence presented in this report suggests otherwise.

The conspiracy of silence also hardened the dialogue among minorities of color, muffled criticism of personal and institutional racism, and rendered mute the discussion of race as a serious subject of concern for Hispanic Americans. It is hoped that this will change.

References

Arce, C. E., Murgia, E., & Frisbie, W. P. (1987). Phenotype and life chances among Chicanos. *Hispanic Journal of Behavioral Sciences, 9*, 19–32.

Berle, B. R. (1959). *Eighty Puerto Rican families in New York City*. New York: Columbia University Press.

Berne, E. (1983). The mythology of dark and fair: Psychiatric use of folklore. *Transactional Analysis Journal, 13*, 261–270. (Paper presented at the San Francisco Psychoanalytic Society, March 13, 1950, and reprinted from the *Journal of American Folklore*, 1959, 1–13.)

Bhatti, B., Derezotes, D., Kim, S., & Specht, H. (1989). The association between child maltreatment and self-esteem. In A. M. Mecca, N. J. Smelser, & J. Vasconcellos (Eds.), *The social importance of self-esteem* (pp. 24–71). Berkeley, CA: University of California Press.

Buriel, R., Calzada, S., & Vasquez, R. (1982). Relationship of traditional Mexican American culture to adjustment and delinquency among three generations of Mexican American male adolescents. *Hispanic Journal of Behavioral Sciences, 1*, 41–45.

Casas, J. M., & Vasquez, M. J. T. (1988). Counseling the Hispanic client: A theoretical and applied perspective. In P. B. Pedersen, J. G. Draguns, W. J. Louner, & J. E. Trimble (Eds.), *Counseling across cultures* (pp. 153–176). Honolulu, HI: University of Hawaii Press.

Codina, G. E. (1990). *Race, class, ethnicity and Chicano mental health: A psychosocioeconomic model*. Doctoral dissertation, University of Michigan.

Codina, G. E., & Montalvo, F. F. (in preparation). *Effects of phenotyping on the mental health and self-esteem of Mexican Americans*.

Codina, G. E., & Roberts, R. (1987). A comparison of well-being in the Mexican origin and general populations using national survey data. In R. Rodriguez & M. T. Coleman (Eds.), *Mental health issues in the Mexican origin population in Texas* (pp. 71–88). Austin, TX: Hogg Foundation for Mental Health, University of Texas.

Comas-Diaz, L., & Minrath, M. (1985). Psychotherapy with ethnic minority borderline clients. *Psychotherapy, 22*, 418–426.

Cota-Robles de Suarez, C. (1971). Skin color as a factor in the racial identification and preference of young Chicano children. *Aztlan, 2*, 107–150.

Covington, M. V. (1989). Self-esteem and failure in school: Analysis and policy implications. In A. M. Mecca, N. J. Smelser, & J. Vasconcellos (Eds.), *The social importance of self-esteem* (pp. 72–124). Berkeley, CA: University of California Press.

De Cordoba, J. (1988, March 11). Think 'family feud' to help figure out politics in Panama. *Wall Street Journal*.

Denton, N. A., & Massey, D. S. (1989). Racial identity among Caribbean Hispanics: The effect of double minority status on residential segregation. *American Sociological Review, 54*, 790–808.

Dworkin, A. G. (1965). Stereotypes and self-images held by native-born and foreign-born Mexican Americans. *Sociology and Social Research, 49*, 214–224.

Erikson, E. H. (1963). *Childhood and society* (2nd ed.). New York: W. W. Norton.

Erikson, E. H. (1968). *Identity: Youth and crisis*. New York: W. W. Norton.

Fitzpatrick, J. P. (1971). *Puerto Rican American: The meaning of migration to the mainland*. Englewood Cliffs, NJ: Prentice-Hall.

Forbes, J. D. (1968). Race and color in Mexican American problems. *Journal of Human Relations, 16*, 55–68.

Frank, D. D., & Marolla, J. (1976). Efficacious action and social approval as interacting dimensions of self-esteem: A tentative formulation through construct validation. *Sociometry, 39*, 41–58.

Garcia Saiz, M. C. (1989). *Las castas Mexicanas; Un genero pictorico Americano* (The castes: A genre of Mexican paintings). Milan, Italy: Olivetti.

Gordon, M. M. (1964). *Assimilation in American life: The role of race, religion and national origin.* New York: Oxford University Press.

Gordon, M. W. (1949). Race pattern and prejudice in Puerto Rico. *American Sociological Review, 14*, 194–301.

Gordon, M. W. (1950). Cultural aspects of Puerto Rico's race problems. *American Sociological Review, 15*, 382–392.

Griffith, J. (1983). Relationship between acculturation and psychological impairment in adult Mexican Americans. *Hispanic Journal of Behavioral Sciences, 5*, 431–459.

Harris, M. (1964). *Patterns of race in the Americas.* New York: Walker and Company.

Hurstfield, J. (1978). Internal colonialism: White, black and Chicano self-conceptions. *Ethnic and Race Studies, 1*, 60–79.

Lewin, K. (1948). *Resolving social conflict.* New York: Harper Brothers.

Longres, J. F. (1974). Racism and its effect on Puerto Rican continentals. *Social Casework, 55*, 67–75.

Massey, D. S., & Denton, N. A. (1990). *Racial identity and the segregation of Mexicans in the United States.* Population Research Center of the National Opinion Research Center, University of Chicago.

Montalvo, F. F. (1984). Making good schools from bad. In *Make something happen, Hispanics and urban high school reform,* vol. 2 (pp. 71–74). Washington, DC: Hispanic Policy Development Project.

Montalvo, F. F. (1987). *Skin color and Latinos: The origins and contemporary patterns of ethnoracial ambiguity among Mexican Americans and Puerto Ricans* (Monograph). San Antonio, TX: Our Lady of the Lake University.

Morner, M. (1967). *Race mixture in the history of Latin America.* Boston: Little, Brown and Co.

Neff, J. A., Hoppe, S. K., & Perea, P. (1987). Acculturation and alcohol use: Drinking patterns and problems among Anglo and Mexican American male drinkers. *Hispanic Journal of Behavioral Sciences, 9*, 151–182.

Padilla, A. M. (Ed.). (1980). *Acculturation: Theory, models, and some new findings.* Boulder, CO: Westview Press.

Padilla, A. M. (1987). Introduction, special issue: Acculturation research. *Hispanic Journal of Behavioral Sciences, 9*, v–vii.

Relethford, J. H., Stern, M. P., Gaskill, S. P., & Hazuda, H. P. (1983). Social class, admixture, and skin color variation among Mexican Americans and Anglo Americans living in San Antonio, Texas. *American Journal of Physical Anthropology, 62*, 97–102.

Rodriguez, C. E. (1980). Puerto Ricans: Between black and white. In C. E. Rodriguez, V. S. Korrol, & J. O. Alers (Eds.), *The Puerto Rican struggle: Essays on survival in the U.S.* (pp. 20–30). Maplewood, NJ: Waterfront Press.

Rodriguez, C. E. (1989). *Puerto Ricans: Born in the U.S.A.* Winchester, MA: Unwin Hyman.

Rodriguez de Laguna, A. (1987). *Notes on Puerto Rican literature: Images and identities—an introduction.* Newark, NJ: Rutgers, The State University of New Jersey.

Rogler, C. (1948). Some situational aspects of race relations in Puerto Rico. *Social Forces, 26*, 72–77.

Ruiz, R. A. (1981). Cultural and historical perspectives in counseling Hispanics. In

E. H. Richardson, R. E. Ruiz, & E. J. Smith (Eds.), *Counseling the culturally different: Theory and practice* (pp. 186–215). New York: John Wiley.

Sereno, R. (1946). Cryptomelanism: A study of color relations and personal insecurity in Puerto Rico. *Psychiatry, 10,* 261–269.

Szapocznik, J., & Kurtines, W. M. (1980). Acculturation, biculturalism, and adjustment among Cuban Americans. In A. M. Padilla (Ed.), *Acculturation: Theory, models, and some new findings.* Boulder, CO: Westview Press.

Tumin, M. M., & Feldman, A. (1969). Social class and skin color in Puerto Rico. In M. M. Tumin (Ed.), *Comparative perspectives on race relations* (pp. 197–214). Boston: Little, Brown & Company.

Vegas-Willis, G., & Cervantes, R. C. (1987). Consideration of psychological stress in the treatment of the Latina immigrants. *Hispanic Journal of Behavioral Sciences, 9,* 315–329.

Wagley, C., & Harris, M. (1958). *Minorities in the new world.* New York: Columbia University Press.

Walsh, M. W. (1987, February 18). Amid dark-haired Mexicans, blonds really have more fun. *Wall Street Journal.*

7

Sensitive Mental Health Services for Low-Income Puerto Rican Families

América Facundo

Nunca perdió vigor en Bernardo la honda raíz isleña;
y nunca incurrió Cesar en la mezquindad de regatear-
le puertorriqueñidad a la gran masa trasplantada.[*]

José Luis González
Prologue to *Memorias de Bernardo Vega*
(Andreu-Iglesias, 1980)

Puerto Rican families come in many forms, structures, and colors. Extended families may have members whose appearance ranges from black skin, dark hair, and dark eyes to blonde hair, blue eyes, and freckled white skin. Within one family, all or some may speak Spanish, all or some may speak English, all may be bilingual, and in some families members may speak three or more languages. More than three million Puerto Ricans live in Puerto Rico, and close to the same number live in the United States. Some listen to Mozart, others to *salsa*; some like rock or jazz and others *jibaro* [peasant] music; some decorate their homes with plastic flowers, others with Dali's paintings; some obtain doctoral degrees, others do not make it beyond primary school; some travel to Europe on vacations, others have not seen the sea; some are Catholics, oth-

---

[*]"Bernardo's deep roots as an Islander never lost strength, and Cesar never descended to the meanness of negating the Puerto Ricanness of the transplanted people."

ers fundamentalists, *santeros*, *espiritistas* [spiritualists], or are not religious; some want independence for Puerto Rico, others statehood; some want the continuation of the commonwealth, others do not get involved in politics; some go to Houston for open-heart surgery, others have no health insurance; some leave their country on their own initiative, others because they have no choice.

In other words, discussing Puerto Ricans, or any other ethnic group, is a complex matter. Should one focus on the similarities or the differences within the group? Should one use generalizations to facilitate understanding by readers not acquainted with the group, or should the complexity of the group always be respected when attempting to describe it? Is there a set of values, beliefs, and behaviors that make up the "culture" of the group, or is the concept of culture too broad to be useful in any way?

Discussing an ethnic group as diverse as Puerto Ricans is further complicated by the fact that Puerto Ricans are divided between two nations. In addition, issues related to national and ethnic identity, language, adherence to values and belief systems, economic resources, educational background, migration patterns, and the clinical implications of these issues must all be considered. This chapter focuses on the delivery of sensitive mental health services to low-income Puerto Rican families in the United States.

Puerto Rican Migration to the United States

The first large wave of Puerto Rican migration to the United States occurred in the period 1899–1940.[1] It began shortly after the invasion of the island by U.S. troops following the Spanish–American war. Landless peasants were thrown into the labor force when the lands used for coffee crops were taken over by sugar corporations bought with U.S. capital; these workers were prime candidates for emigration to the United States (Maldonaldo-Denis, 1982).

Nearly 90,000 workers migrated to the United States during this period, primarily to New York (Vázquez-Calzada, 1979). Because the majority of these workers had no schooling, they became low-wage laborers who were intermittently employed, underemployed, and unemployed as economic conditions dictated (Rodríguez, 1979). Although migration to the United States did not significantly improve their living conditions, it seemed "less bad" than the complete lack of job opportunities in their homeland.

The second large migratory wave occurred after World War II. The Puerto Rican government, in conjunction with the U.S. government, developed an economic strategy designed to attract

U.S. industrial capital to develop the island's economy. Long-term tax exemptions and "cheap labor" were among the incentives offered to U.S. industrialists. This strategy, called "Operation Bootstrap," was formally initiated in 1947.

To deal with what was regarded as an excessive population that would hinder economic growth, as an "escape valve" Operation Bootstrap promoted massive emigration of Puerto Ricans to the U.S. as well as sterilization of low-income women, sometimes without prior consent, through a so-called "family planning" program (Maldonado-Denis, 1969).

Operation Bootstrap did not work as planned. The industries, which were highly mechanized, did not absorb the expected number of people into the work force, particularly during the phase characterized by the establishment of huge petrochemical and pharmaceutical plants on the island. Thus, the "escape valve" —emigration—was left open.

As a result of the promotion of massive emigration, by 1988 the number of Puerto Ricans in the United States had reached 2.5 million (12.7% of the total Latino population) (U.S. Department of Commerce, 1988). As a result of the sterilization strategy, by 1969 35% of Puerto Rican women between 20 and 49 years of age had been sterilized (History Task Force, 1979). Forced exile and sterilization of the poor were considered a reasonable price to pay for the so-called economic growth of Puerto Rico.

The majority of Puerto Ricans who migrated have had to deal with racism and discrimination, not only because they were considered "foreigners" (even though legally they are citizens, due to the colonial relationship between Puerto Rico and the U.S.), but also because they were poor. At present the employment situation has not improved significantly for low-income Puerto Rican migrants; they continue to be offered low-status jobs with low wages.[2] According to the Current Population Survey (U.S. Department of Commerce, 1988), 37.9% of all Puerto Rican families in the United States live *below* the poverty level, despite the fact that their unemployment level is only 9.2%. The median earned income of Puerto Rican families is $15,185, compared with $30,853 for the nation as a whole. Thus, underemployment and underpayment continue to be the norm.

The historical experience of Puerto Ricans has divided them into diverse groups, those who remained on the island after it became a colony of the United States and those who emigrated to the United States. The circumstances of each group have led to significant differences in values, beliefs, and problem-solving strategies, which impede generalizations about the Puerto Rican "culture."

A growing number of Puerto Rican human services profession-als are also leaving the island and are being recruited by agencies and institutions that serve Puerto Ricans in the United States. They are being recruited in the belief that if the "helper" and "client" have the same national origin, the therapeutic relationship is facilitated. In the specific case of community mental health centers, however, dif-ferences in social class[3] between therapists and clients and how cross-cultural differences affect the therapeutic relationship are, with few exceptions, ignored (Comas-Díaz & Griffith, 1988).[4]

Mental Health Sevices

The 1980s have seen significant growth in the mental health lit-erature addressing cultural, socioeconomic, clinical, and develop-mental issues of Puerto Ricans in the United States (García-Coll & Mattei, 1989; Comas-Díaz & Griffith, 1988; McGoldrick, Hines, Lee, & García-Preto, 1986; McGoldrick, Pearce, & Giordano, 1982; Cani-no & Canino, 1980). In addition, a growing literature on cross-cul-tural therapy and counseling applies to Puerto Ricans (Pedersen, 1987; Ibrahim & Arrendondo, 1986; Falicov, 1983; Sue, 1981; Sue et al., 1982). However, a gap seems to exist between the valuable information that is being published and the application of that knowledge. The "pathologization" of Puerto Ricans and other minority groups in the United States continues to be a problem of significant proportion, as are the blaming, judgmental, and moral-istic attitudes of many service providers. Furthermore, some authors still offer heavily stereotypical descriptions of Puerto Ricans, presenting a static rather than an evolutionary, dynamic, transactional view of the culture (e.g., Dillard, 1983).

Low-income Puerto Rican families in the United States may share some characteristics within their social milieu, such as the importance of the extended-family network, of respect and authority within the family and the wider community, child-rearing patterns, religious affiliations, and the clinical symptomatology they may pre-sent in periods of extreme stress. These similarities have been dis-cussed extensively; rather than elaborating upon those themes here, readers are encouraged to consult the sources noted above.

This section focuses on problems that result from performing psychological assessments without accounting for the socioeco-nomic contexts in which the clinical symptoms arise. The guiding paradigm is drawn from a sociopolitical perspective. The political nature of theory and therapy, insofar as they are framed within ide-ologies that either challenge or justify socially structured inequities in social relations, are discussed (Miller & MacKinnon, 1987).

Although it has been stated repeatedly that "cultural awareness" in therapy must include awareness of class differences (Comas-Díaz & Griffith, 1988; Sue, 1981; Canino & Canino, 1980; Minuchin, Montalvo, & Guerney, 1967), such awareness is often absent in family therapy literature and practice. Socially disempowered families or individuals cannot be assessed separate from the position they occupy in the power structure of the society in which they live. Behaviors labeled as "mental illness" or "dysfunction" may be survival strategies in response to poverty, racism, sexism, or other types of oppression. In such instances, the victims end up being blamed. Diagnostic categories become a substitute for understanding problems that may be the result of social entrapment. The "disorder" is ascribed to the individual or the family, but the socioeconomic context of the family is ignored.

Even when therapists and clients share the same ethnic background, if issues related to poverty and migration are not considered, therapy is not likely to be successful. Values and belief systems usually differ significantly across classes, and ideology is usually linked to one's position in the social hierarchy. A common national origin or language does not mean that significant class differences will disappear inside the therapy room; in fact, they may be exacerbated.

The scarcity of bilingual professionals available to offer mental health services to Puerto Ricans increases the difficulties in therapy. Although recruitment in Puerto Rico by U.S. agencies is becoming common, it seldom includes basic orientation and training sessions about the characteristics and socioeconomic environment of the population whom these professionals are to serve. It is often assumed incorrectly that a common national origin will automatically increase the quality of services.

In mental health clinics, newly arrived clinicians from middle-class backgrounds often feel overwhelmed, frustrated, and impotent when they face the types of problems that Puerto Rican migrant clients present. Clients may far outnumber the available bilingual practitioners. Thus, clinicians may be assigned large case loads with no back-up support system provided by the clinic. During their years of study, these practitioners may have never dealt with mental health issues related to poverty and migration. In addition, the number of client "no-shows" may be high for various reasons (Bernal & Flores-Ortiz, 1982), which may be interpreted as a lack of discipline or genuine interest on the part of clients. Despite the literature that explains why absenteeism occurs, practitioners often become frustrated.

Thus, the lack of sound orientation and training before recruited practitioners engage in clinical practice with Puerto Rican immigrants often has devastating results for all parties involved. Clinicians burn out quickly, and the turnover rates for therapists in community mental health clinics are often very high, which places clients in stressful situations when they are separated from clinicians to whom they might have already disclosed a good deal of personal information. Comas-Díaz (1988) states that "cross-cultural mental health training is not only useful where racial and ethnic differences exist between patient and clinician . . . cross-cultural treatment methods are also needed when the clinician and the patient are racially and ethnically similar but have different socioeconomic backgrounds and/or different value systems" (p. 356).

Unemployment, Underpayment, and Clinical Symptoms

Puerto Rican immigrant families often experience stress as a result of the absence of job opportunities, lack of matching skills for jobs that may be available, and/or poor salaries for the jobs that are available.

Such situations may provoke a number of behaviors that may be misdiagnosed as "emotional disorders" and family "dysfunction." The following two case vignettes[5] illustrate how employment-related factors affect families who are relatively new to the United States. Contextual or ecosystemic analyses that facilitate the design of the therapeutic intervention are presented, and survival skills that may be used by Puerto Rican immigrants confronted with lack of employment opportunities are discussed.

Case Vignette 1

The G family comprised both parents, Pedro (49 years old) and Teresa (41) plus seven children. Carmen, the oldest, was 23, and Papo, the youngest, was 10. Pedro, Jr., Jaime, Fernando, Margarita, and Flor ranged in ages from 14 to 21 years. An eighth child had died five years previously at age 4. The circumstances of her death are described below.

The request for mental health and medical services was initiated by the father, who for six years had been the "identified patient." He attended the first therapy session with his older daughter, Carmen. He arrived tearful, head hung low, and depressed. Carmen did most of the talking during the initial stage. She reported that her father's symptoms included depression, crying spells, social withdrawal, insomnia, irritability, lack of appetite, excessive cigarette smoking (two packs a day), and continuous coffee drinking.

To get Pedro to talk, I asked him questions about the history of his present emotional state. Highlights of his report are as follows:

Six years previously, he had suffered an accident while working in Puerto Rico. The accident occurred while Pedro was driving a trailer. The fellow worker who was with him died instantly. Pedro spent three months hospitalized with head and back injuries, the first three weeks of which he was unconscious.

Upon discharge he went back to work, still experiencing visual and memory problems, in addition to back pain. A year later he had a second accident while driving. The company laid him off with a total compensation of less than $2,000. (He had worked for the company for more than 20 years.) Pedro requested help from the Legal Services Corporation (a U.S. federal agency with offices in Puerto Rico), but in his opinion the services offered were not adequate and an appeal of the company's decision never reached the court.

Pedro began experiencing mood swings from severe depression to rage. This created crisis situations for the entire family, who, according to their report, had had a fairly normal life up until then. During this time Pedro underwent eye surgery for lesions caused by the accidents.

Shortly after his lay-off, his four-year-old daughter was hospitalized with a high fever of unknown origin. She died of a generalized infection caused by an infected intravenous tube administered at the public hospital. His daughter's death increased Pedro's depression, sense of despair, and feeling of powerlessness. Moreover, his wife, Teresa, also experienced severe depression as a result of their child's death.

Three years ago the family started to break up. The oldest daughter, Carmen, moved to the East Coast of the United States, followed gradually by her older siblings. Two years later Pedro's wife, Teresa, left him and also migrated to the United States with the two younger children. According to Pedro, she could no longer deal with his mood swings and outbursts of anger. Pedro reported that he often became very irritable, could not tolerate noise, and screamed and threw things when he got very upset. He stated that he had never become physically violent with his family.

Pedro remained in Puerto Rico, living alone in the family's house. Shortly after Teresa left, Carmen was contacted by an uncle who requested that she visit her father because his depression was getting worse and he was becoming physically ill. Carmen complied. She went to see her father and decided to bring him back to the United States with her.

When I started working with the Gs, Pedro and Teresa did not speak to each other and lived in separate apartments. Pedro was living with Carmen and her husband. Margarita, who had already been "adopted" by her older sister, also lived with them. Teresa lived with Papo and Flor in an apartment next to one of the older sons.

Jaime and his wife, who was pregnant, were estranged from the rest of the family. Carmen explained that she thought they avoided the family because her brother's wife, although Puerto Rican, did not speak Spanish and didn't feel comfortable with the family because of the language barrier. (This was a vague response, but I respected their apparent wish to maintain areas of privacy at that point.)

Fernando lived with friends and was also in conflict with his parents. Pedro explained that Fernando had a tendency to get himself in trouble (for example, borrowing more money than he could possibly repay) and then rush to his father requesting help. These requests, Pedro said, made him feel even worse because it made more obvious that he could no longer "support or even help his family economically."

Pedro had "given up." The changes in the family structure from how they lived and functioned in Puerto Rico to their circumstances in the United States were too much for him to handle. Having lost his role as the family provider, he declared himself "terminally disabled" and allowed Carmen to "mother" him by taking care of all his needs except for personal hygiene. His depression continued, and the crying spells occurred more frequently. However, his outbursts of anger, which appeared to have been the only expression of power he had left, disappeared. Carmen even became his "voice" as a result of the language barrier.

The living arrangements gave Teresa a "break" from dealing with Pedro's depression as well as space to let her own depression be expressed. Teresa described herself as being "sick of her nerves" since her daughter died. The younger children, all of whom described Pedro as having been a "very strict" father, found themselves liberated from his "law and order" as well as from his anger, while still maintaining physical closeness to both parents.

The family was experiencing turmoil when they started therapy: the sudden separation and lack of communication of the parents after more than 20 years of marriage; the migration of all family members to the United States, with the consequent difficulties of adaptation to a new land (the parents did not speak English); the organization of the family in the United States; the older daughter as the focus of support for the entire family system; the humiliation of having to request welfare support from local agencies (expressed by both parents in tears in one of the sessions); and the two teenage daughters having to work as wait-resses for the first time due to economic difficulties.

The family's expressed goal in therapy was to get the parents back together: "if father could get his nerves cured!" I interpreted their request for therapy as a sign of readiness to assume control of their lives again. They needed me to facilitate the process by "legitimizing" their emotional reactions to the tragedies they had experienced and to help them obtain financial aid from the disability, welfare, and rent-subsidy programs. Pedro was ill with a kidney infection; as a result of his accident, he still had visual problems and severe back pains. Teresa had never worked outside the home. In addition, their lack of skills in English reduced their job opportunities. Nonetheless, Pedro wanted to be recognized as the family provider, even at the cost of being declared "officially disabled."

Part of the work during therapy was to reframe their sense of shame at having to ask for help from Puerto Rican immigrants already established in the community, while they reestablished themselves as a new immigrant family. A series of family rituals, such as collective dinners and presenting the history of their family through photographs and role playing, were incorporated into the treatment process.

In addition, throughout the process I shared with them my interpretations of their situation and development stages while requesting their feedback. I made it clear that therapy required teamwork and that their input and expertise about themselves were of utmost importance. I have found emphasizing teamwork to be very effective for empowering families: they are the experts, and I am the facilitator.

Family therapy lasted five months, at the end of which Pedro and Teresa were back together, had been granted the diverse financial aids for which they had applied, and had a support system in the community to help them deal with ongoing challenges.

Case Vignette 2

In the late 1970s, at age 16, Javier migrated to the United States from a slum in metropolitan San Juan. He had dropped out of school prior to completing the seventh grade because he felt he "wasn't learning anything and it was a waste of time." He learned auto mechanics while helping a friend who had a garage. His father had left home when Javier was 10 years old, and they sel-dom saw each other. His mother had migrated to the United States the previous year with two younger children. Javier joined them with the intention of getting a job quickly as a mechanic and moving into his own apartment. He acquired basic English language skills within several months.

After a year of searching unsuccessfully for a job, he started to drink and get into fights. In one fight, he mortally stabbed another Puerto Rican. While in prison, he was diagnosed as "schizophrenic" by the consulting psychiatrist, apparently due to his continuous expression of anger, and was transferred to a psychiatric prison. After four years, during which he was medicated with antipsychotic drugs, he was released on probation. He returned to his mother's apartment and resumed his search for a job. Four months later he got a job at a gas station working for minimum wage. He lasted three weeks at this job. Someone informed the owner that Javier had been in a psychiatric prison, and he was fired. Once again, he turned to drinking to work out his frustrations.

Javier was 23 when I first saw him in therapy. He was seeking to be declared "disabled" so that he could get financial assistance. He was willing, he said, to "act crazy if that was necessary—he was already carrying the label anyway." Therapy lasted six months and consisted of several components: individual work with Javier on rebuilding self-esteem; family work, which meant including his mother in some of the sessions in an effort to establish additional support and to plan strategies that could help Javier deal with the stigma of "madness." Together, they decided that moving to another community would help them in obtaining a fresh start.

During therapy, we contacted various agencies until we located one that was willing to train and certify Javier as an auto mechanic. With the certification in hand, Javier started his own business of fixing cars in front of his apartment (not uncommon in Puerto Rican *barrios*). He soon earned a solid reputation; staff from the clinic and other related agencies began going to him with their cars.

Discussion

Although these vignettes may be regarded as extreme cases, they illustrate various elements that are commonly encountered in community mental health centers. In both vignettes, the official label of *disabled* was regarded as a solution to economic difficulties that the "identified patients" were facing.

A rather common perception or interpretation of the situation of low-income Puerto Rican immigrants who present for mental health services is that "if they don't get a job, their emotional condition will not improve." This section presents a more systemic explanation focusing on the similarities in survival skills used by low-income Puerto Rican immigrants in situations of unemployment or insufficient wages.

As happened with the G family, many immigrant families lose the father as family provider. The number of Puerto Rican immigrant families headed by women reached 44,000 by 1988, compared with 51,600 headed by couples (United States Department of Commerce, 1988). The loss or absence of jobs poses a severe problem for both male- and female-headed households. Moreover, a significant number of employed Puerto Rican immigrants continue to work at low-paying jobs. The fact that women receive even lower salaries than do men further complicates the economic survival of immigrant families.

In the United States, minimum-wage employment may work against rather than in favor of a family's economic well-being in that it may make them ineligible for public assistance programs, despite the fact that they are unable to meet the costs of basic needs. Under such stressful circumstances, many heads of households develop symptoms that make them eligible for economic assistance programs. The symptoms may be physical, such as severe back pain, or psychological, such as delusions, hallucinations, anxiety attacks, or, as discussed in the literature, "nerve attacks" (Guarnaccia, De La Cancela, & Carrillo, 1989).

Understanding these phenomena requires knowledge of the impact of socioeconomic conditions on people's lives. Without such knowledge, it is difficult, if not impossible, to understand how illness—either physical or mental—may become an asset. Low-income and poor families confront therapists with issues of economic survival, as opposed to the more "existential" or other clinical issues commonly addressed in graduate training programs.

To illustrate how illness can become an economic asset, one need only examine health insurance and housing subsidies. The salary earned under conditions of underemployment may disqualify a family for Medicaid services yet not be sufficient to pay for private health insurance, particularly if the employer does not assume part of the cost, which is often the case. This alone discourages many people from taking jobs that pay only minimum salaries. Housing subsidies may also be affected if a member of the family becomes employed. In some states, it is calculated that an income of at least $7 per hour is needed for rent (Anderson, 1987). Thus, for many families, a housing subsidy may make the difference between having a home or joining the homeless.

Such situations have a strong impact on therapy. For example, removal of a diagnostic label may be detrimental to the family's economic stability. Even when the situation of the "identified patient," and consequently the family system, improves as a result of therapy, it is often necessary to negotiate the removal of the diagnostic label by securing an adequate substitute for the subsidies that will be lost. The absence of alternatives often works against achieving long-lasting positive outcomes in therapy. There is always the possibility of relapse to symptomatic behaviors if alternative income is lost when the case is reevaluated. Some agencies reevaluate once a year, but others do so more frequently. Thus, in designing the therapeutic process, therapists must account for this variable, which often means engaging in "casework" as opposed to "pure" therapy.

Javier exemplifies a situation occasionally encountered in community mental health centers: the willingness of the head of household to "simulate" symptoms as a means to becoming eligible for subsidy incomes. Upon a thorough assessment, it usually becomes clear that a very thin line exists between "simulated" symptoms and those that actually develop as a result of the environmental and economic stresses to which the person or family is subjected.

In Javier's case, it was possible to help him get job training. Often the clinician may be unsuccessful in placing the client in job training or employment. Immigrants not fluent in English may not qualify for either job-training centers or available jobs. Furthermore, communities or states with a general shortage of jobs provide little opportunity, if any, for employment of minority persons.

In addition to being aware of these environmental circumstances, clinicians also need to be sensitive to the particular situation of each family. Making generalizations about the "unwillingness" of a "people" to work helps no one. The quality of the clinician's interaction with clients is an essential part of how the family's "reality" is constructed, interpreted, and dealt with.

Thus, when working with families who are disempowered within societal structures, it is necessary to perform ecosystemic assessments; that is, the potential support systems in the wider community—including the availability or lack of job opportunities—must be considered early in the therapeutic process.

Unemployment and Domestic Oppression

Domestic oppression and violence are not uncommon problems in the context of mental health services for low-income Puerto Rican immigrant families. The family member who discloses information about an abusive situation may be any member of the family: a child, a mother (with or without a partner) who is experiencing difficulty disciplining her children, or an abusive father or husband who is aware of and concerned about his behavior (see Velez, 1989; Vázquez-Nuttall & Romero-García, 1989). The following discussion, however, assumes that the male is the perpetrator and that the abuse is disclosed by a female.

Puerto Rican women who adhere to more traditional female roles within the culture may disclose the oppression or abuse in a matter-of-fact manner, whereas women who are subjected to excessive abuse or who may be searching for alternative relationship styles may use a more direct accusatory manner and may openly request help. Although abuse and violence against a spouse or children should never be condoned or justified, the practitioner must clearly understand the causes of the abusive behavior before relevant, effective, and helpful clinical interventions can be undertaken.

Assessment of the nature and extent of the oppression or violence must proceed cautiously in order to avoid imposing the clinician's own values on the clients' interpretation and handling of the situation. As stated by Canino and Canino (1980):

> In the Puerto Rican culture the man has the final word in many family transactions not overtly delegated to the wife. Therapeutic approaches that undermine or fail to acknowledge male authority usually end in failure. This is especially true in cases . . . where the father's authority has already been undermined by unemployment and discrimination (p. 540).

Indeed, careful assessment, using the input of both spouses, often discovers a link between the poor self-esteem of male partners as a consequence of their unemployed or underpaid status. As illustrated in the G family, the loss of family-provider status may diminish the husband/father's sense of self-esteem, which may in turn lead to his seeking other ways of maintaining authority within the family. Abusive behavior is frequently the result. Exploitation and discrimination at the workplace, during search for a job, or in the culture in general may lead the man to develop hostile and aggressive survival skills. Often, it is difficult for the male perpetrator to draw a line between the external environment and his family, and the hostility and aggression are turned toward the family (Fanon, 1963; Memmi, 1965).

Cultural and social norms within the Puerto Rican culture that sanction the absolute authority of men facilitate patterns of abuse. The phenomenon, of course, does not occur exclusively in low-income immigrant families. Amaro, Felipe-Russo, and Johnson's (1987) study of Hispanic women professionals revealed that Puerto Rican professional women who had Puerto Rican male partners were more likely to experience psychological distress symptoms than were their Mexican American and Cuban counterparts.

Other explanations for the phenomenon of abusive behaviors associated with unemployment or underemployment of Puerto Rican men, both immigrants and on the island, must not be overlooked in the clinical context. These include the "learned helplessness" hypothesis associated with the impact of five centuries of subjugation, first by Spain and then by the United States, in addition to the unresolved question of whether Puerto Rico should become independent. The national identity crisis provoked by political controversies has been found to affect the developmental process of Puerto Ricans as well as their attitudes and problem-solving strategies (Rivera-Ramos, 1984; Rogler & Hollingshead, 1985; Maldonado-Denis, 1982; Longres, 1974; History Task Force, 1979). Thus, in therapy it is usually necessary to deal with issues of identity and self-esteem to help clients develop a sense of *ableness*.

No easy solution exists for the mental health problems associated with the impact of unemployment and underemployment on low-income and poor Puerto Rican immigrants. In my experience, family and group approaches are more effective than are individual approaches. However, it should be kept in mind that some dimensions of the problem are outside the realm of psychotherapy because they are political in nature.

Strengths

Despite the multiplicity of problems that affect low-income and poor Puerto Rican families in the United States, for the most part they retain values, attitudes, and behaviors that can be used constructively in the context of mental health services. Such strengths include the affective bonds among extended family members, the value placed on the community in providing diverse types of support to its members, and *personalismo* as a commonly shared character trait.

From the perspective of family therapy, the bonds among extended family members can often be used in treatment. When deemed necessary, clinicians may request the presence of family members outside the nuclear unit without fear of altering the family's structure.[6] Open discussion among family members can resolve many problems, some of which may be related to conflicts caused by the close bonds of the extended system. It also facilitates the design of therapeutic strategies in situations in which the family unit needs external supports. Such strategies may range from help with child care to scheduled visits during periods when the identified patient may need hospitalization or heavy medication to control severe psychotic states.

The willingness of members of the community to serve as supports, which is sometimes enhanced by shared religious affiliations, can also be helpful in treatment. In my experience, it is not uncommon for families to attend a therapy session with a neighbor or friend to show him or her that they are improving.

Finally, the concept of *personalismo* as a cultural trait of Puerto Ricans refers to the willingness of Puerto Picans to be warm and sharing in relationships. In the context of therapy, it allows the clinician to take a warmer stance in his or her treatment approach. In addition, it facilitates the discretionary use of humor as a therapeutic tool. Clients, in turn, frequently express their appreciation to the therapist by bringing gifts of Puerto Rican foods or objects dear to them.

Knowledge of the family's specific cultural, socioeconomic, and religious background, together with sound intuitive skills, help clinicians use the strengths of Puerto Rican families.

Some Recommendations

It is difficult to recommend specific ways to approach an ethnic group. Perhaps the best way to approach this task is to recommend ways to learn more about Puerto Rican clients.

1. Always ask clients directly what you want to know about them. For the most part they will be your best teachers, helping you to understand their problems and strengths. Always treat your clients as individuals as opposed to representatives of a national, social, religious, or ethnic group.

2. Read extensively about Puerto Ricans while exercising your critical judgment. As with all cross-cultural literature, information may be excellent and useful or filled with stereotypical, useless descriptions and attributions. Generalizations are usually inadequate, inaccurate, and often encourage prejudices that will work against both you and your clients.

3. Develop an awareness of the values and paradigms that stem from your own cultural, racial, ethnic, religious, and social background. Never assume that clients share your world view.

The following guidelines may be helpful throughout the initial assessment and subsequent therapy process.

1. Ask clients about their background and how their move to the United States is affecting the family. More specifically, ask the following:

 ◆ Are they first-, second-, or third-generation immigrants?
 ◆ Were the reasons for their move economic, health-related, or other?

- Did they come from an urban or rural background?
- Did the family migrate together? Were they separated during the initial stage, and did they eventually reunite?
- Does the family have language-related problems? Do the parents speak Spanish and the children English?

If the therapist is also a Puerto Rican immigrant, it is helpful to compare how all of the above are similar to or different from his or her own circumstances. Personal biases that influence the therapeutic relationship may become clearer through self-exploration.

2. The "no soy de aquí ni soy de allá" syndrome (I'm neither from here nor from there) should be considered. Assess the following:

- Do your clients feel a sense of belonging either in the United States or in Puerto Rico?
- Have they support systems in both countries, in one of the two, or in neither?
- Do they hope to return to their homeland or do they feel permanently settled in the United States?
- Have they attempted to return to the island and felt discriminated against in Puerto Rico as "returning migrants?"

3. Ask about how they have coped with racism, discrimination, and cultural differences in the United States.

- What is their employment status? What skills do they possess and how well are they paid if employed?
- How does their income compare with potential income from public assistance programs such as welfare, housing subsidies, AFDC?
- Do language barriers affect work?
- Whom do they consider their first resource when in crisis: the extended family, the priest, the minister, the *santero*, the spiritualist, the physician, the therapist?

4. If you must use the *Diagnostic and Statistical Manual of Mental Disorders* (American Psychiatric Association, 1987), be aware that diagnostic categories may be inadequate or invalid in cross-cultural contexts.

Conclusion

Mental health services in cross-cultural contexts must always account for multiple components beyond those that pertain specifically to "culture." Issues related to the differences in social class within an ethnic group, which have been the focus of this chapter regarding low-income Puerto Rican migrant families, are part of those components. Other components include the effect of becoming part of a minority group on immigrants and the stages of cross-cultural transitions that immigrants go through. The many changes involved in making transcultural moves are bound to affect immigrants' behaviors, feelings, values, and cognitions. Thus, cross-cultural mental health treatment requires that culture be viewed as a dynamic, transactional, and evolving process rather than as a static entity. A process view of culture helps prevent the detrimental practice of stereotyping minority groups in the United States

Finally, mental health professionals who work with Puerto Rican immigrants or other minority groups should always be clear about whether their professional practice promotes conformity and dependence in clients or the *empowerment* of their clients. This ethical issue must never be forgotten.

Notes

1. For detailed analysis of the history of Puerto Rican migration to the United States, see History Task Force (1979); and Maldonado-Denis (1969, 1982).

2. A growing number of Puerto Rican professionals have been migrating to the United States since the 1970s (Petrovich, 1983; Turner, 1982). The employment conditions of the middle-class sector of Puerto Ricans in the United States (although this population has not been formally studied) are bound to be different from those of the low-income sector, which are the focus of this chapter.

3. Eloquent analyses of social class differences among Puerto Ricans are offered by González (1981, 1987).

4. Exceptions to the practice of ignoring social class differences between therapists and clients in mental health centers are represented by the Roberto Clemente Family Guidance Center in New York and the Worcester Youth Guidance Center in Worcester, Massachusetts. Both of these centers have incorporated training components for therapists that include discussion of social class issues.

5. Names and other identifying information have been changed to ensure confidentiality. Both assessments and therapy processes were conducted in Spanish; the vignettes are based on translations.

6. Canino and Canino (1980) used the concept "normal enmeshment" to describe bonds among extended family members. Although I agree with their description, I chose not to use the concept of enmeshment in order to avoid misinterpretations that have been discussed in the family therapy literature.

References

Amaro, H., Felipe-Russo, N., & Johnson, J. (1987). Family and work predictors of psychological well-being among Hispanic women professionals. *Psychology of Women Quarterly, 11*(4), 505–521.

American Psychiatric Association. (1987). *Diagnostic and statistical manual of mental disorders* (3rd ed., rev.). Washington, DC: Author.

Anderson, D. (1987). When the bough breaks: Homelessness in America. *The Family Therapy Networker, 11*(6), 18–29.

Andreu-Iglesias, C. (1980). *Memorias de Bernardo Vega*. Río Piedras, Puerto Rico:

Ediciones Huracán, Inc.

Bernal, G., & Flores-Ortiz, I. (1982). Latino families in therapy: Engagement and evaluation. *Journal of Marital and Family Therapy, 8*, 357–365.

Canino, I., & Canino, G. (1980). Impact of stress on the Puerto Rican family. *American Journal of Orthopsychiatry, 50*, 535–541.

Comas-Díaz, L. (1988). Cross-cultural mental health treatment. In L. Comas-Díaz & E. Griffith (Eds.), *Clinical guidelines in cross-cultural mental health* (pp. 335–361). New York: John Wiley.

Comas-Díaz, L., & Griffith, E. (Eds.). (1988). *Clinical guidelines in cross-cultural mental health.* New York: John Wiley.

Dillard, J. M. (1983). *Multicultural counseling: Toward ethnic and cultural relevance in human encounters.* Chicago: Nelson-Hall.

Falicov, C. (Ed.). (1983). *Cultural perspectives in family therapy.* Rockville, MD: Aspen Press.

Fanon, F. (1963). *The wretched of the earth.* New York: Grove Press.

García-Coll, C., & Mattei, M. L. (Eds.). (1989). *The psychosocial development of Puerto Rican women.* New York: Praeger.

González, J. L. (1981). *El país de cuatro pisos y otros ensayos.* Río Piedras, Puerto Rico: Ediciones Huracán.

González, J. L. (1987). *Nueva visita al cuarto piso.* Santurce, Puerto Rico: Collección del Flamboyán.

Guarnaccia, P. J., De La Cancela, V., & Carrillo, E. (1989). The multiple meanings of ataque de nervios in the Latino community. *Medical Anthropology, 11*(1), 47–62.

History Task Force, Centro de Estudios Puertorriqueños. (Eds). (1979). *Labor migration under capitalism: The Puerto Rican experience.* New York: Monthly Review Press.

Ibrahim, F. A., & Arrendondo, P. M. (1986). Ethical standards for cross-cultural counseling: Counselor preparation, practice, assessment, and research. *Journal of Counseling and Development, 64*, 349–352.

Longres, J. F., Jr. (1974). Racism and its effects on Puerto Rican continentals. *Social Casework, 55*, 67–75.

Maldonado-Denis, M. (1969). *Puerto Rico, Una interpretación histórico social.* Mexico, D.F.: Siglo XXI Editores.

Maldonado-Denis, M. (1982). Puerto Rican emigration: Proposals for its study. *Contemporary Marxism, 5*, 19–26.

McGoldrick, M., Hines, P., Lee, E., & García-Preto, N. (1986). Mourning rituals: How cultures shape the experience of loss. *The Family Therapy Networker, 10*(6), 28–36.

McGoldrick, M., Pearce, J. K., & Giordano, J. (Eds.). (1982). *Ethnicity and family therapy.* New York: Guilford Press.

Memmi, A. (1965). *The colonizer and the colonized.* Boston: Beacon Press.

Miller, D., & MacKinnon, L. K. (1987). The new epistemology and the Milan approach: Feminist and sociopolitical considerations. *Journal of Marital and Family Therapy, 13*, 139–155.

Minuchin, S., Montalvo, D., & Guerney, B. (1967). *Families of the slums: An exploration of their treatment.* New York: Basic Books.

Pedersen, P. B. (1987). Ten frequent assumptions of cultural bias in counseling. *Journal of Multicultural Counseling and Development, 15*, 16–24.

Petrovich, J. (1983). Contradictions of educational expansion in Puerto Rico. *Homines, 7*(1–2), 140–146.

Rivera-Ramos, A. N. (1984). *Hacia una psicoterapia para el Puertorriqueño.* Río

Piedras, Puerto Rico: Cedepp.

Rodríguez, C. (1979). Economic factors affecting Puerto Ricans in New York. In History Task Force, Centro de Estudios Puertorriqueños (Eds.), *Labor migration under capitalism: The Puerto Rican experience*. New York: Monthly Review Press.

Rogler, L. H., & Hollingshead, A. B. (1985). *Trapped: Puerto Rican families and schizophrenia* (rev.). Maplewood, NJ: Waterfront Press.

Sue, D. (1981). *Counseling the culturally different*. New York: John Wiley.

Sue, D., Vázquez-Nuttall, E., Bernier, J., Durran, A., Feinberg, L., Pedersen, P., & Smith, E. J. (1982). Cross cultural counseling competencies. *The Counseling Psychologist, 10*(2), 45–52.

Turner, H. (1982, January 31–February 1). Brain drain: New kind of migration from Puerto Rico heads North. *San Juan Star.*

United States Department of Commerce, Bureau of the Census. (1988). *The Hispanic population in the United States: March 1988* (advance report). Washington, DC: United States Government Printing Office.

Vázquez-Calzada, J.L. (1979). Demographic aspects of migration. In History Task Force, Centro de Estudios Puertorriqueños (Eds.), *Labor migration under capitalism: The Puerto Rican experience*. New York: Monthly Review Press.

Vázquez-Nuttall, E., & Romero-García, I. (1989). From home to school: Puerto Rican girls learn to be students in the United States. In C. García-Coll & M. L. Mattei (Eds.), *The psychosocial development of Puerto Rican women*. New York: Praeger.

Velez, D. (1989). Cultural constructions of women by contemporary women authors. In C. García-Coll & M. L. Mattei (Eds.), *The psychosocial development of Puerto Rican women*. New York: Praeger.

8

Mental Health Services
And the Hispanic Elderly

Manuel R. Miranda

Currently, among all Americans, mental health is not being adequately promoted and mental illness is not being adequately treated. According to the National Institute of Mental Health (1987), nearly 30 million Americans require professional treatment for mental illness during any six-month period. Tragically, the problem of mental illness has now reached the point where "the personal and social costs of mental illness are similar in scale to those for heart disease and cancer" (National Institute of Mental Health, 1987). And compared with the general population, racial and ethnic minorities face even greater economic, social, and psychological costs.

America's elderly, unfortunately, have not been spared from the destructive effects of mental illness. Research suggests that between 15% and 25% of the 28 million Americans older than 65 suffer from significant mental health problems (Flemming, Richards, Santos, & West, 1986). In other words, as many as 7 million of our elderly Americans may currently need professional mental health services.

The mental health needs of elderly Americans are not being adequately met (Flemming et al., 1986; U.S. General Accounting Office, 1982). Only a fraction of elderly persons with mental health problems are currently receiving professional treatment. Elderly persons, who make up 12% of the American population, represent only approximately 6% of the persons served by community mental health centers and about 2% of those served by private therapists (Flemming et al., 1986). In addition, less than 1.5% of all expenditures for mental health care are allocated for community-based services to older individuals. Sixty percent of those elderly who are admitted to state mental hospitals have not received prior mental health care (White House Conference on Aging, 1981). This finding indicates that little primary prevention is directed toward increasing the aging individual's coping skills and support systems. Most mental health facilities are poorly equipped to deal with the problems of the elderly; thus this portion of our population must seek support from family members (who may already be overburdened) and/or from board-and-care homes. The lack of existing outpatient mental health services that allow the elderly to deal with their problems on a here-and-now basis results in the elderly being severely isolated from general communal life.

Although the situation is troublesome for all elderly Americans, minority elderly experience "multiple jeopardy": being elderly, from a racial or ethnic minority group, and, in many instances, poor. As such, minority elderly persons are more likely to experience psychological and social stress than is the elderly population as a whole. The situation is made worse by the fact that racial and ethnic minorities are much less likely to have the institutional and social resources (which are more readily available to the cultural majority) necessary to deal with mental health problems.

Despite the unprecedented explosion in scientific knowledge and the phenomenal capacity of medical science to diagnose, treat, and cure physical diseases and mental illnesses, minority Americans of all ages have not benefited fully or equitably from such technology. The tremendous scientific achievement and steady improvement in overall health status for the nation are sadly counterbalanced by the persistent, significant health inequities for minority-status persons of all ages.

The lack of data on psychological problems among the Hispanic elderly restricts the efforts of mental health professionals in developing effective intervention programs for this population (Miranda & Ruiz, 1981). The few studies conducted tend to employ psychosocial explanations that do not consider behavioral difficulties in terms of the societal barriers that the Hispanic elderly confront in adjusting to old age. This exclusion or deemphasis of explanatory factors external to the individual is a major obstacle to developing insight into the experiences of the Hispanic elderly.

As more Hispanics enter their senior years, programs for the Hispanic elderly may require drastic revision within the next 15 to 20 years. It is critically important to identify and measure with precision those variables that affect mental health within this population. For example, how is adjustment to aging influenced by differences in the country/area of origin or residence (United States vs. Central or South America, Southwest vs. other regions, urban vs. rural); by differences in language skills (monolingual vs. bilingual, language dominance, variable literacy); by differences in years and quality of education; by general life experiences (including both common and unique stress and the resulting coping mechanisms developed); by physical health; and by a host of other variables that directly affect the validity of diagnostic and treatment procedures for the Hispanic elderly?

Certainly, some of these issues apply universally to most elderly individuals. The specificity of these issues in relation to the Hispanic elderly, however, stems from the interactional patterns of Hispanic elderly persons. More specifically, cultural expression is affected by three major variables. First, in times of stress, support is available from members of the same culture, from problem solving in a familiar social environment, and from thinking or talking about problems in one's native tongue. Second, any factor that interferes with the way in which a culture functions simultaneously reduces the individual's ability to resist stress. Third, and this variable illustrates the complexity of research and theory development in relation to culture, a single variable can support cultural continuity or contribute to cultural discontinuity, depending on the influence of other variables. For example, migration from Central or South America to the United States initiates the process of acculturation; that is, it weakens identification with the birth culture and promotes identification with the U.S. culture. However, migration back to the country of origin can strengthen ties to the birth cultures ("the good old days") or can weaken them ("how times have changed"). In other words, variables can have diverse effects on how well membership in a cultural group helps a Hispanic elderly person resist stress and adjust to old age.

A question remains, however: What constitutes an adequate definition of mental health? In the author's opinion, mental health should be viewed as a theoretical construct that has no meaning outside a cultural context. Behaviors such as cognition, perceptions, emotions, sentiments, attitudes, and values may be adaptive and acceptable in one culture, yet maladaptive and prohibited in a second (Madsen & Shapira, 1970). Thus, the mental health status of Hispanic elderly must be evaluated within the context of their existing cultural practices before a meaningful assessment of pathology can be obtained.

The Double-Jeopardy Hypothesis

Environmental variables reflecting the interaction between the dominant culture and the Hispanic culture affect the mental health needs of Hispanics. Key among these interactions is the double-jeopardy hypothesis, which places Hispanic elderly persons in a vulnerable position due to their ethnic status and advanced age (Dowd & Bengtson, 1978).

Current conceptualizations of Hispanic aging extend a stratification perspective in that race or minority status added a dimension of inequality together with age, socioeconomic class, and gender. When several of these factors are experienced simultaneously, the elderly person's well-being is jeopardized in multiple ways. Thus elderly Hispanics may, in fact, experience "multiple jeopardy."

Dowd and Bengtson (1978) attempted to develop a testable double-jeopardy hypothesis in their study of older blacks, Mexican Americans, and Anglo-Americans living in Los Angeles.

> Like other older people in industrial societies, they experience the devaluation of old age found in most modern societies. . . . Unlike other older people, however, the minority aged must bear the additional economic, social, and psychological burdens of living in a society in which racial equality remains more myth than social policy (p. 427).

Dowd and Bengston suggested that double jeopardy could be demonstrated if the effects of being disadvantaged at earlier ages were found to worsen in old age for minority persons compared with nonminority persons.

Recent literature on the double-jeopardy hypothesis points out that ethnic-minority elderly persons, such as Hispanics, experience more psychological distress not only because of greater exposure to stressful events but because they have fewer psychological and social resources with which to cope with stress (Kessler & Cleary, 1980). Resource deficits are experienced by the elderly in general but are even more acute among the Hispanic elderly. Not only are they exposed more frequently to stress than are non-Hispanic elderly persons, but they also have fewer culturally appropriate coping resources as a result of financial deprivation, subordination to other groups, and systematic exclusion from access to social and economic opportunities.

In testing the applicability of the double-jeopardy hypothesis to the Hispanic elderly, Dowd and Bengtson (1978) found that even when socioeconomic status, gender, and income were held constant, older Mexican Americans in Los Angeles were more likely to report poorer physical health than were older Anglo-Americans. Because the racial and ethnic differences in self-ratings were higher among older persons than among middle-aged respondents, the authors concluded that the double jeopardy-hypothesis was supported regarding health. Interestingly, however, results did not support the double-jeopardy hypothesis with regard to primary-group relations. Mexican Americans reported greater contact with relatives during middle age than did Anglo-Americans. This difference was somewhat less evident with advancing age, although the decrease was not statistically significant. It should be noted, however, that Anglo-Americans tended to have a wider social network than did Mexican Americans, which increased significantly with age. Thus as Anglo-Americans get older and become increasingly separated from their families, they have the option of turning to nonfamilial support networks in meeting their needs. Hispanics are less likely to have this resource.

Family relationships among the elderly are significant, although gerontologists disagree about the extent of family support of minority elderly persons. In the 1950s and 1960s, for example, it was customary to describe the Hispanic family as extremely warm and supportive of the individual. The lower incidence of psychiatric treatment among Hispanics was explained by the "supportive" qualities of the Hispanic family (Jaco, 1957). Similarly, Madsen (1966) argued that stress more negatively affects Anglo-Americans because they lack family support as opposed to Hispanic elderly whose stresses are shared and counteracted by the family. Studies of elderly Mexican Americans in San Antonio (Carp, 1968; Reich, Stegman, & Stegman, 1966) also described the Hispanic family as extremely warm and supportive of older people.

Recent literature on the Hispanic family, however, strongly criticizes the stereotype of a strong, cohesive Hispanic family unit capable of fending off all external threats to individual well-being (Galarza, 1981). The Hispanic tradition of moral obligation toward the elderly has been strained by mobility and urbanization. Many Mexican Americans with rural roots have become an urban minority in the United States. Mobility and acculturation have separated the Hispanic family from the elderly, who frequently end up living isolated lives in urban *barrios*. Within these neighborhoods, cultural traditions, which are of special significance to Hispanic elderly, have been weakened by disuse, institutional neglect, and increased distance between generations. For the Hispanic elderly, the question has become: How much of their past will they be allowed to enjoy, relative to the growing conviction among their children and grandchildren that the elderly have little to contribute to a society with different values and beliefs (Korte, 1981; Galarza, 1981)?

One hundred fifty years of changes in sovereignty, ethnic ratios, property ownership, and employment opportunities are eroding the cultural roots of the Hispanic elderly.

> The environment of the *barrio* has changed drastically from rural to urban. The extended family yielded more and more to the extenuated family. Tradition loosened its hold on individual and institutional roles in group life. Mobility of the family unit and of the individual became frequent, indeed necessary. The elderly ceased being the preservers and transmitters of valued customs and beliefs. These values and beliefs declined in currency as helpful guides to conduct and model of public life. Becoming old was not the same thing as becoming experienced in commanding respect and holding authority in a community (Galarza, 1981, p. 243).

Social Support Networks as Intervention Models

To achieve and maintain mental health, basic human needs, including a sense of usefulness, a sense of control over one's life, and the ability to express and accept love and friendship, must be satisfied. This is true regardless of an individual's degree of physical and economic well-being. The loss of loved ones, increased physical disability, depleted economic resources, and loss of societal roles that occur during one's later years clearly work against the satisfaction of these basic needs.

Fulfillment in one's elderly years and prevention of mental illness can be aided by a strong social support system, improved or expanded coping skills, and reduction of unnecessary stress. If preretirement planning, social support programs, and education are initiated during the years leading up to and immediately following retirement, the need for acute and long-term mental health care for older persons may be substantially reduced. Self-help or peer-help groups can aid in planning for one's elderly years, understanding illnesses, dealing with personal disabilities, and coping with widowhood or ongoing parenting responsibilities. Religious institutions, senior centers, and social service organizations can serve as vehicles for programs and services. Group programs facilitate social interaction and interpersonal support, thereby protecting the individual from emotional and behavioral problems. The development of natural support systems (e.g., noninstitutional support systems such as extended family or informal community groups) in lieu of expanding existing institutional programs is beneficial for elderly persons from diverse cultural backgrounds. Natural support networks or self-help groups incorporate and enhance the cultural life-style of the ethnic elderly person, thus maintaining a sense of identity and belonging. Too frequently, institutions and agencies fail to respond to the diverse cultural needs of their clientele (e.g., language, preferred styles of receiving and giving assistance) as a result of economic limitations and the need to focus on cost–benefit issues.

Most natural networks involve a process of reciprocity (Valle & Martinez, 1981). The Hispanic elderly find it very difficult to accept assistance unless the opportunity exists for them to provide assistance or service in turn. To increase reciprocity in the area of mental health service, it is necessary to reduce the discrepancy in status between the client and therapist and to redefine the relationship as one of mutual assistance. The restructuring of the therapist–client relationship has implications for mental health agencies. For example, can reciprocity cut across levels of acculturation or social class? Do different expectations on how one receives and gives help exist among low, medium, and higher socioeconomic status members?

A key issue regarding natural networks concerns the development of cooperative relations between agencies and natural networks. Miranda and Ruiz (1981) suggested that a collaborative relationship is beneficial in meeting the emotional and physical needs of the elderly. Clearly, documentation of the effectiveness of such collaborative relationships is needed. Questions remain regarding the most effective settings or conditions. Do collaborative arrangements flourish only in agencies staffed predominantly by bilingual–bicultural personnel? Or can Anglo-oriented agencies develop effective working relationships with Hispanic clients? Are certain types of emotional problems, such as psychosis, terminal illness, and drug abuse, more responsive to collaborative relationships?

These issues obviously require more study. Research indicates that Hispanics have a low utilization rate for mental health services. Natural networks have been offered as a possible explanation for this phenomenon in that such networks are relevant and functional for Hispanics because they are culturally appropriate and historically based. Hispanic elderly are attracted to these natural networks because they respond to the cultural patterns with which they are familiar. Whether these systems have a significant effect upon the lives of younger Hispanics is not clear.

Natural support systems must be studied to identify how they can be enhanced to provide even more mental health benefits for the Hispanic elderly. Interactive factors must be analyzed: urban versus rural features of the networks, cross-class factors that influence the giving and receiving of help, and intergenerational differences.

Mental Health Services to Hispanic Elderly

Any discussion of social support systems and their effectiveness in alleviating stress for the Hispanic elderly requires a consideration of mediating variables such as coping styles and personal assets. Although these mediating variables are important in understanding the relationship between life stress and mental health status in any population, they are critical to understanding the impact of cultural values and behaviors on mental health status on Hispanic elderly persons.

In studying the relationship between stress, mental health status, and coping style and personal assets, it is important to identify potential risk factors that create stress (e.g., life events such as discrimination, immigration status, poverty) among the Hispanic elderly. One needs to determine how risk factors are mediated by social support networks, coping responses, and personal resources as reflected in mental health status, help-seeking behavior, and therapeutic intervention strategies. In so doing, one gains insight into preventive techniques as determined by a thorough examination of the significant interactional processes.

The relationship between life-events stress and mental illness among the Hispanic elderly has implications for the delivery of mental health services. The relationship of sociocultural variables with mental illness as indicated by coping responses, personal assets, and social support networks can be analyzed in terms of (1) how the elderly client might be changed and/or (2) how the health service delivery system might be changed to meet the needs of the elderly. The elderly client might change personal habits, behaviors, perceptions, and/or seek a different environment or modify the current environment. A general finding, for example, that life events are related to psychiatric disorders might suggest that the elderly client should be helped to choose less change or to improve his or her coping abilities. The client might find a less demanding social environment that requires less change. For example, the practitioner may need to help an elderly Hispanic who lives in the *barrio* to make personal or environmental changes in a culturally appropriate manner. To do so, the practitioner needs to remain sensitive to the client's social and cultural support systems by, for example, identifying key individuals (link persons) in the client's community capable of helping the client and family locate community resources in the rehabilitation process (Valle, 1985). These link persons frequently serve as cultural brokers in bringing the ethnic client in contact with institutional resources.

To deal effectively with psychiatric disorders linked to life change, the mental health system can change in two ways. First, the service provider should develop a more empathic understanding of the life changes experienced by elderly Hispanic clients and the ways in which mental illness symptoms may be related to cultural factors. Similarly, the service delivery system might target services to persons who are experiencing change, for example, those about to retire, those who have lost a spouse, recent migrants, persons who are separated from their family, and those suffering from physical disabilities.

In terms of the relationship between life events and mental status, interesting interactions have been noted between the ethnicity variable and life changes. For example, events that occur to significant others (outside of spouse and children) are more likely to affect the psychological and physical status of Mexican Americans than they are likely to affect Anglo-Americans (Hough, McGarvey, Graham, & Timbers, 1982). This finding supports the traditional stereotype that Mexican culture places more emphasis on an extended social network outside the immediate nuclear family. Clinicians need to be keenly aware of the differences among the life events of their culturally different clients. For example, the clinician must distinguish between the Anglo-American retiree who seeks escape from his or her urban existence by moving outside the city and the Hispanic elderly person who is forced from his or her cultural enclave or *barrio* as the result of increased industrial growth and urbanization (Galarza, 1981).

Although the mental health professional needs to understand how life changes affect elderly Hispanics' social support network and how these may be linked to mental health problems, such empathy is only one dimension of the relationship between client and service provider. The mental health service system itself may need to use extended social networks as an aid to mental health maintenance. Establishing new or supporting existing social networks can be an important intervention tool for mental health professionals. The intervention strategy may encourage more group participation as opposed to individual treatment. Valle (1985) elaborated on how this might be done with Hispanic clients in an effort to restructure the fragmented familial and extended-kin networks. The ability to deal effectively with stress as dictated by coping styles and personal assets bears directly on the availability of culturally based support systems (e.g., informal support systems with strong ties to the traditional culture, such as the extended family).

Similarly, elderly Hispanic clients should be encouraged to acknowledge the importance of extended social networks and to recognize the potentially health-damaging effects of severing themselves from these networks by moving to new environments. If a move to a new environment is necessary, assisting clients to form new networks can be an effective preventive strategy for health care providers.

Reworking the System: Problems and Solutions

The lack of specialized mental health services for the elderly is problematic in general. MacDonald (1987) demonstrated that participation by the elderly in community mental health center programs would more than double if services were specially designed for the elderly and staffed with trained mental health professionals. Unfortunately, the consolidation of federal support of mental health services into a block grant as mandated by the Omnibus Budget Reconciliation Act of 1981 resulted in a dramatic decrease in funding. As of 1985, nearly 40% of the community mental health centers surveyed reported reductions in service delivery to older persons (Flemming et al., 1986). Almost half of these centers lacked staff with specific training in geriatric mental health, and a similar number reported having no specialized services for the elderly.

Current Medicare psychiatric benefits are outmoded and markedly inferior to benefits for physical illness. Inpatient care in psychiatric hospitals under Part A of Medicare is limited to 190 lifetime days, an arbitrary limitation that ignores the chronic and/or recurring nature of many mental disorders. Outpatient mental health benefits under Part B of Medicare are restricted to a $1,100 cap and require 50% co-payment by the beneficiary. Intermediate-care nursing facilities, which are appropriate for persons with chronic disorders such as Alzheimer's disease, are not covered under Medicare. The current Medicare mental health benefit structure is also grossly inadequate and fails to encourage the most psychiatrically appropriate and cost-effective forms of care. Although the inpatient psychiatric benefit in itself is quite limited, the outpatient benefit is restrictive and encourages costly hospitalizations at a time when the most advanced therapeutic approaches emphasize outpatient community-based care. Moreover, treatment by many mental health professionals is discouraged because Medicare does not recognize most nonmedical professionals as independent providers.

Medicaid mental health benefits, which vary considerably from state to state, also fail to meet the mental health needs of the elderly population. Community-based mental health services are optimal rather than mandatory under the Medicaid program. Two Medicaid requirements that affect nursing home treatment are particularly detrimental to elderly nursing home residents with mental health problems. First, by statute, Medicaid denies reimbursement of services for nonelderly patients of institutions for mental disease (IMDs). Medicaid regulations, in effect, define IMDs as facilities that engage primarily in care provision for mental diseases for more than 50% of their residents, regardless of age. The threat of being classified as an "IMD" and the subsequent loss of Medicaid reimbursement for nonelderly patients provides a strong incentive for nursing homes to avoid providing mental health services to any of their patients. Little mental health assessment is provided, despite growing research indicating that a significant proportion of elderly nursing home residents suffer from mental health problems (National Institute of Mental Health, 1987). Second, Medicaid eligibility requirements, even in states with the most generous benefit structures, are so stringent that both the patient and the patient's spouse must literally be impoverished before Medicaid nursing home benefits are made available. Such a system is detrimental not only to the patient but also to the healthy spouse, who is placed at risk physically, mentally, and financially.

The health care system in this country must be strengthened and restructured to encourage the improved delivery of mental health services to the elderly in general and the Hispanic elderly in particular. Services should include a variety of support systems, particularly as they relate to informal systems (e.g., community link persons) in helping the elderly and their families or caregivers. Mechanisms are needed to ensure that elderly persons and their families not only have access to the full range of needed services but that these services are appropriately modified to meet the special needs of various elderly populations. Current research (Light, Lebowitz, & Bailey, 1986) demonstrates that increased cooperation between federally funded Area Agencies on Aging and community-based mental health centers can dramatically improve service utilization rates even among the most difficult-to-reach elderly. Coordination and cooperation among federal, state, and community agencies whose responsibilities include provision of aging, health, and mental health services must be ensured if elderly persons with mental health needs are to be served adequately.

Congressional action should expand the federal government's role in mental health services in three critical areas: (1) the development of an effective mental health service system to adequately care for elderly persons, (2) modification of Medicare and Medicaid mental health service coverage and cost containment, and (3) improvement in quality assurance and access protection. Clearly, implementation of this three-part agenda must be accompanied by strong research efforts and model programs. Identification of intervention strategies and service-delivery methods capable of effectively meeting the mental health needs of the elderly must be undertaken. Education and training efforts are needed to ensure that the mental health problems of the elderly are accurately identified and appropriately treated. In recognition of these needs, future congressional actions should require the development of a federal research plan on elderly mental health to be implemented through the National Institute of Mental Health, the National Institute on Aging, and the Administration on Aging. Such an agenda would be a significant landmark in sensitizing the mental health field to the service needs of the elderly. Paradoxically, attempts to improve mental health services for the elderly have been channeled through appeals to the mental health organizations that have shown minimal interest in the elderly as well as aging organizations that have shown minimal interest in mental health. These organizations need to become sensitized to the various needs of the elderly. Movement of proposed legislation into the form of law requires the united and intensified efforts of both.

References

Carp, F. (1968). *Factors in utilization of services by Mexican Americans.* Palo Alto, CA: American Institute for Research.

Dowd, J. J., & Bengtson, V. L. (1978). Aging in minority populations: An examination of the double jeopardy hypothesis. *Journal of Gerontology, 33,* 427–436.

Flemming, A. S., Richards, L. D., Santos, J. F., & West, P. R. (1986). *Report on a survey of community mental health centers,* vol. 3. Action Committee to Implement the Mental Health Recommendations of the 1981 White House Conference on Aging. Washington, DC: American Psychological Association.

Galarza, E. (1981). Forecasting future cohorts of Mexican elderly. In M. R. Miranda & R. A. Ruiz (Eds.), *Chicano aging and mental health.* Washington, DC: U.S. Government Printing Office.

Hough, R. L., McGarvey, W., Graham, J., & Timbers, D. (1982). *Cultural variations in the modeling of life change-illness relationships.* Unpublished manuscript, Department of Sociology, San Diego State University, San Diego, CA.

Jaco, E. G. (1957). Social factors in mental disorders in Texas. *Social Problems, 4,* 322–329.

Kessler, R. C., & Cleary, P. D. (1980). Social class and psychological distress. *American Sociological Review, 45,* 463–478.

Korte, A. O. (1981). Theoretical perspectives in mental health and the Mexican elders. In M. R. Miranda & R. A. Ruiz (Eds.), *Chicano aging and mental health.* Washington, DC: U.S. Government Printing Office.

Light, E., Lebowitz, B. D., & Bailey, F. (1986). CMHC's and elderly services: Analysis of direct and indirect services and service delivery sites. *Community Mental Health Journal, 22,* 294–302.

MacDonald, D. I. (1987). *ADAMHA testimony before the U.S. House of Representatives Committee on Appropriations, Subcommittee on Labor, Health and Human Services.* Washington, DC.

Madsen, M. (1966). Anxiety and witchcraft in Mexican American acculturation. *Anthropology Quarterly, 39,* 110–127.

Madsen, M. C., & Shapira, A. (1970). Cooperative and competitive behavior of urban Afro-American, Anglo-American, Mexican-American village children. *Developmental Psychology, 3,* 16–20.

Miranda, M. R., & Ruiz, R. A. (Eds.). (1981). *Chicano aging and mental health.* Washington, DC: U.S. Government Printing Office.

National Institute of Mental Health. (1987, May 19). *Testimony of Dr. Frank J. Sullivan, Acting Director, before the United States House of Representatives, Committee on Government Operations, Subcommittee on Human Resources and Intergovernmental Relations.* Washington, DC: Author.

Reich, J. M., Stegman, M. A., & Stegman, N. (1966). *Relocating the dispossessed elderly: A study of Mexican Americans.* Philadelphia: Institute of Environmental Studies, University of Pennsylvania, Philadelphia.

U.S. General Accounting Office. (1982). *The elderly remain in need of mental health services.* Washington, DC: U.S. Government Printing Office.

Valle, R. (1985). Social networks and social supports: Their meaning for research and service delivery. In W. Vega & M. R. Miranda (Eds.), *Stress and Hispanic mental health: Relating research to service delivery.* Washington, DC: U.S. Government Printing Office.

Valle, R., & Martinez, C. (1981). Natural networks of Latinos of Mexican heritage: Implications for mental health. In M. R. Miranda & R. A. Ruiz (Eds.), *Chicano aging and mental health.* Washington, DC: U.S. Government Printing Office.

White House Conference on Aging. (1981). *Report of the mini-conference on the mental health for older Americans.* Washington, DC: U.S. Superintendent of Documents.

9

Older Hispanic Women: A Decade in Review

Elena Bastida and Rumaldo Juárez

Research on the aging experience of Hispanic Americans began in earnest more than a decade ago. In 1976, little information was available on this subject, except for the pioneering work of Sotomayor (1973) on Chicano grandparents and that of Maldonado (1975). Since then, a handful of authors have contributed much to our knowledge about this population.

During the 1980s, much research was focused on elderly Hispanic women. Various authors have made gender-related contributions in their work with older Hispanics (Markides & Vernon, 1984; Zuniga, 1984; Sanchez-Ayendez, 1984, 1986; Bastida, 1987, 1988; Facio, 1989; Mahard, 1989). However, it is difficult to obtain a demographic profile of older Hispanic women. Most studies currently available report on the demographic characteristics of the Hispanic elderly in general and do not note gender differences. This chapter attempts to bridge this gap by presenting a profile of older Hispanic women based on a decade of research and broad statistical categorizations.

Size of the Population

In 1980, 553,612 Hispanic-origin women 60 years of age and older lived in the United States (U.S. Department of Commerce, 1981). Nine years later, conservative estimates, due to a great

TABLE 1.
Distribution of the older Hispanic population by age and sex, 1980.

Age (years)	Men	Women
60–64	145,161	169,696
65–69	109,479	143,916
70–74	80,382	103,459
75 and older	98,780	136,510
Total	433,802	553,581
65 and older	288,641	383,916

Adapted from U.S. Department of Commerce, Bureau of the Census. (1981, May). *Persons of Spanish origin in the United States: March 1980 (advance report).* Population Characteristics, Series P-20, No. 361. Washington, DC: U.S. Government Printing Office.

many undocumented persons living in the United States, indicate their numbers at more than 660,000 (Valle, 1983). In 1980, 433,002 Hispanic males older than 60 were living in the United States (Table 1). Moreover, in 1980 there were 288,441 males to 393,916 females 65 years and older, a ratio of 75 men for every 100 women. Further examination of sex ratios among these older cohorts indicates that the ratio narrows considerably for the 60-to-64 age group, with a ratio of 86 men for every 100 women. As expected, the gap widens for the 75-years-and-older age group, with a ratio of 72 men for every 100 women (Table 2).

TABLE 2.
Ratio of older Hispanic men to older Hispanic women by age, 1980.

Age (years)	Men	Women
60–64	86	100
60 and older	78	100
65–75	76	100
65 and older	75	100
75 and older	72	100

TABLE 3.
Total Hispanic population by sex and origin, 1980.

Spanish origin	Males	Females
Mexican	4,076,000	3,856,000
Puerto Rican	838,000	985,000
Cuban	414,000	417,000
Other Spanish	1,269,000	1,390,000
Total	**6,597,000**	**6,648,000**

Adapted from U.S. Department of Commerce, Bureau of the Census. (1981, May). *Persons of Spanish origin in the United States: March 1980 (advance report).* Population Characteristics, Series P-20, No. 361. Washington, DC: U.S. Government Printing Office.

For all older Hispanic categories, the ratio of older men to older women is significantly narrower for Hispanics than it is for the total population, and narrower than for whites and blacks separately. This narrow gap may be explained in part by the lower life expectancy of Hispanic women and by earlier patterns of emigration, whereby it was customary for men, rather than women, to emigrate to the United States for economic reasons. For the Mexican American population, this immigration pattern may be even more pronounced when one takes into account patterns of illegal entry. It is speculated that men are more likely than are women to take the risks associated with illegal entry. However, current patterns (post-1970) of legal immigration to the United States do not reflect the significant difference between the number of men and women legally entering the United States. Of all Spanish-origin populations, Mexican Americans are the only subpopulation in which men are slightly overrepresented. For other Spanish-origin populations, the reverse is the case, with women accounting for a larger proportion of the population (Table 3).

As indicated in Table 3, in the 65-years-and-older age group, Mexican-origin women make up the largest portion, followed by other Hispanic-origin women. Cubans make up the third-largest number of women and Puerto Ricans the fewest. When subgroup variations are examined, interesting results are obtained. Older Hispanic women make up 6% of all Hispanic women in the United States. However, different proportions are obtained when each subgroup is compared with its respective base population. Older Cuban-origin women are overrepresented. In 1980, the percentage

TABLE 4.
Distribution of persons 60 years and older by years of school completed and sex, 1980 (%).

Years of school completed	60–64		65–69		70–74		75 and older	
	Men	Women	Men	Women	Men	Women	Men	Women
None	8	9	11	13	15	16	22	22
1–6 (%)	33	36	37	38	40	41	39	40
7–8(%)	17	17	18	18	17	17	16	16
9–11 (%)	13	14	12	11	9	9	7	7
12 (%)	15	15	12	13	0	12	9	10

Note: totals do not add to 100% due to rounding.
Adapted from U.S. Department of Commerce, Bureau of the Census. (1981, May). *Persons of Spanish origin in the United States: March 1980 (advance report)*. Population Characteristics, Series P-20, No. 361. Washington, DC: U.S. Government Printing Office.

of Cuban women 65 years and older was 13%, exceeding that of all other Hispanic subgroups as well as whites and blacks. Within the other subgroups, percentages ranked as follows: 6% for other Hispanic-origin females, 5% for Mexican origin, and 4% for Puerto Rican origin.

Education

Education is usually indexed by the number of years of school completed. When referring to educational attainment, it is important to take into account differences among cohort. Younger Hispanic women are more likely to be high school graduates than is the 65-years-and-older cohort. However, the education gap between the young and the old is significantly larger among Hispanic women than it is for the total U.S. female population. For the total population, women age 20–24 are twice as likely to be high school graduates as are women 65 years of age and older; Hispanic women age 20–24, however, are three times as likely to be high school graduates.

Surprisingly, the educational differences between older Hispanic men and women are not as pronounced. In fact, for some age categories, older women exceed older men in the number of years of formal schooling completed (Table 4). Even though the difference is small, 10% of women aged 75 years and older had completed four years of high school in 1980, compared with 9% of the men (U.S. Department of Commerce, 1981). For other age categories, as may be observed in Table 4, the similarities in educational attainment are striking.

In Mahard's (1989) study of older Puerto Ricans in New York City, slightly different educational characteristics were found among older Puerto Rican men and women. She notes that "the data on education indicate a low level of formal schooling, with 44% of the sample having completed four years of schooling or less." Only 12% of Mahard's sample had completed high school. "Women and men differ significantly in terms of education, with proportionately fewer women having completed eight or more years of schooling and proportionately more women being in the lower education categories" (Mahard, 1989, p. 248).

Health Status

National data on general mortality and health for Hispanic Americans are fragmented. Recently, however, the National Center for Health Statistics has begun to gather national data on this

TABLE 5.
Condition of illness reported by gender.

Condition/Illness	Male (n = 371)		Female (n = 651)	
	n	%	n	%
Hardening of arteries				
Yes	48	14.1	132	22.0
No	292	85.9	468	78.0
Total	340	100.0	600	100.0
No information	31		51	
High blood pressure				
Yes	128	36.1	280	44.4
No	227	63.9	350	55.6
Total	355	100.0	630	100.0
No information	16		21	
Stroke				
Yes	36	10.2	41	6.6
No	316	89.8	577	93.4
Total	352	100.0	618	100.0
No information	19		33	
Cancer				
Yes	8	2.3	29	4.8
No	336	97.7	574	95.2
Total	344	100.0	603	100.0
No information	27		48	
Arthritis				
Yes	172	47.8	387	61.1
No	188	52.2	246	38.9
Total	360	100.0	633	100.0
No information	11		18	
Blindness				
Yes	139	38.9	276	44.7
No	218	61.1	342	55.3
Total	357	100.0	618	100.0
No information	14		33	
Glaucoma/cataracts				
Yes	57	16.2	146	23.9
No	294	83.8	466	76.1
Total	351	100.0	612	100.0
No information	20		39	

Adapted from Juarez, R., Lopez, M., Bastida, E., Ballejos, M., Garza, K., Glassman, C., & Huff-Hinkle, C. (1989). *Innovative approaches toward prevention of institutionalization of Mexican American elderly*. Final report, U.S. Administration on Aging. Edinburg, TX: Pan American University.

TABLE 6.
Self-assessment of health status by gender.

Health status	Male (*n* = 371)		Female (*n* = 651)	
	n	%	*n*	%
Excellent	9	2.5	14	2.2
Good	92	25.1	135	21.0
Fair	183	49.9	352	54.7
Poor	83	22.6	142	22.1
Total[a]	367	100.1	643	100.0
No information	4		8	

[a]Totals do not add to 100% due to rounding.

Adapted from Juarez, R., Lopez, M., Bastida, E., Ballejos, M., Garza, K., Glassman, C., & Huff-Hinkle, C. (1989). *Innovative approaches toward prevention of institutionalization of Mexican American elderly.* Final report, U.S. Administration on Aging. Edinburg, TX: Pan American University.

population. Moreover, little specific attention has been focused on the health statistics of older Hispanics. The data obtained by a few southwestern states afford better comparability because many of these states (e.g., Texas) have collected health data on the Hispanic population over a long period (Markides & Coreil, 1988). For example, Ellis's (1962) work with data from the period 1949–1951 in San Antonio and Houston showed that Spanish-surname whites had considerably higher mortality rates and lower life expectancy than did Anglos, particularly women.

In a more recent study of 1,022 elderly Hispanics in south Texas, women were more likely than were men to suffer multiple illnesses (Juarez et al., 1989). In general, a higher proportion of women reported suffering from hardening of the arteries, high blood pressure, cancer, and arthritis, whereas men reported a higher incidence of stroke (Table 5).

In the same study, women were less likely than were men to self-assess their health as good. For example, although 25% of the men self-assessed their health as good, only 21% of the women did so. More women than men self-reported their health as poor or fair (Table 6) (Juarez et al., 1989).

Although findings from the Juarez at al. study are limited to a south Texas Mexican American population, data from a recent national study of the Hispanic elderly living alone confirm their results. This study, based on a national sample of 2,299 respondents, included members of all four major Hispanic subgroups—Mexican American, Puerto Rican, Cuban, and other Hispanic. Data obtained from 1,477 female respondents were similar to the Texas findings, with 56% of these women reporting their health as fair or poor. The mean number of physician visits for this population during the past year was 8.0 for women and 6.8 for men (Commonwealth Fund Commission on Elderly People Living Alone, 1989). Other studies corroborate the above findings: Hispanic American women consistently score the poorest health status in self-assessment responses (East Los Angeles Task Force, 1975; Markides, Martin, & Gomez, 1983).

Mortality Rates

As with health statistics, data on mortality rates for Hispanics are not readily available. Mortality rates for New Mexico and Texas indicate that Hispanic females fare slightly worse than do white and nonwhite females in that they have higher cancer mortality rates, particularly in malignancies of the cervix, uterus, trachea, and lungs. These higher cancer mortality rates are present in the 45–64 age group as well as in the 65-and-older group (Markides & Coreil, 1988). However, Hispanic females have lower rates of breast cancer.

Income

In general, the poverty rate of elderly Hispanics is nearly double that for all elderly (22% compared with 12% for all elderly) (Commonwealth Fund Commission on Elderly People Living Alone, 1987). Elderly persons were classified as poor in 1987 if their incomes were $5,393/year or less. Among the Hispanic elderly, women living alone have the highest poverty rates. Data from the Social Security Administration (1987) indicate that in 1985, 88% of nonmarried Hispanic women were receiving Social Security benefits of less than $5,000 a year compared with 83% of nonmarried Hispanic men. In 1986, the poverty rate for Hispanic males was 18.8% compared with 25.2% for females. The poverty rate for elderly Hispanic women was almost twice as high as the 13.3% rate for elderly white women. Moreover, Hispanic elderly women living outside metropolitan areas were the most impoverished of all. In 1980, 38% of rural Hispanic women lived in poverty, compared with 21% of white rural women (Agree, 1986).

More recent data reveal a similar economic profile of Hispanic women. Of 1,022 subjects studied in south Texas, 85% of the men but only 75% of the women received Social Security. Whereas 69%

of the women reported receiving Supplemental Security Income (SSI), only 50% of the men were SSI recipients (Juarez et al., 1989). A smaller number of women received Social Security benefits; thus a larger number received SSI and were more likely to live on incomes below the poverty line.

These findings lend further support to the existence of poverty among elderly Hispanic women who live in nonmetropolitan areas. In south Texas, where agriculture is still a major source of employment and income, annual incomes of the 641 elderly women respondents were very low. For example, 23.2% had incomes below $3,000, and 67% reported incomes between $3,000 and $5,999. Only 9% of the women reported incomes between $6,000 and $9,999, and a meager 1% indicated an income higher than $10,000. Moreover, when asked about their sources of income, women overwhelmingly reported only one source. Four hundred and six (77.6%) indicated only one source, compared with 61.7% of the men in the study. Only 3.5% of the women, as opposed to 8% of the men, indicated three or more sources.

Mahard's (1989) study of older Puerto Ricans supports the results of Juarez et al. In her study, one-third of all respondents reported a 1985 pretax annual income for self and spouse of less than $5,000: "Income distributions show a pronounced sex difference. Women are considerably more likely than men to be represented in the lower income category" (Mahard, 1989, p. 248). Moreover, the major source of income for these older people was Social Security, with men and women being approximately equally likely to receive income from this source. In addition to being overrepresented in the lowest income category, women were also more likely than were men to receive income from public assistance programs such as SSI and food stamps. Mahard concludes that two characteristics, probably interrelated, distinguish older Puerto Rican women from men: "[T]hey show a considerable income disadvantage relative to men and they are much less likely than men to be currently married" (p. 252).

To summarize, Hispanic men aged 65 and older had a median per-capita income of $7,369, compared with $4,583 for Hispanic women, $6,757 for black males, $4,508 for black females, $12,131 for white males, and $6,738 for white females (Cubillos & Prieto, 1987).

Living Arrangements

As might be expected, Hispanic elderly are more likely to live in the community and less likely to be institutionalized than are white and black elderly. Agree (1986) observed that as of 1980

97% of the Hispanic elderly lived in households in the community (either alone, with family members, or with nonrelatives), compared with 96% of the black population and 94% of the total elderly population. According to the 1980 census, elderly Hispanics were far less likely than were elderly whites to live in homes for the elderly. Only 1% of Hispanic males and .9% of women in the 65–74-year-old category were living in nursing homes. Among the 75-years-and-older cohort, only 4.3% of the males and 5.4% of the females were nursing home residents in 1980.

Cubillos and Prieto (1987) suggested that Hispanic elderly were much more likely than were whites or blacks to live with their children in situations wherein the children, not the elderly persons, were the householders. In 1980, Hispanic women aged 65–74 years were four times as likely as were whites to live with their children. Of the 37% of elderly Hispanics who were not householders in 1980, 14% of the men, compared with 54% of the women, lived in families.

Data from the Juarez et al. study present a different pattern of living arrangements for older Hispanic women. Clear differences were noted in that study by gender. Of the subjects living alone, 78% were females. Of these, more than two-thirds were widowed and, for the most part, lived alone (Juarez et al., 1989).

Coping

As noted by Gonzalez (1988), two personality variables serve as predictors of adaptive coping among the elderly: perceived mastery and self-esteem. *Mastery* generally refers to the degree to which one feels in personal control of one's circumstances and environment, the extent to which one's actions determine rewards and punishments. Self-esteem, another important component of coping, generally examines self-worth and psychological adjustment. Gonzalez (1988) notes that "although mastery and related variables tend to be viewed as lineally related to one's development (i.e., mastery increases with age), the relationship may in fact be curvilinear. That is, perceived personal control in the elderly may diminish for assorted reasons" (p. 35). Similarly, Gonzalez (1988) further notes that self-esteem may also have a curvilinear effect with respect to age. Given the emphasis that our society places on personal autonomy and individual mastery, the Hispanic elderly, in particular older Hispanic women, who confront gender-related, cultural, and linguistic barriers, may experience a considerable decline in self-esteem.

A recent study conducted by the National Hispanic Council on Aging (Sotomayor & Curiel, 1988) examined mastery and self-esteem in a national sample of elderly Hispanics from four communities: Hartford, Connecticut; northern New Mexico; San Antonio, Texas; and the Rio Grande Valley of south Texas. Findings were examined by several authors, which provided an interdisciplinary perspective on this set of data. In general, the authors found similar levels of self-esteem among men and women (Curiel & Rosenthal, 1988). Contrary to the findings of Blau and Stephens (1978) in their Texas comparative study, elderly Hispanic women were not found to be more isolated from peer relationships. Older women had the same (and sometimes more) sources of support as did the men in the sample. Moreover, the older women in the study did not appear to be more vulnerable to depression and alienation, scoring similar to men in scales of self-esteem, life satisfaction, and mastery (Curiel & Rosenthal, 1988; Gonzalez, 1988; Korte & Villa, 1988). Curiel and Rosenthal (1988) suggested the need to examine variables other than those traditionally related to feminine traits in studying self-esteem in older Hispanic women.

In a gender analysis of depressive symptoms in older Mexican American women based on the south Texas sample of Juarez et al., Lueders (1989) found that 13.5% of the women in the study had no family support and 14.3% responded that they "did not know" whether family support was available to them. Widowed women reported the highest levels of depressive symptoms. Lueders's findings are similar to those of Markides and Farrells (1985), who found widowed subjects had higher scores than did married subjects and that women who were divorced/separated had lower scores than did the married women. Lueders notes that "discrete marital statuses have differential influence as a factor in the existence of depressive symptoms" (p. 22).

> Moreover, the speculated trend that disrupted marital status might have little effect in older Mexican American women may require modification. . . . For instance, widowed women would have no choice in regard to the disruption of the marital state, while for divorced/separated women the disruption may have involved more choice and, thus, may be less psychologically distressing (Lueders, 1989, p. 41).

Self-assessments of mental health were obtained by Juarez et al. (1989) in their study of a small number of homebound elderly Hispanics in south Texas. The latter were part of the larger Juarez et al. (1989) study of older Hispanics in south Texas discussed above. This smaller subsample, referred to as the "demonstration subjects" in the study, consisted of 13 men and 29 women ranging in age from 64 to 95 years. The subjects were asked to self-rate

TABLE 7.
Demonstration subjects:
Overall self mental health rating by gender.

Rating	Male (n = 13)		Female (n = 29)	
	n	%	n	%
Present Time				
Excellent	2	15.4	0	0.0
Good	3	23.1	1	4.5
Fair	5	38.5	15	68.2
Poor	3	23.1	6	27.3
Total[a]	13	100.1	22	100.0
No information	0	*	7	*
Relative to 5 years ago				
Better	3	23.1	1	4.0
About the same	6	46.2	12	48.0
Worse	4	30.8	12	48.0
Total[a]	13	100.1	25	100.0
No information	0	*	4	*

[a]Totals do not add to 100 percent due to rounding.

Adapted from Juarez, R., Lopez, M., Bastida, E., Ballejos, M., Garza, K., Glassman, C., & Huff-Hinkle, C. (1989). *Innovative approaches toward prevention of institutionalization of Mexican American elderly.* Final report, U.S. Administration on Aging. Edinburg, TX: Pan American University.

their mental health at the time of the interview. Whereas 5 of the 13 men rated their mental health as good or excellent; only 1 of 29 women in the subsample reported her mental health as good. The largest number of women indicated fair mental health (*n* = 15); six of the women reported it as poor. When asked to compare their mental health with what it had been five years previously, 48% of the women (*n* = 12) but only 30% (*n* = 4) of the men responded that it was "worse" than it had been five years ago (Table 7).

A second set of questions asked the subjects about their worries and satisfaction with life (Table 8). Whereas 20% of the men reported that they "never" worried about life, only 5% of the women indicated "never." Most women did not find life exciting, with the largest number finding life to be "pretty routine" or "dull." To summarize, whereas only a small number of subjects

TABLE 8.
Demonstration subjects: Attitudes about life by gender.

Attitudes	Male (*n* = 13)		Female (*n* = 29)	
	n	%	*n*	%
Frequency of worry				
All of the time	4	40.0	9	45.0
Sometimes	4	40.0	10	50.0
Never	2	20.0	1	5.0
Total	**10**	**100.0**	**20**	**100.0**
No information	3	*	9	*
Life generally is . . .				
Exciting	2	18.2	2	10.5
Pretty routine	8	72.7	14	73.7
Dull	1	9.1	3	15.8
Total	**11**	**100.0**	**19**	**100.0**
No information	2	*	10	*
Satisfaction with life				
Very satisfied	1	8.3	3	14.3
Somewhat satisfied	9	75.0	15	71.4
Not very satisfied	2	16.7	2	9.5
Very unsatisfied	0	0.0	1	4.8
Total	**12**	**100.0**	**21**	**100.0**
No information	1	*	8	*

Adapted from Juarez, R., Lopez, M., Bastida, E., Ballejos, M., Garza, K., Glassman, C., & Huff-Hinkle, C. (1989). *Innovative approaches toward prevention of institutionalization of Mexican American elderly.* Final report, U.S. Administration on Aging. Edinburg, TX: Pan American University.

were satisfied with their life, a fact that is not surprising given their poor health, a larger number of men than women appeared to be very satisfied. Given the small size and special conditions of this demonstration sample, findings must be treated with a great deal of caution. However, this small subset points to gender differences in self-ratings of mental health and general life satisfaction.

Finally, Mahard (1989) noted that both migration and the experience of living in a culture that differs from their culture of origin have been sources of chronic stress for elderly Puerto Ricans: "Chief among these, and particularly important for the women in our sample, is the physical separation from loved ones in Puerto Rico" (p. 255). Sixty percent of Mahard's sample indicated that during a typical week they thought about absent relatives and friends on the island very often or fairly often. Women were considerably more likely than were men to report such frequent thoughts (67% vs. 50%, $\chi^2 = 23.44$, $d.f. = 1$, $p < .0001$). Mahard further noted that many of these older people also felt considerable nostalgia for the island of Puerto Rico, with such feelings also being more common among women. Women were significantly more likely than were men to report having "many" problems with the English language. Mahard noted that women were more likely than were men to report bringing a translator with them when they had to deal with bureaucracies such as hospitals, clinics, or government agencies.

Conclusion

The data presented here are consistent with the literature on aging that points to the "triple jeopardy" (being old, part of a minority, and a woman) condition of older minority women, especially as it applies to their socioeconomic and health status. In general, this brief review indicates that the triple-jeopardy hypothesis is particularly applicable to the socioeconomic situation of older Hispanic women.

Data on other dimensions of the aging condition are not as clear or as supportive of the triple-jeopardy hypothesis for this population. In fact, our review of research findings points to several inconsistencies with regard to psychological dimensions and family support. Some studies find older Hispanic women more likely to be depressed and unhappy than their male counterparts, whereas other studies do not find significant gender differences. Moreover, some studies indicate that older Hispanic women are more likely than other older women in our society to live in intergenerational households in which the children are the householders. Other studies find that older Hispanic widows, like other older widows, are likely to live alone.

Clearly, more gender-specific research is necessary, in particular research that addresses the special circumstances of older Hispanic women. For example, Bastida (1984) observed that older Hispanic women tend to report greater difficulties than do men with transportation, because they are less likely to know how to drive. In general, Bastida concludes from her field-work experience that older Hispanic women have been forced to become more resourceful than men due to the adversities in their lives.

Hence their coping strategies, especially in daily situations, were different from those of the men she studied. Bastida found that women were more likely to rely on interpersonal skills as a way of coping with many of their situational adversities. Thus interpersonal skills appeared more polished among the women (Bastida, 1984, 1987). For example, women were very successful in manipulating and in exchanging their limited resources for needed services and support. Her findings also indicate that married men gained from their wives' interpersonal skills, because wives were eager to use their skills to negotiate on behalf of their husbands.

In closing a decade of fruitful research on older Hispanics, the general characteristics of this population have been outlined and our knowledge base enhanced from its meager beginnings in 1970. Still, much remains to be investigated in the decade ahead. As in other scientific research, we must build on the foundation laid during the past decade. However, our research should follow a more clearly delineated path. In the 1980s, research on the Hispanic elderly followed either a spontaneous direction, spearheaded by the professional interests of the investigator, or specific goals, clearly specified by the pragmatic interests of funding agencies. Research in the 1990s should be directed at closing the gaps left by a decade of exploratory investigations. It should help advance our knowledge of Hispanic aging by building bridges that will begin to answer the many questions raised during the 1970s and 1980s. Clearly, research needs to explore gender differences among Hispanics in the next decade.

References

Agree, E. (1986). *The AARP minority affairs initiative: A portrait of older minorities.* Washington, DC: Center for Population Research, Georgetown University.

Bastida, E. (1984). Reconstructing the world at sixty: Older Cubans in the U.S.A. *Gerontologist, 24,* 465–470.

Bastida, E. (1987). Sex-typed age norms among older Hispanics. *Gerontologist, 27,* 59–65.

Bastida, E. (1988). Age- and gender-linked norms among older Hispanics. In S. Applewhite (Ed.), *Hispanic elderly in transition: Theory, research and practice.* New York: Greenwood Press.

Blau, Z., Oser, G., & Stephens, R. (1978). Aging, social class and ethnicity: A comparison of Anglo, black and Mexican-American Texans. *Pacific Sociological Review, 22,* 501–525.

Commonwealth Fund Commission on Elderly People Living Alone. (1987). *Old, alone and poor.* Washington, DC: Commonwealth Fund.

Commonwealth Fund Commission on Elderly People Living Alone. (1989). *Pover-*

ty and poor health among Hispanic elderly. Washington, DC: Commonwealth Fund.

Cubillos, H., & Prieto, M. (1987). *The Hispanic elderly: A demographic profile.* Washington, DC: National Council of La Raza.

Curiel, H., & Rosenthal, J. (1988). The influence of aging and self-esteem: A consideration of ethnicity, gender and acculturation-level differences. In M. Sotomayor & H. Curiel (Eds.), *Hispanic elderly: A cultural signature.* Edinburg, TX: Pan American University Press.

East Los Angeles Task Force. (1975). *Feasibility study to assess the health needs of the Spanish-speaking elderly in an urban setting.* Unpublished manuscript, The Community Health Foundation, Los Angeles.

Ellis, J. (1962). Spanish surname mortality differences in San Antonio, Texas. *Journal of Health and Human Behavior, 3,* 125–127.

Facio, E. (1989, August). *Age, gender and culture: The social construction of widowhood among Hispanic elderly women.* Paper presented at the Annual Meeting of the Society for the Study of Social Problems, San Francisco.

Gonzalez, G. (1988). Psychological strengths of the Hispanic elderly: A comparison of four communities. In M. Sotomayor & H. Curiel (Eds.), *Hispanic elderly: A cultural signature.* Edinburg, TX: Pan American University Press.

Juarez, R., Lopez, M., Bastida, E., Ballejos, M., Garza, K., Glassman, C., & Huff-Hinkle, C. (1989). *Innovative approaches toward prevention of institutionalization of Mexican-American elderly.* Final report, U.S. Administration on Aging. Edinburg, TX: Pan American University.

Korte, A., & Villa, R. (1988). Life satisfaction of older Hispanics. In M. Sotomayor & H. Curiel (Eds.), *Hispanic elderly: A cultural signature.* Edinburg, TX: Pan American University Press.

Lueders, L. (1989, December). *Marital status as a factor in the occurrence of depressive symptoms in older Mexican-American women.* Unpublished thesis, Pan American University.

Mahard, R. (1989). Elderly Puerto Rican women in the continental United States. In C. Garcia Coll & L. Mattei (Eds.), *The psychosocial development of Puerto Rican women.* New York: Praeger.

Maldonado, D. (1975). The Chicano aged. *Social Work, 20,* 213–216.

Markides, K., & Coreil, J. (1988). The health status of Hispanic elderly in the Southwest. In S. Applewhite (Ed.), *Hispanic elderly in transition: Theory, research, policy and practice.* New York: Greenwood Press.

Markides, K., & Farrell, J. (1985). Marital satisfaction in three generations of Mexican Americans. *Social Psychiatry, 20,* 86–91.

Markides, K., Martin, H. W., & Gomez, E. (1983). *Older Mexican Americans: A study in an urban barrio.* Unpublished manuscript, Center for Mexican American Studies, University of Texas, Austin.

Markides, K., & Vernon, S. (1984). Aging, sex-role orientation, and adjustment: A three-generations study of Mexican-Americans. *Journal of Gerontology, 39,* 586–591.

Sanchez-Ayendez, M. (1984). *Puerto Rican elderly women: Aging in an ethnic minority group in the United States.* Unpublished doctoral diss., University of Massachusetts.

Sanchez-Ayendez, M. (1986). Puerto Rican elderly women: Shared meanings and informal supportive networks. In G. Cole (Ed.), *All American women.* New York: Free Press.

Social Security Administration. (1987). Unpublished data on the economic status of Hispanic elderly. Washington, DC: U.S. Department of Health and Human Services.

Sotomayor, M. (1973). *A study of Chicano grandparents in an urban barrio.* Unpublished doctoral diss., School of Social Work, University of Denver.

Sotomayor, M., & Curiel, H. (Eds.). (1988). *Hispanic elderly: A cultural signature.* Edinburg, TX: Pan American University Press.

U.S. Department of Commerce, Bureau of the Census. (1981). *Persons of Spanish origin in the United States. Current population reports.* Series 20, No. 351. Washington, DC: U.S. Government Printing Office.

Valle, R. (1983). The demography of Mexican-American aging. In R. L. McNeely & J. Colen (Eds.), *Aging in minority groups.* Beverly Hills, CA: Sage Publications.

Zuniga, M. (1984). Elderly Latina mujeres stressors and strengths. In R. Anson (Ed.), *The Hispanic older women.* Washington, DC: National Council on Aging.

10

Culturally Relevant Services for Hispanic Elderly

Joseph S. Gallegos

From a gerontological perspective, Hispanic elderly persons face issues that are germane to all elderly persons: access to services, the changing family structure, and an increasingly frail population that requires more health care services. The size, composition, and future trends of this population are considered in this chapter, and a model for the development of culturally relevant services for Hispanic elderly is discussed.

The Population

In the early 1970s, the federal government adopted the term "Hispanic" to refer to Spanish-speaking people from North and South America who were of Hispanic or Latin descent. Mexican Americans, Cuban Americans, Puerto Rican Americans, and other citizens from Central and South America are included in this group. Because of their numerous countries of origin and because of intermarriage and the mixing and blending of Spanish, African, and American Indian cultures, Hispanics as a group are difficult to identify, describe, and summarize, in that they display a broad range of physical and cultural characteristics. Added to this are a number of self-imposed and externally imposed terms of definition that make it difficult to generalize about Hispanics.

TABLE 1.
Selected characteristics of Hispanic elderly by major groups.

	Mexican Americans (%)	Cuban Americans (%)	Puerto Ricans (%)
Age of arrival in continental U.S. (years)			
Younger than 25	50	6	26
25–44	25	22	44
45 and older	20	70	23
Speak Spanish only	32	57	37
75 years and older	39	45	31
8th grade or less education	75	57	77
Receive Social Security	85	66	74
Receive pension	22	11	20
Poverty status			
Poor	43	35	42
Not poor	32	38	31
Receive SSI	36	48	46
Fair/poor health	54	46	63

Adapted with permission from Andrews, J. (1989). *Poverty and poor health among elderly Hispanic Americans.* Baltimore, MD: Commonwealth Fund Commission on Elderly People Living Alone.

To begin with, there is no one Hispanic culture. Not only are Mexican, Cuban, and Puerto Rican American groups different, but substantial cultural differences exist within these groups as well. Growing up and growing old are as influenced by social and economic strata as they are by geography and individual preferences. Diversity exists even within Hispanic subgroups, for example, The "Manito" Mexican American from New Mexico is different from Mexican Americans from south Texas or Yakima, Washington. Yet, despite the many differences that exist, commonalities in Latino culture exist. Commonalities in language and family values cut across these groups. In fact, some consideration is being given to the use of the term "Latino" in place of Hispanic because it seems to convey more cultural commonality than does "Hispanic," which seems to emphasize ethnic differences.

Population Diversity

Andrews (1989) provides the following profile of the major elderly Hispanic groups (see Table 1).

Mexican American elderly. Despite the fact that Mexican American elderly are more likely to have been born in the United States and speak English than are Cuban and Puerto Rican American elderly, 75% of Mexican American elderly have less than an eighth-grade education. Related to this lack of education, they are more likely to have performed low-wage farm work (17%) or service-sector work (20%) than are either Cuban or Puerto Rican American elderly. Moreover, because of their longevity in the United States and long work history, Mexican American elderly are more likely to receive Social Security benefits, including Medicare. Oddly, however, even though they have a higher poverty rate, Mexican American elderly are less likely to be covered by Medicaid and Supplemental Security Income (SSI).

Cuban American elderly. Most Cuban American elderly (98%) are first-generation immigrants. Of the Hispanic American elderly, they are oldest group; 45% are 75 years of age or older. They are less likely to speak English than are members of the other Hispanic groups, despite the fact that 43% have achieved higher than an eighth-grade education. Among elderly Hispanic Americans, elderly Cuban Americans are least likely to receive Social Security or pension income and to be covered by Medicare; most, however, are likely to be receiving Medicaid and SSI. Some of these differences can be explained by the fact that most Cuban Americans (70%) came to the United States after the age of 45. Thus they have a shorter work history and are more likely to have been employed in professional, managerial, or proprietary jobs (16%) than are their Mexican American and Puerto Rican counterparts.

Puerto Rican American elderly. Similar to the immigrant status of Cuban Americans, most Puerto Rican elderly (98%) were born in Puerto Rico. However, most Puerto Ricans entered the United States before the age of 45. They also have the lowest level of education (77% with eighth grade or less). Regarding the likelihood of poverty, eligibility for receipt of pensions, Social Security, and SSI, as well as Medicare and Medicaid coverage, Puerto Rican elderly rank between Cuban American and Mexican American elderly. However, 63% report poor or fair health.

Age considerations. For government purposes, the term elderly refers to people 65 years and older eligible for Social Security program benefits and 60 years and older for Older American Act programs. However, Newton (1980) refers to several studies in which the issue of defining "old" leads to the conclusion that, for Mexican Americans, onset of old age can begin as early as age 45. These studies argue for a "functional" rather than a "chronological" standard for defining age, which would allow members of some minority groups to receive social services earlier in their lives based upon ability to function. This consideration is particularly important to Mexican and other Hispanic elderly, who suffer from the correlates of low income, poor health, and consequently early old age as a result of years of menial and hard labor, exposure to agricultural pesticides, and other adverse work conditions.

Census data. A common position taken with regard to the census is that the count of Hispanics is inadequate. Language barriers and the difficulty of counting migrant populations contribute to the undercount. Nonetheless, census data continue to be the basis for the allocation of resources and services in many states. Despite their inadequacy, the census data at least provide a general picture of the Hispanic population and, more particularly, the Hispanic elderly.

The U.S. Census Bureau reported that in 1988 19.4 million Americans of Spanish origin were living in the United States (8.1% of the U.S. population) (U.S. Department of Commerce, 1988). In 1988, 55% of all Hispanics in the United States lived in California and Texas, and 73.7% lived in California, Texas, New York, and Florida. The number of Hispanic people of all ages in the United States is increasing, with an increase of 34% between 1980 and 1988. The median age of Hispanics in the United States in 1980 was 21.4 years (U.S. Department of Commerce, 1980), but has since risen to 25.5 years (U.S. Department of Commerce, 1988). Projections made by the U.S. census indicate that the percentage of Hispanic elderly will increase in the coming decades (see Tables 2 and 3).

Currently, nearly one million elderly (older than age 65) Hispanics live in the United States. They are the most rapidly growing elderly population in the United States, although they presently comprise only 3% of the entire elderly population and approximately 5% of the Hispanic population. It is projected that Hispanic elderly may quadruple by 2020 (Andrews, 1989). More significantly, the 85-and-older segment of this group is growing at an even faster rate than that of other elderly in the group as well as elderly persons in the United States in general. This growth has important implications for increased health-care costs and for the dependency of elderly Hispanics on families as well as for the economic and cultural issues that surround the topic of long-term care. The frail elderly who reach the age of 85 are likely to incur as

TABLE 2.
Distribution of the elderly population.

	% of total population 65+	% of ethnic minority population 65+	Median age (years)
Whites	89.8	12.2	31.3
Blacks	8.2	7.9	24.9
Asian American	0.6	5.9	28.7
Native American	0.3	5.2	22.8
Hispanic American	2.3	4.9	23.2

much in health care expenses during their remaining life as they incurred during all previous years. Couple this issue with the changing family structure and economic status of the Hispanic population as a whole and one begins to realize the enormity of the problems that lie ahead if proactive steps are not taken soon. The issues that need to be addressed can be summarized as access to services, implications of the changing family structure, and health care.

Education. Nearly one-third of Hispanics 65 years and older lack a fifth-grade education (Select Committee on Aging, 1989). Hispanic elderly had a lower educational level than did other minority groups. The average number of school years completed for Hispanics age 65 and older was 7.6 for males and 7.3 for

TABLE 3.
Distribution of the Hispanic elderly population 65 years and older in 1987.

	N	%
Mexican	491,000	54.2
Puerto Rican	81,000	8.9
Cuban	123,000	13.6
Other	211,000	23.3

Adapted from Select Committee on Aging, House of Representatives. (1989). *Demographic characteristics of the older Hispanic population* (Comm. Pub. No. 100-696). Washington, DC: U.S. Government Printing Office.

females, compared with 7.8 and 8.8 for black elderly and 12.1 and 12.1 for white elderly.

The lack of formal education of many Hispanic elderly may constitute a barrier to access to services. Many are illiterate in both English and Spanish and consequently do not benefit from written outreach and media materials (Guttmann & Cuellar, 1982; Lacayo, 1982; Torres-Gil, 1982; Garcia, 1985). In addition, Hispanic elderly may lack knowledge about services, a further barrier to receiving help (Starrett & Decker, 1984). Moreover, eligibility requirements and complicated procedures can prevent the use of services, even if their existence is known (Guttmann & Cuellar, 1982).

Language. Even when the elderly Hispanic uses services, language may be an obstacle to receiving appropriate help. Hispanic elderly may have difficulty communicating with English-speaking social service and health care providers. They often tend to use health care services only when the health care facility has bilingual staff (Toma, 1985; Jette & Reimen, 1989). Mark's (1987) survey found that the availability of Spanish-speaking health care providers increased the Hispanic elderly woman's tendency to use health care services. A study by Starrett and Decker (1984) found that Hispanic elderly people's knowledge of social services had a direct effect on use of services. Not surprisingly, English literacy was a predictor of greater knowledge about services. These difficulties can be overcome through the use of translators, Spanish-speaking staff, and innovative outreach marketing strategies.

Economic barriers. It is difficult to separate the various factors that contribute to economic barriers to service for Hispanic elderly. The Hispanic elderly person's limited education and history of low-income jobs are likely intertwined. Nonexistent or inadequate education frequently contributes to a lifetime of low-paying farm work and service jobs that do not offer pensions (Andrews, 1989) or Social Security coverage (72% of this population receives Social Security compared with 92% of all elderly). Lack of Social Security coverage in turn may be associated with the Hispanic elderly's low usage of Medicare. Low income itself is a deterrent to use of services in that low-income persons may be without transportation or may be afraid that services will not be affordable. The median annual income for Hispanic elderly in 1986 was 64% of that of white elderly ($5,510 vs. $8,544). In that same year, the annual income of elderly Hispanics was below $5,000 for 48.5% of the population vs. 24% for white elderly. Ninety percent of elderly Hispanic women had incomes of less than $10,000 (Select Committee on Aging, 1989).

Unemployed, low-income Hispanic elderly commonly rely on SSI for their primary source of income (Cubillos & Prieto, 1987). However, Hispanic elderly are twice as likely as are white elderly to be without coverage by either SSI or Social Security. Lack of cultural awareness of the service system contributes to this situation because service providers are not likely to have cross-cultural experience or training to equip them to meet the special needs of Hispanic elderly (Green, 1982). Culture and economic status play a part in service utilization in other ways as well. Pride, reluctance to admit need, and fear of being poorly received have been mentioned as barriers to using social services (Garcia, 1985; Guttmann & Cuellar, 1982).

Minority status. Hispanic elderly persons' minority status is another factor that influences their health care and social service utilization. Hispanics, especially the elderly, have historically experienced discrimination and racism. Patterns stemming from white ethnocentricism and from job competition have placed Hispanics in a generally precarious economic position. As a result, the Hispanic elderly population has faced greater educational and employment barriers than have persons from other elderly groups (Andrews, 1989).

Minority status, coupled with age, makes this group doubly disadvantaged. Lacayo (1982) suggests a triple-jeopardy status based on the high percentage of Hispanic persons who have an annual income of less than the poverty level, are members of a minority group, and are old. Guttmann and Cuellar (1982) use the phrase "multiple jeopardy" to describe other disadvantages, such as lack of education and poor health.

The long history of societal discrimination and racism directed at Hispanics in America, which has adversely affected their economic and social status, has in part influenced this group's utilization of social services. Further, Guttmann and Cuellar (1982) cite a lack of Hispanic persons' involvement in community service planning and delivery as having a deterrent effect on minority participation.

Issues

The role of the family and its changing structure have significant implications for service access and health care. Living arrangements as well as the degree of acculturation and assimilation influence the structure and function of the family. For example, if social services are not available, the needy elderly Hispanic will likely have to depend on relatives for support. Hispanic elderly use fewer services than do elderly Anglo people because

Hispanics tend to have strong networks of informal caregivers within the extended family (Greene & Monahan, 1984). One study found that the oldest generation in Mexican American families tended to rely for help chiefly on their own adult sons and daughters (Markides, Boldt, & Ray, 1986). The Commonwealth Fund Commission report (Andrews, 1989) indicates that 77% of all Hispanic elderly who had been hospitalized reported that they were cared for by a family member or a spouse. Although many Hispanic families care successfully for their older family members, it is not known how long these families will be able to meet the elders' physical, emotional, and financial requirements.

Living arrangements. Although Hispanic elderly are more likely to live in multigenerational families than are other elderly (Cubillos & Prieto, 1987), assuming that the extended family can meet all needs is a disservice to both the elderly and their families. If an older person's needs are met through the family only, rather than through some direct contact with the outside world, isolation and dependency can result (Rathbone-McCuan & Hashimi, 1982). Furthermore, caring for elderly relatives can be a heavy burden on a family's resources, which may already be stretched. Evidence also suggests that extended-family patterns are being broken down by urbanization and that Hispanics are beginning to adopt the middle-class American custom of not expecting family members to support their relatives (Newton, 1980), which means that Hispanic elderly will require social services more than ever in the future.

Cultural norms and values have also influenced the Hispanic older person's utilization of health care and social services. Older Hispanic people offer reciprocal help to the family by providing child care. Thirty-six percent of the Hispanic elderly care for the family's children (Andrews, 1989). Unless service facilities accommodate children as well, elders may be unwilling or unable to use the facilities. Cultural norms and values that lead to the Hispanic elderly's reliance on family for emotional, physical, and financial support also affect the Hispanic elderly's use of long-term facilities (Jette & Reimen, 1989). The same reluctance may extend to the use of senior centers that discourage use by grandparents with children.

Acculturation. Acculturation has had adverse effects on the traditional Hispanic family. In Hispanic culture, the family traditionally provides support for its members. The elderly played an important role in the maintenance of the family while relying on the family to take care of them. The relationship was reciprocal, mutually beneficial, and geared toward maintenance of the family system. Various pressures have taken their toll on the Hispanic family in America, however, and have disrupted the balance, leaving the elderly without the natural system of support on which they have traditionally relied. The exposure of children and other relatives to acculturation processes has challenged values, especially traditional values of familial support for the elderly (Zuniga de Martinez, 1981).

Assimilation. Changes in the Hispanic family have also occurred as a result of assimilation. For some Hispanics, it is relatively easy to "pass" as white and thus blend into the mainstream culture. As younger Hispanics become upwardly mobile, they move away from the neighborhoods where their older relatives live, leaving the elderly physically isolated (Zuniga de Martinez, 1981). Lack of financial security also puts pressure on the traditional family system: the elders are reluctant to ask for support from the younger family members because of the strain it puts on the younger persons' finances. These factors disrupt the reciprocal system of family support; elders in need of help are not likely to turn to outsiders except as a last resort (Zuniga de Martinez, 1981).

Legal status may also affect the help-seeking process of a Hispanic family. If a family member is in the United States illegally, or even if the person feels vulnerable to being considered illegal, he or she may avoid reaching out for assistance. Recent naturalization laws will no doubt increase service utilization by individuals who previously resisted services out of fear.

Social Service Access

The past decade has witnessed the publication of a number of significant needs assessments and reports on the Hispanic elderly: Asociación Nacional Pro Personas Mayores (1980; The National Council on Hispanic Elderly (Sotomayor & Curiel, 1988); The University of Michigan (Lindemann & Benavidez, 1988); The National Council of La Raza (1987); and the Commonwealth Fund (Andrews, 1989). These important studies provide a consistent record of the needs of elderly Hispanic persons, centering on access.

Hispanic elderly have never received adequate attention regarding their needs and problems, despite the mandate of the Older Americans Act (OAA) of 1965. In the early 1970s, barriers to service were recognized, and policies were put in place by the federal government to address this service problem (Torres-Gil, 1982). In 1973, amendments to the OAA recognized the heterogeneity of the elderly population. Low-income and minority elderly were targeted as requiring services different from those needed by the mainstream population. Various specialized programs were developed and implemented across the country, and overall, public and elected officials became more sensitive to problems of the Hispanic elderly. In 1980, however, the Reagan administration brought a halt to the progress that had been made. Budget cuts and decentralization of oversight of these programs reversed the attention previously given to minority elderly (Torres-Gil, 1982). For example, nationally, the number of Hispanic elderly making use of services has decreased by at least 20% since 1980.

Health Care Issues

As mentioned in the section on economic barriers, the older Hispanic population's lack of education, poor income, and inadequate participation in the Social Security system is associated with their lack of coverage by Medicare (Andrews, 1989). Whereas 96% of all elderly are covered by Medicare, only 83% of Hispanic elderly are covered. The Commonwealth Fund Commission's report found that 8% of Hispanic elderly had no health insurance, compared with only 1% of all elderly (Andrews, 1989). The report also indicated that 21% of the Hispanic elders had Medicare and SSI, compared with 69% among all elderly. For the small percentage of Hispanic elderly who have supplemental health insurance, coverage is insufficient to offset the high cost of health care. Seventy-six percent of Hispanics receive their allotted Social Security benefits, compared with 92% of whites (Andrews, 1989).

Additionally, the Commonwealth Fund Commission's report found that 28% of Hispanic elderly relied only on Medicare, compared with 19% of all elderly. The report points out that low-income Hispanic older people tend to suffer from the high cost of health care and insurance premiums. Finally, the Commission's report indicated that 33% of Hispanic elderly have Medicaid and Medicare, compared with 8% of all elderly. This figure is a function of the higher poverty rate among the Hispanic elderly.

When looking at health issues, one also needs to consider that the health of older Hispanics is generally worse than that of non-minority elders (Rathbone-McCuan & Hashimi, 1982). Harsh working conditions may contribute to shorter life spans for farm workers of both sexes (American Association of Retired Persons, 1988). Under these circumstances, accelerated aging may occur, forcing persons who do farm work for a living to leave the work force at a relatively young age.

Other factors need to be addressed concerning catastrophic health care and long-term care for Hispanic elderly. These factors include the impact of modernization upon the traditional family support system, the increased dependency ratio (of both dependent children and elders) for the already hard-pressed Hispanic head of household, and increasing health care costs. The Catastrophic Health Care bill repealed in 1989 would have benefited the Hispanic elderly community directly; as low-income elderly, they would have borne the least of the cost for expanded health care services. Unfortunately, those who would have paid the larger portion of the sliding-fee formula, the elderly with substantial resources, were also the elderly with the political clout to repeal the short-lived law.

Even though the Catastrophic Health Care bill would have been an important first step toward universal health care, the bill did not fully address the issue and costs of long-term care. It is commonly assumed, perhaps because of romantic notions about the Hispanic family and its extended caregiving system, that Hispanic children would not choose to place elderly parents in a nursing home. As noted earlier, assimilation of Hispanics into the U.S. mainstream appears to have affected the extended family, which in turn has obvious implications for the use of long-term care facilities. A little more than a decade ago, the life expectancy of Hispanics was 60.9 years for males and 74.1 for females. Hispanic elderly generally did not live long enough to enter nursing homes, in which the average age of residents is 85. It should be noted that in terms of functional age, some research supports the notion that Hispanics age faster than do others. Thus elderly Hispanics much younger than 85 might actually be candidates for nursing homes. However, cultural values of pride and self-reliance may have created barriers to nursing home placement. Regardless, in light of the changing family structure, the economic realities of health care costs, and the increasing numbers of Hispanic elderly, the Hispanic community must prepare psychologically and financially for increased utilization of long-term care services. Culturally appropriate alternatives to institutionalization, such as Hispanic adult foster homes or Medicaid waivers, which allow payment to family members for in-home care of disabled relatives, are some options.

Cultural Diversity

In an analysis of barriers to service for Hispanic elderly, one ultimately confronts the various concepts of ethnicity and cultural diversity. Depending upon how diversity is viewed, the perceived needs of a specific ethnic group will also vary.

Green (1982) examines two concepts of ethnicity: categorical and transactional. A categorical view of cultural diversity defines specific groups according to the traits the members hold in common. Emphasis is placed on the differences between groups. The transactional concept of ethnicity is concerned with the communication between individuals and groups and the way communication maintains a sense of cultural distinctiveness.

Categorical View

Labeling and stereotyping are extensions of the categorical concept of ethnicity. The existence of a strong familial and social support system is a common stereotype about Hispanic culture. The belief that all of the needs of the elderly will be satisfied within these systems effectively removes pressure from the social service system to establish a network of support for the Hispanic elderly (Torres-Gil, 1982). This belief also ignores the possibility that the same support system can be used to cover up family dysfunction, such as alcoholism or elder abuse.

Transactional View

The transactional approach to ethnicity emphasizes the relations between the larger society and the group in question. It is a systems-based view of cultural diversity:

> [W]hat is critical to the transactional conception of ethnicity is not the inventory of cultural traits as such. Rather, it is the boundaries that groups define around themselves, using selected cultural traits as criteria or markers of exclusion or inclusion. Social boundaries, then, not categorical bundles of specific cultural traits, define ethnic groups (Green, 1982, pp. 11–12).

The interface of the boundaries of an ethnic group and the larger society is what is important, not the specific differences between the two groups. In applying this idea to the lack of services for Hispanic elderly, the functions of the boundaries are taken into consideration. The boundaries serve a positive function in defining the ethnic group and providing a sense of group and individual identity. However, if the boundaries are too inflexible to adjust to cultural change, they become barriers. With the changes in the Hispanic family structure described earlier, the perception of the Hispanic family-support network (on the part of both the Hispanic community and the larger society) has actually become a barrier to the elderly in gaining access to the help they may need.

Power-Based View

The boundaries defining ethnic minority groups are protective ones erected to maintain the integrity of the group from the threat of assimilation posed by the more powerful majority population. For the Hispanic elderly, the issue of power becomes important. Hispanic elderly have little voice in the political system (Torres-Gil, 1982). The strength of the senior lobby lies in its retired, white, middle-class constituency, which does not advocate for the needs of elderly Hispanics and other minority groups. For the Hispanic elderly, traditional roles in the family are weakening (Zuniga de Martinez, 1981), and these elderly are physically and culturally isolated from the service system. These power differentials are more pronounced for Mexican and Puerto Rican American elderly than they are for Cuban and newly arrived South American immigrants, whose socioeconomic status is more similar to that of white America. Nonetheless, from the power perspective, empowerment should be the goal for all treatment of and services for Hispanic elderly.

Cultural Competence Intervention Model

Models of cultural competence in human service intervention combine the transactional concept of interaction between majority and ethnic minority groups and the power-based concept of ethnicity. Key concepts of cultural competence include respect for cultural diversity, understanding of social realities of oppression and discrimination, and empowerment of the groups or individuals concerned (Gallegos, 1984; Cross, Bazron, Dennis, & Isaacs, 1989). Although models of cultural competence have not been tested to the point of defining the interventions necessary for improving the access of Hispanic elderly to services, such models appear to offer the best approaches to examining problems and developing intervention strategies.

Cultural awareness is the first major component necessary in achieving cultural competence. The first level of cultural awareness requires sensitivity and respect for cultural diversity. For social service professionals working with Hispanic elderly, this means knowledge of and appreciation for Hispanic culture as well as family and community institutions. The second level of cultural awareness assumes not only awareness of Hispanic culture but also the ability to apply that knowledge in planning and delivering services for Hispanic elderly. For example, although a service planner or provider may be aware of the traditional family helping role, he or she must also be able to assess a Hispanic family or individual in relation to this traditional family model in order to propose appropriate interventions.

A culturally competent approach to service incorporates practice principles and concepts that demonstrate an understanding of the realities of oppression and discrimination. Another practical concept of cultural competence is the application of knowledge about help-seeking behavior. In the help-seeking behavior model, five aspects are noteworthy: (1) Definitions of a problem are influenced by one's culture, that is, elderly Hispanics will diagnose and label their own problem within their own framework of understanding; (2) labels, terms, or concepts familiar and acceptable to elderly Hispanics must be used when successful intervention is sought; (3) the culturally competent service planner or provider should apply these labels, terms, and concepts when planning intervention strategies; (4) the human service worker must assess his or her own level of cultural competence and knowledge of resources in order to acquire needed competencies; (5) the expectations and values of the community need to be considered for assessing the outcomes of intervention because treatment can be considered successful only if the elderly Hispanic client or the Hispanic community views it as such.

The final component of the cultural-competence approach requires a practice approach that incorporates empowerment of elderly Hispanics as the ultimate intervention goal. As an intervention goal, the aim of empowerment is to increase the exercise of interpersonal influence and effective social functioning of individuals and communities.

Efforts to apply the ideas of culturally competent services have gained support in concept, if not in practice, in services for the elderly. Currently, the development of culturally competent and appropriate services to minority elderly is in the hands of applied gerontologists who are conducting research from which to develop practice models and testable hypotheses. Examples of this work include studies on self-esteem of elderly Hispanics aimed at helping one understand the dynamics of sociocultural dissonance and the impact of self-esteem and self-concept upon coping skills and help-seeking behavior (Sotomayor & Curiel, 1988; Paz, 1989). Sociocultural dissonance refers to the discordant stress imposed upon the bicultural individual who is forced to choose between values of the minority culture and the dominant culture. Thus this line of investigation in ethnogerontology seeks to learn how history and life experiences have influenced Hispanic elders' self-esteem and their capacity to endure and survive.

On a community level, the cultural-competence approach has been demonstrated and replicated with minority elderly. Beall (1978) noted the inability of services for the elderly to adequately address the needs of elderly Hispanics. He notes in particular that in addition to linguistic, cultural, and other barriers that go hand

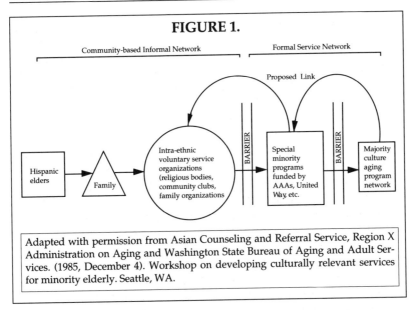

FIGURE 1.

Community-based Informal Network | Formal Service Network

Proposed Link

Hispanic elders → Family → Intra-ethnic voluntary service organizations (religious bodies, community clubs, family organizations) → BARRIER → Special minority programs funded by AAAs, United Way, etc. → BARRIER → Majority culture aging program network

Adapted with permission from Asian Counseling and Referral Service, Region X Administration on Aging and Washington State Bureau of Aging and Adult Services. (1985, December 4). Workshop on developing culturally relevant services for minority elderly. Seattle, WA.

in hand with minority status, elderly Hispanics are unable to relate to the service system and the service system is unable to relate to elderly Hispanics. Beall addresses the need for research that will affect the priority-setting process of the Agency on Aging (AoA) in OAA fund allocations. Unfortunately, despite support for assessment of the needs of minority elderly, OAA funding of minority-targeted programs remained primarily in the area of nutrition—that is, in the promotion of ethnic meals programs—and senior centers, neither of which have incorporated culturally syntonic strategies in a significant way. This problem is not so much a reflection of the intentions of the AoA but rather of the aging-service system. The OAA funds were designed to empower local development and delivery of services through the Area Agency on Aging (AAA) system. The power behind aging services, however, still remains with the state offices on aging, which are driven by Medicare/Medicaid funds and not OAA funds and local priorities.

As noted earlier, AoA has supported applied research on the development of culturally competent services for elderly minorities. One such model specifically addressed linkages between minority elderly, minority service networks, and the mainstream aging-services network. This project, titled "Developing Culturally Relevant Services for Minority Elderly," was implemented under the auspices of the Asian Counseling and Referral Service (1985) in Seattle, Washington. The project design incorporated the concepts and principles of cultural competence by allowing the community to define its problems and solutions as well as by engaging the community in the search for empowering goals. In addition to empowering individual elderly and their families, the project promoted the competency and effectiveness of minority service agencies as well as those of the mainstream. Figure 1 graphically presents the project design, modified for application to a Hispanic elderly community.

The model presented in Figure 1 is currently being applied with elderly Hispanics in the state of Oregon. The project has two components: needs assessment and outreach. Five counties in Oregon are participating in the project. Area Agencies on Aging in these counties have committed Volunteers in Service to America (VISTA) workers to implement a general needs-assessment survey of older (more than 50 years old) and disabled Hispanics. In the process of conducting a needs-assessment interview, the interviewer also obtains information about immediate needs and makes an appropriate referral to the agency case manager.

Currently, only one county has completed its process; its findings were consistent with those of national studies regarding service barriers and needs. Interestingly, the rural nature of the reporting county meant that the respondents were primarily (98%) migrant or former migrant workers. The elderly Hispanics in this sample were more likely to be from Mexico, whereas 10 years ago this population was likely to be Mexican American from south Texas. In addition to being from Mexico, clusters of migrants from different states in Mexico as well as respondents who identified themselves as Mexican Indians were in evidence. Thus, among the elderly Mexican-heritage population, there is increasing diversity.

Special populations in need of information on options or in need of services can be effectively served if the modalities evolve from the population and its cultural context. In Washington County, Oregon, the AAA had no data on local Hispanic elders, no liaison with Hispanic organizations, no bilingual case-management staff, no relationship with Hispanic elders, and approximately four Spanish-surname households on its case load. The Washington County AAA attempted to develop culturally relevant services with the assumption that the population had in some manner met its needs in the past, and if these experiences were integrated in a culturally appropriate manner, the population would use the services. Expected products of the project include culturally appropriate service modalities, a resource plan, an advocacy plan, an implementation plan, and a technical assistance plan designed by the population with agency assistance.

Each plan outlines goals, objectives, and responsibilities for the population and the agency.

Summary

As we approach the 21st century, Hispanics have become the fastest growing minority population and Hispanic elderly the fastest growing subgroup of it. The simple conclusion is that unless the needs and issues of Hispanic elderly are recognized and addressed, problems among this group will increase in proportion to their numbers. Such a situation would be especially traumatic for a community whose traditional culture places high regard on respect for elders and family interdependence. It is important to mainstream society that such problems be averted. Moreover, by studying and understanding the coping mechanisms within the Hispanic community, problems that plague our society as a whole, such as family disintegration and isolation, may be solved.

References

American Association of Retired Persons. (1988). *Directory of minority agencies and organizations serving mid-life and older persons in the Northwest.* Long Beach, CA: Author.

Andrews, J. (1989). *Poverty and poor health among elderly Hispanic Americans.* Baltimore, MD: Commonwealth Fund Commission on Elderly People Living Alone.

Asian Counseling and Referral Service, Region X Administration on Aging, and Washington State Bureau of Aging and Adult Services. (1985). *Developing culturally relevant services for minority elderly.* Seattle, WA: Administration on Aging.

Asociación Nacional Pro Personas Mayores. (1980). *A national study to assess the service needs of the Hispanic elderly.* Principal translator C. G. Lacayo. Los Angeles: Author.

Beall, T. (1978). Establishing a basis for assessing the responsiveness of Older Americans Act programs to Hispanic and other minority elderly. In M. Montiel (Ed.), *Hispanic families: Critical issues for policy and programs in human services.* Washington, DC: National Coalition of Hispanic Mental Health and Human Services Organizations.

Cross, T. L., Bazron, B. J., Dennis, K. W., & Isaacs, M. R. (1989). *Towards a culturally competent system of care.* Washington, DC: CASSP Technical Assistance Center, Georgetown University Child Development Center.

Cubillos, H. L., & Prieto, M. (1987, October). *The Hispanic elderly: A demographic profile.* Washington, DC: National Council of La Raza.

Gallegos, J. S. (1984). The ethnic competence model for social work education. In B. W. White (Ed.), *Color in a white society.* Silver Spring, MD: National Association of Social Workers.

Garcia, J. L. (1985). A needs assessment of elderly Hispanics in an inner city senior citizen complex: Implications for practice. *Aging and ethnicity, 4*(1), 72–85.

Green, J. W. (1982). *Cultural awareness in the human services.* Englewood Cliffs, NJ:

Prentice-Hall.

Greene, V. L., & Monahan, D. J. (1984). Comparative utilization of community-based long-term care services by Hispanic and Anglo elderly in a case management system. *Journal of Gerontology, 39,* 730–735.

Guttmann, D., & Cuellar, J. (1982). Barriers to equitable service. *Generations, 6,* 31–33.

Jette, C. C., & Reimen, R. (1989). Hispanic geriatric residents in a long term setting. *Journal of Applied Gerontology, 7,* 350–366.

Lacayo, C. G. (1982). Triple jeopardy: Underserved Hispanic elders. *Generations, 6,* 25–58.

Lindemann, M. M., & Benavidez, J. (1988, June). *1987 needs assessment of the Hispanic 60 and over population in the State of Michigan.* Lansing, MI: Office of Services to the Aging.

Markides, K. S., Boldt, J. S., & Ray, L. A. (1986). Sources of helping and intergenerational solidarity: A three-generations study of Mexican Americans. *Journal of Gerontology, 41,* 506–511.

Marks, G. (1987). Health behavior of elderly Hispanic women: Does cultural assimilation make a difference? *American Journal of Public Health, 77,* 1315–1319.

National Council of La Raza. (1987, October). *The Hispanic elderly: A demographic profile.* Washington, DC: Author.

Newton, F. C. (1980). Issues in research and services delivery among Mexican American elderly: A concise statement with recommendations. *Gerontologist, 20,* 208–213.

Paz, J. (1989, October). *The empowered Hispanic elderly: An analysis of self-esteem and mastery.* Paper presented at the annual meeting of the National Association of Social Workers, San Francisco, CA.

Rathbone-McCuan, E., & Hashimi, J. (1982). The Hispanic elderly: Cuban, Puerto Rican, and Mexican. In E. Rathbone-McCuan & J. Hashimi (Eds.), *Isolated elders.* Rockville, MD: Aspen Systems Corporation.

Select Committee on Aging, House of Representatives. (1989). *Demographic characteristics of the older Hispanic population* (Comm. Pub. No. 100-696). Washington, DC: U.S. Government Printing Office.

Sotomayor, M., & Curiel, H. (Eds.). (1988). *Hispanic elderly: A cultural signature.* Edinburgh, TX: Pan American University Press.

Starrett, R. A., & Decker, J. T. (1984). The utilization of discretionary services by the Hispanic elderly: A causal analysis. *California Sociologist, 7*(2), 159–180.

Toma, J. (1985, December). *Technical assistance guide for area agencies on aging: Minority elderly* (rev.). Seattle, WA: Washington State Area Agency on Aging Operations.

Torres-Gil, F. M. (1982). *Politics of aging among elder Hispanics.* Washington, DC: University Press of America.

U.S. Department of Commerce, Bureau of the Census. (1980). *General social and economic characteristics: Oregon.* Washington, DC: U.S. Government Printing Office.

U.S. Department of Commerce, Bureau of the Census. (1988). *The Hispanic population in the U.S.: March 1988.* Washington, DC: U.S. Government Printing Office.

Zuniga de Martinez, M. (1981). The Mexican American family: A weakened support system? In E. P. Stanford (Ed.), *Minority aging: Policy issues for the '80s* (Proceedings of the Seventh National Institute on Minority Aging). San Diego, CA: Campanile Press.

11

Juvenile Delinquency among Hispanics: The Role of the Family in Prevention and Treatment

Arturo T. Río, Daniel A. Santisteban,
and José Szapocznik

Hispanics are the nation's youngest and fastest growing population (U.S. Department of Commerce, 1986, 1988). Recent population estimates indicate that 22 million Hispanic Americans live in the United States (U.S. Department of Commerce, 1987), which represents approximately 9% of the total U.S. population. The breakdown by Hispanic subgroups is as follows:

Mexican origin	11.8 million
Puerto Rican origin (in P.R.)	3.2 million
Puerto Rican origin (on mainland)	2.3 million
Central/South American origin	2.1 million
Cuban origin	1.0 million
Other Hispanic origin	1.6 million

Since the 1980 census, the rate of growth of the Hispanic community has been 30%, or roughly five times the general population growth rate in America. In addition, this population is relatively young; 33% of Hispanics are younger than 15, compared with 20% of the general population. Approximately 1.7 million Hispanic adolescents (ages 15–19) lived in the United States in 1986. The Hispanic adolescent population is expected to increase by 29.4% by the end of the century, compared with a projected 6.4% increase in the white non-Hispanic adolescent population.

The fact that Hispanics are a young and fast-growing population has important implications in terms of delinquency prevention program development. This is especially true in that 40% of Hispanic youth are growing up in poverty and approximately half drop out of school before completion of the 12th grade. Clearly, any effort made in the area of prevention should allocate substantial resources to understanding and developing culture-specific interventions that are sensitive to the needs of this population (Rogler, Malgady, Costantino, & Blumenthal, 1987). Efforts to adapt existing "mainstream" programs to the Hispanic population should take into account the issue of population generalizability (Laosa, 1990), which refers to the applicability of research findings across different populations.

Before proceeding further, it must be noted that the term Hispanic does not represent a homogeneous group. With any broad classification, as many within-group differences exist as do between-group differences (U.S. Department of Commerce, 1988). Perhaps the term Hispanic is best understood when it is compared with the term European. Although commonalities across European groups exist, important differences are evident. The same is true among Hispanics. Unfortunately, this diversity is not always conveyed in the literature on Hispanic families. As in any broad group classification, there is variation due to factors such as national origin, socioeconomic status, educational level, urban versus rural life, employment status, number of years or generations in the United States, level of acculturation, geographical residence, etc.

As Laosa (1990) notes, some children from Hispanic immigrant families adapt rather well, but many do not. In fact, some evidence suggests that the prevalence of adjustment problems in Hispanic children and adolescents increases as a function of length of stay in the United States (Borjas & Tienda, 1985; Canino, Early, & Rogler, 1980).

Because sociodemographic variables affect family functioning, any intervention used should assess the contribution of each of these factors and evaluate its compatibility with the proposed interventions. Taking within- and between-group differences into account will enhance the likelihood of cultural sensitivity, thus avoiding the possibility of appearing culturally offensive to a Hispanic family. With adolescents and their parents, ethnic identification must be carefully evaluated. As Galan (1988) suggests, we need to know something about each family member in terms of his or her level of cultural integration or biculturality. An individual's Hispanic surname says very little about the extent to which the adolescent identifies and is involved with any particular Hispanic culture.

Delinquency among Hispanics

Rogler (1984) noted that "very little is known about Hispanic delinquency in general, and about those factors that may influence Hispanic behavior . . . the existing literature is virtually silent on delinquency about Hispanic youth, and there are no data which explain why Hispanic youth engage or do not engage in delinquent activity" (p. 1). Little information about Hispanic delinquency has appeared in the five years since Rogler made this statement. In terms of aggregate national data, the situation is not expected to improve, because the FBI has stopped collecting crime and delinquency statistics by ethnicity.

The most recent (and last) national delinquency statistics for Hispanics found in the 1986 FBI Uniform Crime Reports (1987) present arrest data for Hispanic minors (younger than 18). The data reported allow for comparison of Hispanics age 18 and older with Hispanics younger than 18 and for comparisons between Hispanics and non-Hispanics. These data are not presented in a way that allows comparison between Hispanics and other subgroups (e.g., blacks, whites, and so forth). These data show that Hispanics committed 14.7% of violent crimes and 12.9% of nonviolent (property) crimes. Overall, Hispanics committed 12.7% of all crimes. With regard to Hispanics older than 18 versus those younger than 18, the statistics are similar concerning the crime index for violent offenses (13.5% vs. 11.8%) and total offenses (12.9% vs. 11.8%).

Incarceration data, however, are more alarming. Between 1977 and 1983, the number of Hispanic youth incarcerated in detention centers increased 62% and the number of Hispanics in "training schools" increased 71% (Schwartz, 1984). In 1983, 15% of all incarcerated youth were Hispanic. In relation to white Americans, Hispanics are overrepresented in facilities for juvenile delinquents, tend to be placed in more secure facilities, and tend to have higher rates of incarceration than are warranted by the frequency or type of offenses committed (Morales, Fergusen, & Munford, 1983; Krisberg, Schwartz, Fishman, Eisikovits, & Guttman, 1986). It should be noted that incarceration records do not reflect the true nature and rates of juvenile delinquency (Kazdin, 1987). In fact, according to Empey (1982), 90% of illegal acts are either not detected or if detected are not pursued by the juvenile justice system.

Recently completed and yet unpublished research was conducted on a random population sample of more than 1,000 male

Hispanic adolescents (ages 12–19) in the South Bronx area of New York City. Information on self-reported criminal offenses was obtained with use of Elliot's National Youth Survey. The results of the study (O. Rodriguez, personal communication, August 8, 1989) indicated that Hispanic adolescents (primarily of Puerto Rican origin) reported the same level of offenses as that found in Elliot's national sample. Rodriguez indicated that there is no reason to believe that Hispanic adolescents commit more offenses than do Anglo adolescents, although evidence suggests that the Hispanic juvenile arrest rate is higher than that of Anglo adolescents in the South Bronx.

In work recently conducted in the Miami area with 100 regular and heavy drug-using Hispanic adolescent males (ages 14–17), Inciardi (personal communication, July 15, 1989) found that 49% were involved in a major felony at least once per month and 87% were involved in petty property crimes at least once per week. Seventy-four percent of the total Hispanic sample had committed at least one major felony in the past 12 months. Of these, 47% had been involved in robbery, 58% in a burglary, and 52% in motor vehicle theft. Furthermore, the 74 adolescents who admitted to engaging in at least one major felony in the past 12 months accounted for 2,781 felonies in that same period. Of these 2,781 felonies, only 27 resulted in arrest (0.97%). These findings support the findings of Empey (1982) that arrest records do not accurately reflect the extent of the delinquency problem.

Further review of the literature on Hispanic juvenile delinquents reveals that relatively little research has been conducted directly on delinquency (Rogler, 1984). Most of the published work has focused on alcohol/drug abuse (Humm-Delgado & Delgado, 1983) and on gang membership (Moore, 1978; Stumphauzer, 1979; Adler, Ovando, & Hocevar, 1984).

Antecedents of Juvenile Delinquency: Social and Family Factors

Social Factors

Environmental stressors have long been identified as sources of psychosocial dysfunction among Hispanic children, adolescents, and their families (Canino, 1982). Two important categories of stressors that are hypothesized to lead to mental health problems and delinquency in Hispanic family members are stressful social conditions (e.g., poverty, educational deprivation, inner-city life) and acculturation stressors (culture shock, language barriers, ethnic-identity conflicts). Demographic variables that may contribute to delinquency include neighborhood status, community values, community disorganization, discrimination, and unemployment.

Much of the literature on delinquency among Hispanics has focused on broad sociodemographic factors such as culture and poverty. These factors presumably affect family functioning and are often said to be correlated with delinquency. Although little doubt exists that environmental and extrafamilial stressors contribute to the risk of delinquency, one must look into the family to find out what characteristics make families most vulnerable to these stressors and what family characteristics serve as protective factors that attentuate environmental stressors. As Adler, Ovando, and Hocevar (1984) state, it is still quite popular to blame delinquency and related problems of Hispanic youth on the "culture of poverty," making it difficult to move away from this simple explanation to more complex models that account for rates of juvenile delinquency and nondelinquency across social classes and ethnic groups. We agree with Kumpfer (in press) that "the final pathway in which family factors influence delinquency in the child is the way that the family functions, rather than external demographic variables."

Family Factors

The literature has identified both "protective" and "risk" factors associated with adjustment and maladjustment of children and families (Rutter, 1979; Garmenzy, 1985). Although most of the literature is reported from the perspective of high risk for the emergence of delinquency, some researchers have reported on those factors that help the Hispanic family respond to stressors in an adaptive fashion.

Protective factors. It has long been known that some children raised in very stressful and deprived environments somehow manage to overcome the "high risks" and adjust well to the environment. These "resilient" children (Werner, 1984; Werner & Smith, 1982) may provide clues for prevention, although the reasons for such heartening outcomes are not yet known (Laosa, 1990). Still, these children provide some clues for Laosa's interdisciplinary, multivariate model of adaptation among children of Hispanic immigrants. The model considers the family unit to be of paramount importance in how stressors are dealt with in the home.

The extent and degree to which parental and family variables affect the adjustment outcome of Hispanic children and adolescents have important implications in the field of delinquency. By focusing on the "successes" of resilient children, researchers can learn more than they can by continuing to focus on the "failures" of high-risk children and families. Factors that help mitigate adjustment problems of high-risk children are as important to study as are factors that "push" or "pull" children into problems.

Early studies (Jaco, 1959; Madsen, 1964a, 1964b) suggested that protective factors in the Hispanic family are instrumental in the adjustment process and that the Hispanic family protects its members through its support structure. It has been argued that the close-knit family system and community networks help protect Mexican American families from the development of dysfunctional behavior. Even before problems crystalize, Hispanic families unite to solve emerging problems within the existing structure and resources of the family.

In our work (Szapocznik & Kurtines, 1989), we found that several characteristics of families helped them respond to stressors in an adaptive fashion and stimulate the growth of their members. First, parents or parent figures demonstrate good family-management skills. They are able to provide effective leadership (behavior control and guidance) and are capable of supporting one another and working together *vis-à-vis* the child or adolescent. Second, communication among family members is characterized by directness and specificity—the ability of family members to communicate effectively. Third, family members demonstrate a certain level of flexibility in terms of handling familial and extrafamilial stressors in adaptive rather than rigid, automatic ways. Finally, these families allow important conflicts to surface and are able to achieve some resolution. Functional families realize that all problems cannot be resolved and so prioritize them in order to deal with those problems that are most important to adaptive functioning.

High-risk factors. A number of studies have investigated the relationship between high-risk family factors and delinquency. These studies have attempted to predict juvenile delinquency from a set of factors considered antecedents or correlates of anti-social/delinquent behavior. Family functioning is evaluated in relationship to antisocial/delinquent behaviors such as drug abuse and gang membership in particular and to the behavior-problem syndrome in general. The behavior-problem syndrome refers to a constellation of problem behaviors such as dropping out of school, severe conflicts with parents, trouble with police, and teenage pregnancy as well as behaviors often associated with drug abuse. Family functioning is thus an antecedent of a cluster of co-occurring behavior problems. An overview of some of the more significant findings is presented below.

A comprehensive review of parent and family factors associated with antisocial behavior and delinquency indicated that parents of these youths, when compared with parents of "normal youths," (1) show less acceptance of their children, (2) show less warmth, affection, and emotional support, (3) report less attachment to their children, (4) have family relations that are less supportive and communication that is more defensive, (5) participate in joint family activities to a lesser degree, and (6) have poor marital relationships (characterized by unhappiness, conflict, and aggression) (Kazdin, 1987). Further, families of antisocial youth generally have one member who clearly dominates the others. In terms of behavioral control, Patterson (1982) found that parents of antisocial children use behavioral modification (reinforcement) techniques inappropriately. Thus, some evidence suggests that juvenile-delinquency prevention should focus on the development of good parenting skills, which consist of effective monitoring and disciplining of children (Patterson, 1986). Parental monitoring, according to Patterson and Dishion (1985), refers to the extent to which the parent is aware of the child's whereabouts and behavior and the degree to which the parent supervises the child.

A review of prediction studies of juvenile delinquency by Loeber and Dishion (1983) revealed that parents' family-management techniques are a principal predictor of juvenile delinquency. These techniques include how parents handle supervision and discipline of their children. Other predictive factors, in order of importance, included the child's level of conduct problems (particularly lying, stealing, and/or truancy), parental criminality or antisocial behavior, and poor academic performance. Interestingly, the lowest-ranking predictors of juvenile delinquency were socioeconomic status and separation from parents. These two factors are often included as high-risk factors associated with or predictive of delinquency.

It has been further postulated that lack of appropriate parental supervision and the presence of social-skills deficits in the child increase the likelihood that the child will associate with deviant peers (Patterson & Dishion, 1985). These three variables, when present along with poor academic skills, have been related to an adolescent's engagement in delinquent behavior. Delinquent behavior often occurs in two stages. The first stage, a breakdown in family management, consists of increased antisocial behavior by the child and impaired development of his or her social and academic skills. These behavioral and skill deficits lead to rejection by "normal" peers and academic failure. The second stage, characterized by continued disruptions in parent-monitoring practices and poor social skills, places the adolescent at further risk for contact with deviant peers. Elliot, Huizinga, and Ageton

(1982) found that involvement in a deviant peer group is the strongest correlate of delinquency.

A recent study by Rodriguez (personal communication, August 8, 1989) compared delinquency-predictor variables obtained on a sample of Hispanics in the South Bronx with National Youth Survey (NYS) results (Elliot, Huizinga, & Ageton, 1989). The NYS indicated a direct effect for peer involvement (operationalized as "time spent with") and an indirect effect for family involvement and school involvement. Interestingly, the Hispanic data obtained by Rodriguez indicate a *direct effect for peer and family involvement* and an indirect effect for school involvement, suggesting that family involvement may be a more important factor for Hispanic families than for non-Hispanic families.

In a related study, Rodriguez (personal communication, August 8, 1989) studied delinquency levels and family composition of Hispanics in the South Bronx. He compared delinquency rates of three types of families: (1) intact (original two-parent), (2) single female head of household, and (3) broken families in which a male figure had been reintroduced. Results indicated that intact families had lower levels of adolescent delinquency than did either single-parent female-headed families or families in which a male figure had been reintroduced. No significant difference was found in delinquency rates between single-female-headed families and families in which a male figure had been reintroduced.

Edelman (1984) conducted an exploratory study on avoidance of delinquency by male Puerto Rican adolescents considered at high risk in the South Bronx. He noted that youth whose parents enforced isolation from delinquent peer involvement were unlikely to become involved in delinquency. On the other hand, a delinquent orientation (spending time with delinquents or wishing to do so) and the possession of handguns (even for "protection" purposes) played a role in delinquent behavior.

In a study of family correlates of gang membership among Mexican American youth, Adler, Ovando, and Hocevar (1984) found several characteristics that seem to differentiate the families of gang members from the families of non-gang members. Consistent with the literature in this area, the authors found that gang members' families were much less likely to socialize together (eating together, going out together) than were the families of non-gang members. Parents of gang members were less likely to share responsibility for disciplining and were less likely to discipline consistently than were parents of non-gang members. Interestingly, although the study did not measure level of parental acculturation, the data suggest significant differences between groups on many variables related to acculturation. Mothers of gang members, for example, were much more likely to have been born in Mexico, were much less likely to speak English at home, and were much more likely to label their husbands as *machista* (male chauvinist). In addition, the values reported in relation to parental expectations concerning a son's future and parents' beliefs about the extent to which life is predetermined are consistent with lower levels of acculturation in families of gang members. Although not reported, it would be interesting to know whether significant differences existed between parent acculturation and the adolescents' acculturation in the families of gang members that could help explain the rift between the generations (Szapocznik & Kurtines, 1980).

A study conducted by Buriel, Calzada, and Vasquez (1982) focused directly on the question of acculturation and maintenance of traditional Mexican American culture as it relates to delinquency. The authors' data failed to support the assumption that adherence to a Mexican American culture can be "damaging" and promote delinquency. In fact, the results suggest that first- and second-generation Mexican Americans who were more firmly grounded in the Mexican American culture showed less delinquent behavior (theft, drug use, vandalism, fighting) than did third-generation adolescents. Based on their findings, the authors concluded that "in response to pressures to assimilate, Mexican Americans may fare better if they maintain ties with their traditional culture while simultaneously incorporating aspects of the cultural mainstream. The outcome is a bicultural person capable of functioning in two cultural worlds" (p. 53). These findings are consistent with the theory of bicultural adjustment postulated by Szapocznik and Kurtines (1980).

Studies of families of drug abusers have generally reported a high rate of family pathology, including alcohol and/or drug abuse by parents. Profiles of abusers show that their families tend to be fragmented and in conflict (Austin, Macari, & Lettieri, 1979; Green, 1979; O'Donnell & Clayton, 1979; Stanton, 1979). In many cases, mothers are overinvolved in the rearing of their children, whereas fathers are distant, marginally involved in the family, or absent and may apply harsh and/or inconsistent discipline (Austin et al., 1979).

Thus a number of studies show that maladaptive family patterns may lead to and maintain acting-out behaviors as children pass into adolescence (Stanton, 1979; Austin et al., 1979). This evidence suggests that the family is one of the most important aspects of life context influencing delinquent behaviors. More specifically, the most significant aspect of family functioning affecting acting-out behavior can be defined in terms of maladaptive family interactional patterns (Minuchin, 1974; Santisteban, 1979; Szapocznik, Kurtines, Foote, Perez-Vidal, & Hervis, 1983).

The Behavior-Problem Syndrome

Research on delinquency often includes illegal drug abuse as a major category. Because delinquency and drug abuse tend to coexist and reinforce each other (Jessor, 1983), the two sets of literature are linked. Our research (Szapocznik, Santisteban, Rio, Perez-Vidal, & Kurtines, 1986) as well as that of others suggests that delinquency is frequently a part of a more complex syndrome of antisocial behaviors that often includes drug use. For these reasons, this chapter draws from both the antisocial and drug literature in an attempt to explore the underlying factors that contribute to the emergence and maintenance of both types of antisocial behaviors.

As is evident in the research literature, drug use is often correlated with delinquency, family disorganization, alcoholism, and emotional disturbances (Lund, Johnson, & Purviens, 1978). Considerable research suggests that both adolescent drug abuse and delinquency are part of a more general syndrome of acting-out behaviors. Jessor and Jessor (1977) surveyed a series of studies on the nature of problem behaviors during adolescence, including delinquency, drug abuse, sexual intercourse, drinking problems, and general deviant behavior. Their research with high school students supported a model in which various problem behaviors coexist. Jessor (1983) postulated that such behaviors constitute a syndrome because they arise from an underlying, antecedent set of variables. This constellation of antecedent variables is hypothesized to give rise to a variety of normative transgressions.

The Behavior-Problem Syndrome Among Hispanic Adolescents

Research at the Spanish Family Guidance Center with Hispanic adolescents (Szapocznik, Scopetta, & King, 1978) suggested that Jessor and Jessor's findings (1977) were generalizable to the Hispanic adolescent population of Miami, Florida. Substance abuse appears to be part of a more general "behavior-problem syndrome," which includes alcohol and drug abuse as well as other antisocial and delinquent activities.

In addition to drug use and delinquency, the behavior-problem syndrome in Hispanic adolescents also includes high levels of acculturation (relative to their parents) and a rejection of the culture of origin. Earlier studies conducted at the Spanish Family Guidance Center (Szapocznik & Kurtines, 1980) found that problem behavior in Hispanic adolescents was usually most prevalent among highly acculturated youth with relatively unacculturated parents. These youths tended to reject their culture of origin and the values expressed by their parents, whereas the parents tended to reject the culture adopted by their children. These findings are consistent with reports in the literature that suggest that rejection of parents by children as well as rejection of children by parents is strongly related to delinquency (Kazdin, 1987). Thus, our findings are consistent with those reported by Jessor and support the view that delinquency and drug abuse can be conceptualized as part of a larger behavior-problem syndrome that includes a variety of acting-out behaviors. Our work extends the work of others in that it addresses problems and characteristics particular to Hispanic families, adding rejection of culture of origin to the pattern of behaviors that constitute the behavior-problem syndrome in the youth and a broad cultural intergenerational gap to the family antecedents of the behavior-problem syndrome.

The framework outlined here is similar to Jessor's model in suggesting that the behavior-problem syndrome arises from a set of antecedent factors, but it differs in how the antecedent factors are conceptualized. Rather than emphasizing a more or less fixed personality structure as the pivotal antecedent factor, our model conceptualizes the adolescent's "personality" as a set of habitual behaviors that occur within the interactive context of family dynamics. These habitual adolescent behaviors are cogs in the wheel of interactive patterns of behavior within the family. Consequently, the adolescent's habitual behavior tends to maintain the family's habitual interactional patterns, and the family interactive patterns in turn tend to maintain or promote the adolescent's patterns of behavior (Szapocznik & Kurtines, 1989).

Once adolescent personality proneness to behavior problems has been redefined as adolescent behaviors that occur within the context of family interactions, the locus of intervention becomes apparent. It is a logical consequence that interventions oriented toward the prevention and treatment of behavior problems would shift from individually oriented interventions directed toward personality change to interventions aimed at changing habitual patterns of family interactions that promote and maintain behavior problems in the adolescent. The logic suggests that efforts to prevent the behavior-problem syndrome require targeting habitual patterns of family interactions that may later promote or maintain the behavior-problem syndrome. Our emphasis on family interactions is akin to concepts raised by other authors such as Kumpfer (in press), who has labeled such interactions "functional family factors."

High-Risk Syndrome in Hispanic Families

Both Jessor's work and our own suggest that the behavior-problem syndrome arises from a set of common antecedent factors defined in terms of particular family conditions. The adolescent's antisocial behavior problems are viewed within the context of the family system. We have postulated that certain conditions (Szapocznik, Santisteban, Rio, Perez-Vidal, & Kurtines, 1986), which we have labeled "the high-risk syndrome," place some families at risk for future behavior problems in adolescents. The constellation of family variables that comprise the "high-risk" syndrome in Hispanic adolescents consists of three sets of factors: (1) current family structural dysfunction, (2) potential for future intergenerational conflict, and (3) potential for future intercultural conflict. We have further postulated that family structural dysfunctions represent the necessary conditions and family intergenerational and intercultural conflicts the added stressors that, when combined, tend to give rise to high rates of behavioral-problem syndromes in adolescents. Level of current family dysfunction thus serves as a moderator of future family stressors that come into play as the child enters the difficult stage of adolescence. As a moderator, it can function to either minimize or exacerbate the effect of these sources of stress.

Repetitive maladaptive family interaction. Families are at risk for the behavior-problem syndrome when family functioning displays maladaptive interactional patterns. These repetitive maladaptive family interactions are described in detail in Szapocznik and Kurtines (1989). Specific patterns include an enmeshed or overinvolved mother–son relationship with a peripheral father and a family organization incapable of resolving conflicts. When pathology occurs along these interrelated dimensions of family functioning, it is hypothesized that families with preadolescents are predisposed to serious family dysfunctions that may become manifest in adolescent behavior problems.

Intergenerational conflict. Intergenerational conflict is exacerbated by family developmental transitions such as the transition to adolescence. As Stanton (1979) notes, it is helpful to view the family in terms of its place in the family developmental life cycle. Most families encounter a number of similar stages as they progress through life, such as the birth of first child, adolescence, and separation. These are natural developmental crisis points that are normally weathered by the family system without inordinate difficulty. On the other hand, some families develop problems because they are not able to adjust to a particular transition. They become "stuck" at a point or stage of development because the family continues to interact in its habitual manner and fails to adapt to the changed needs of the adolescent child. Thus intergenerational conflict is a potential source of stress for all families with preadolescents and is not in itself a sufficient condition for the behavior-problem syndrome. However, it is an additional source of stress for families whose current level of functioning is inadequate, and thus serves to exacerbate the already existing dysfunction.

Intercultural conflict. In the Hispanic population, acculturational differences between generations can exacerbate intergenerational conflict. One of the most consistent and significant findings of the research at the Spanish Family Guidance Center (Szapocznik & Kurtines, 1980) has been that acculturation presents the migrant family with special problems and difficulties. Our observations and data reveal that because youngsters acculturate more rapidly than do their parents (Szapocznik, Scopetta, Kurtines, & Aranalde, 1978), the substantial differences that develop in the family may either precipitate or exacerbate intergenerational familial disruption (Szapocznik & Truss, 1978). Our model of acculturation (Szapocznik & Kurtines, 1980) explicitly recognizes a normative component of the acculturation process that is closely related to amount of exposure to the host culture and a pathological component that deviates from the normative component and is reflected in excessive over- or underacculturation. We hypothesize that this deviation from the normative component is maladjustive in the bicultural setting because it renders the individual inappropriately monocultural in a bicultural context. The most important implication for family functioning is that, in Hispanic families, culturally related differences across generations compound the typical sources of stress resulting from the developmental transition to adolescence.

Intervention Strategies in Juvenile Delinquency

Interventions can be divided roughly into the two broad categories of prevention and treatment. Delinquency prevention addresses risk factors in an attempt to avoid the later emergence of these problem behaviors. Treatment aims to correct the problem once it has emerged.

The past three decades have seen an increase in interest in programs that focus on prevention. This has been particularly true in the area of alcohol and drug abuse (Delgado & Rodriguez-Andrew, 1989). However, many of the prevention efforts that utilized interventions such as educational and psychosocial prevention approaches were shown to be effective primarily with white, middle-class populations. The more recent prevention strategies, which aim at the reduction of high-risk syndromes and correlates of drug use and delinquency, have yet to be tested with high-risk minority adolescents. Thus, more work remains to be done in the area of examining the relationship between risk factors and the development of prevention interventions for Hispanic youth (Delgado & Rodriguez-Andrew, 1989).

As in the area of prevention, much work remains to be done in the conceptualization and testing of interventions aimed specifically at the treatment of delinquency of Hispanic youth. All too often, treatment approaches used with Hispanics have applied presumed cultural values inappropriately and ineffectively (Sue & Zane, 1987). In addition, many of these treatment approaches have been based on stereotypical, unfocused, and untested assumptions, thus yielding interventions that lack power and specificity (Rio, Santisteban, & Szapocznik, 1990).

As outlined above, the strategic structural systems approach hypothesizes the existence of a constellation of family structural characteristics that constitute important antecedent conditions for future behavior problems in adolescents. This approach is strategic in that interventions focus on specific problems. It is termed structural because interventions are aimed at changing current and potential structural maladaptive patterns of family functioning. It is a systems approach because the work is done at the family system level, not at the individual level. Placed in the context of the research findings reviewed above, the approaches presented below were specifically designed to modify the types of family interaction patterns (structure) that promote and maintain behavior problems in children and adolescents.

Two intervention approaches are described. The first, *family effectiveness training*, was designed as a prevention/early intervention strategy for families whose children were at risk for the development of problem behaviors. The second, *strategic structural engagement and treatment*, was designed to intervene in the families of adolescents who showed more advanced stages of behavior-problem development such as current delinquency, acting-out behavior, and drug abuse.

Both treatment and prevention were based on the premise that fundamental changes can be made in the family system, which unwillingly maintains the behavior problems. Regardless of the stage of behavior-problem development at which the intervention takes place, treatment targets maladaptive family patterns that permit the emergence or maintenance of behavior problems.

Prevention

Our research with Hispanic families suggested that the aim should be prevention or reduction of the three factors that comprise the high-risk syndrome outlined earlier. In practice, this amounts to promoting more adaptive patterns of interactions that serve as strengthening and protective factors when the family is confronted by intrafamilial and extrafamilial stressors. The preventive intervention (family effectiveness training) was designed to help prepare the family to move effectively from being a family with a child to being a family with an adolescent.

In order to help the family make the transition more smoothly, parents were taught interactive skills that allowed the youngster to take on new roles. Both parents and youngsters learned to listen and to take responsibility for their own behaviors. In addition, youths were allowed to participate in the decision-making process, thereby encouraging a transition from a rigidly autocratic to a more flexible democratic relationship. These new skills allowed parents to change their habitual interactive patterns; they learned to become leaders through skill rather than force. By using leadership skills rather than coercive authority the parents minimized the likelihood of arousing rebelliousness, which seems to be at the crux of the behavior-problem syndrome.

Efforts aimed at minimizing intergenerational culture conflict were achieved by teaching the family bicultural skills and a transcultural perspective that could be applied to all areas of family functioning. Like family-strengthening interventions, the cultural component seeks to prevent future intergenerational conflict, but does so by focusing on the elements of conflict that are most culturally related. Interventions also provide the family with a broad understanding of the cultural/developmental factors that impinge on Hispanic families. Thus, structural changes are brought about in the family by focusing primarily on cultural content, with particular emphasis on the disruptive effects of intergenerational cultural conflict. This goal is achieved by establishing a transcultural, shared world view as a means for moderating the effects of future intergenerational/intercultural conflict.

The parenting and cultural components are also structural in that they tend to prevent the development of maladaptive patterns in the future as well as enhance the likelihood of developing more adaptive patterns. They focus on moderating the likelihood that certain maladaptive patterns of interactions will emerge. However, not all families have the flexibility to integrate this information in order to change their existing maladaptive patterns of family interaction. Once maladaptive interactions become established, they are not easily modified by the family itself. Therapeutic interventions are required to bring about structural (interactional) change directly to these maladaptive patterns of interactions.

Treatment

Unfortunately, most Hispanic families do not seek treatment until the adolescent consistently behaves in a fashion that is bothersome to either the family or to society. Our research indicated that Hispanic families are typically mobilized for treatment by the onset of a crisis and not by preventive or growth concerns (Scopetta, King, Szapocznik, & Tillman, 1977; Rio et al., 1990). Consequently, a large portion of Hispanic families seek treatment after delinquent behavior has surfaced or has become deeply ingrained. Family conflicts are frequently manifested by the adolescent's overt rejection of parental authority and, conversely, by the parents' ineffective behavior-control efforts. As we have found and as was evident in the body of literature presented earlier, ineffective parental functioning in the families of delinquents includes poor behavior control and monitoring of the adolescent, inconsistent discipline, rejection of the adolescent, and few joint family activities.

Treatment interventions aimed at eliminating delinquent and other acting-out behaviors must target those family dysfunctions that both maintain and are exacerbated by the delinquent behavior. In addition, the treatment of Hispanic families must address the intercultural/intergenerational factors that play such an important role in the development of delinquent behavior.

In practice, the first barrier confronted by the treatment provider is the engagement of the entire family in treatment. Delinquent adolescents seldom self-refer to treatment programs. They tend to deny delinquency-related problems and feel that delinquent peers help them to cope with personal and family problems as well as provide them with a strong source of identity, support, and belonging. As Rio et al. (1990) note, once in treatment, delinquent adolescents tend to attribute family-related problems and not their own behavior problems as the primary reason for being in treatment.

A substantial proportion of clients are lost prior to the first treatment session, thus confirming the difficulty of engaging families of behavior-problem adolescents in treatment. Our data show that a very large proportion (78%) of cases seek help but never enter treatment. Of the 22% who enter treatment, half (49.7%) drop out before the completion of treatment. Thus, only 11% of all families who sought help for a conduct-disordered adolescent actually achieved clinically approved termination.

The powerlessness of the parental subsystem manifests itself in both its inability to control effectively the adolescent's behavior (delinquency) and in its inability to organize the family to come to therapy. From this perspective, confronting and dealing with the initial resistance to treatment must become an integral part of the therapist's responsibility. This approach differs drastically from most treatment philosophies, in which patients are considered responsible for bringing themselves to treatment. Ironically, the families that most need therapy are families in which patterns and habits interfere with effective help-seeking behaviors. *When the family wishes to get rid of the symptom, the same interactive patterns that maintained the symptom also act to prevent the family from seeking professional help.* Within this framework, resistance is nothing more than the family's display of its inability to adapt effectively, to help itself, or to seek help. The focus during the early engagement phase is on working with the initial contact person in order to bring about the changes necessary to engage the entire family in therapy. By using the contact person as a vehicle for joining with other family members, the therapist can eventually establish a therapeutic alliance with each member and thereby elicit the cooperation of the entire family in the engagement effort. A more detailed description of engagement strategies can be found in Rio et al. (1990) and Szapocznik and Kurtines (1989). In the process of engaging resistant families, the therapist often sees only one or a few of the members of the family initially. It is still possible, through these individuals, to bring about changes in interactive patterns that will allow the family to come for therapy (Szapocznik, Kurtines, Perez-Vidal, Hervis, & Foote, 1990; Szapocznik, Foote, Perez-Vidal, Hervis, & Kurtines, 1985).

In our work at the Spanish Family Guidance Center, we have identified four patterns often seen in resistant families. The most frequently observed type of resistance to entering treatment is characterized by the *powerful adolescent.* In these families, parents are hierarchically positioned at a lower level of power relative to the adolescent. The adolescent typically resists therapy because (1) it threatens his or her position of power by moving him or her to a "problem-person" position and (2) entering therapy is part of the parent's agenda and, if followed, will enhance the parent's power. The second most common type of resistance to entering treatment is characterized by a *parent who protects the existing fami-*

ly structure. This parent gives a double message—expresses a desire for help while at the same time "protecting" the family by giving "excuses" for not involving the family in treatment. The *disengaged parent* represents the third type of resistance. This family structure is characterized by little or no cohesiveness between the parents. As a result, one of the parents (usually the father) refuses to come to therapy. This parent typically remains uninvolved. The fourth type of resistance involves *family secrets.* In these cases, family members refuse to seek treatment out of a fear that family secrets will be revealed. Although such fears may be unfounded, they are, at times, based on real issues.

The effectiveness of strategic structural systems engagement was evaluated by means of an experimental design (Szapocznik et al., 1988) in which client families were randomly assigned to counselors using one of two approaches: "strategic structural systems engagement" or "engagement as usual." Engagement as usual served as the control condition, wherein clients were approached in a way that resembled as closely as possible the kind of engagement that usually occurs in outpatient centers. In the strategic structural systems engagement condition, on the other hand, client families were engaged with techniques developed specifically for use with families that resist therapy. The difference between the two conditions was highly significant, indicating that 77% of cases in the strategic structural systems engagement completed treatment versus 25% of cases in the control condition.

As noted earlier, working with Hispanic delinquents and their families requires an approach that addresses intergenerational/intercultural differences as well as maladaptive family functioning. Structural family therapy is particularly suited for use with Hispanic American families because it addresses maladaptive family functioning within the content of intergenerational/intercultural realities. The primary focus of structural family therapy is at the process level: the way family members relate to and interact with one another. This approach allows work at the *content* level to take many forms. Content focuses on *what* people talk about while process focuses on *how* people talk to one another. Specifically, in treating families showing intergenerational/intercultural conflict, the content of therapy may be issues of culture differences, differences in rates of acculturation, and so forth. Work at the process level is aimed at changing the manner in which family members relate to one another.

As an example, take a family in which the mother and father are not united on how they view the adolescent's behavior. The father's more autocratic leadership style has become incompatible with the adolescent's adherence to a more democratic style as a result of more rapid acculturation. The mother, on the other hand, may be sympathetic to her son's position, which the father perceives as an act of betrayal or sabotage. With this type of scenario, it is not uncommon to see the father become disengaged from the family and encourage the mother and son to "fend for themselves." At the same time, the mother is likely to encourage the father's peripheral stance because she disagrees with his parenting style. The adolescent, on the other hand, further rejects parental values and overidentifies with his peer group and their values. At this stage the adolescent may begin to act out in a delinquent fashion. In this case example, we see a tenuous parental unit whose weaknesses and conflicts are exposed when confronted by intergenerational/intercultural stressors. This disruption in the family's organization effectively leaves the family without a parental or executive system. No one is left to monitor the adolescent's activities or to provide guidance and leadership. The result is a state of family functioning that further exacerbates the adolescent's behavior problems.

Effective treatment in the family described requires addressing the father–son conflict and promoting an atmosphere in which conflicts can emerge, be negotiated, and ultimately resolved. At the process level, the father's disengagement from his son and the husband–wife failure to work together must be the target of intervention. Although treatment must improve the father's ability to communicate effectively and provide leadership for his son, the spousal system must begin to negotiate and present a united front with regard to the adolescent and his delinquent behavior. By promoting a dialogue and negotiations between father and son around cultural issues such as leadership style (content), the therapist attempts to change the father–son impasse and provide them with tools for working out future disagreements (process). By helping the husband and wife to outline specific disciplinary rules (content), they are taught to work effectively as a parental unit and support each other (process).

This example highlights the adaptability of structural family therapy to the special stressors confronting the immigrant family (primarily at the content level) while also bringing about the type of changes in interaction patterns (process) that have been shown to result in effective treatment outcome. As noted earlier, researchers in the area of culture-specific treatment have argued that novel treatment approaches are all too often "watered-down" versions of traditional approaches (DeLaCancela & Martinez,

1983). A watered-down approach might emphasize cultural conflict but overlook the maladaptive family interactions that serve to maintain problems such as delinquent behavior. The approach outlined here is culture-specific, but the major component is changing the basic maladaptive patterns of interactions.

The effectiveness of structural family therapy was tested in a controlled treatment outcome study (Szapocznik, Kurtines, Foote, Perez-Vidal, & Hervis, 1983, 1986) in which clients consisted of Hispanic American families with conduct-disordered drug-abusing adolescents. Client families were tested extensively at the time of intake and at termination. A subsample underwent a six-month follow-up. The results indicated that client families displayed significant improvement in family functioning and a significant reduction of drug abuse and related behavioral disorders among adolescents. The results thus demonstrated the effectiveness of a structural family therapy approach to this population.

In addition, we recently completed a study comparing brief structural family therapy with individual psychodynamic child therapy (Szapocznik et al., 1989). The sample consisted of elementary-school-age boys with clinically significant emotional and/or behavioral problems. The results indicated that both treatment groups demonstrated overall improvement with regard to child symptomatology. However, between termination of treatment and the one-year follow-up assessment, the family therapy cases showed significant improvement in family functioning, whereas the individual child therapy cases showed a significant deterioration in family functioning. Thus family therapy contributed improvement in both the child and the family. Individual child therapy, on the other hand, had a positive impact on child symptoms but a negative impact on family functioning. It was concluded that family therapy contributes to the protection of family integrity. The finding that brief structural family therapy strengthens the family structure has important implications for prevention with regard to younger siblings in the home.

Conclusion

The literature has shown a close link between family functioning and delinquency. The link appears to be even stronger for Hispanic families than for non-Hispanic families. Our data are consistent with these findings and have shown that, among Hispanics, problems in acculturation affect family functioning and increase the risk of behavior problems in adolescence. When families show preexisting maladaptive patterns of interaction, they are unable to work successfully through stressors such as cultural conflicts and the transition into adolescence. From a prevention perspective, an approach that aims at improving family functioning and prepares the Hispanic family for future stressors is needed. It has been argued here that the manner in which families work together either insulates their members from stressors (protective factors) or exacerbates their effects (high-risk factors).

Often, Hispanic families cannot be reached at the stage when preventive efforts might be helpful and seek treatment only after a full-blown crisis erupts. At this point, the Hispanic delinquent adolescent presents a major challenge to those who attempt to deliver effective treatment. First, considerable evidence indicates that Hispanic families are extremely difficult to engage in treatment. In order to deal effectively with the problem of engagement, the therapist must focus on overcoming adolescent/family resistance to treatment. Second, treatment of delinquency is difficult and requires a well-developed family-based approach whose efficacy is supported by research. Cultural sensitivity is a necessary but not sufficient condition for successful treatment outcome. The task of the therapist is to integrate well-established interventions with a culturally sensitive treatment approach.

Knowledge of the structural family characteristics that provide the context in which delinquent behaviors emerge is necessary for prevention and treatment of delinquency. Our work has demonstrated that knowledge of family characteristics, resulting from and supported by research findings, can be used in developing specific prevention and treatment approaches. In addition, research efforts must continue to shed light on protective and high-risk family factors involved in the problem of delinquency.

References

Adler, P., Ovando, C., & Hocevar, D. (1984). Familiar correlates of gang membership: An exploratory study of Mexican-American youth. *Hispanic Journal of Behavioral Sciences, 6*(1), 65–76.

Austin, G. A., Macari, M. Z., & Lettieri, D. J. (Eds.). (1979). *Research issues update, 1978* (Research Issues 22) (79–808). Washington, DC: National Institute of Drug Abuse.

Borjas, G. J., & Tienda, M. (Eds.). (1985). *Hispanics in the U.S. economy.* New York: Academic Press.

Buriel, R., Calzado, S., & Vasquez, R. (1982). The relationship of traditional Mexican-American culture to adjustment and delinquency among three generations of Mexican-American male adolescents. *Hispanic Journal of Behavioral Sciences, 1*, 41–55.

Canino, I. A. (1982). The Hispanic child: Treatment considerations. In R. M. Becerra, M. Karno, & I. I. Escobar (Eds.), *Mental health and Hispanic Americans— clinical perspectives.* New York: Grune & Stratton.

Canino, I. A., Early, B. F., & Rogler, L. H. (1980). *The Puerto Rican child in New York City: Stress and mental health.* Bronx, NY: Hispanic Research Center, Fordham University.

DeLaCancela, V., & Martinez, I. Z. (1983). An analysis of culturalism in Latino mental health: Folk medicine as a case in point. *Hispanic Journal of Behavioral Sciences, 5,* 251–274.

Delgado, M., & Rodriguez-Andrew, S. (1989). *Hispanic adolescents and substance abuse.* School of Social Work, Boston University.

Edelman, M. (1984). *Exploratory study of delinquency and delinquency avoidance in the South Bronx.* New York: Hispanic Research Center, Columbia University.

Elliot, D. S., Huizinga, D., & Ageton, S. S. (1982). *Explaining delinquency and drug use: The national youth survey* (report No. 2). Boulder, CO: Behavioral Research Institute.

Elliot, D. S., Huizinga, D., & Ageton, S. (1989). *Understanding delinquency: A longitudinal multilateral study of developmental patterns.* Boulder, CO: University of Colorado.

Empey, L. T. (1982). *American delinquency: Its meaning and construction.* Homewood, IL: Dorsey.

Federal Bureau of Investigation. (1987). *Crime in the United States: Uniform crime reports.* Washington, DC: U.S. Government Printing Office.

Galan, F. J. (1988). Alcoholism prevention and Hispanic youth. *Journal of Drug Issues, 18*(1), 49–58.

Garmenzy, N. (1985). Broadening research on developmental risk: Implications from studies of vulnerable and stress-resistant children. In W. K. Frankenburg, R. N. Erde, & J. W. Sullivan (Eds.), *Early identification of children at risk: An international perspective* (pp. 45–58). New York: Plenum.

Green, J. (1979). Overview of adolescent drug use. In G. M. Beschner & A. S. Friedman (Eds.), *Youth drug abuse.* Lexington, MA: D. C. Heath.

Humm-Delgado, D., & Delgado, M. (1983). Assessing Hispanic mental health needs: Issues and recommendations. *Journal of Community Psychology, 11,* 363–375.

Jaco, E. G. (1959). Mental health of Spanish Americans in Texas. In M. F. Opler (Ed.), *Culture and mental health: Cross cultural studies.* New York: Macmillan.

Jessor, R. (1983, November 2) *Adolescent problem drinking: Psychosocial aspects and developmental outcomes.* Paper presented at the Alcohol Research Seminar, National Institute on Alcohol and Alcoholism, Washington, DC.

Jessor, R., & Jessor, S. L. (1977). *Problem behavior and psychosocial development: A longitudinal study of youth.* New York: Academic Press.

Kazdin, A. E. (1987). *Conduct disorders in childhood and adolescence.* Newbury Park, CA: Sage Publications.

Krisberg, B., Schwartz, I., Fishman, G., Eisikovits, Z., & Guttman, E. (1986). *The incarceration of minority youth.* Minneapolis: Hubert H. Humphrey Institute of Public Affairs.

Kumpfer, K. L. (in press). Family function factors associated with delinquency. In K. L. Kumpfer (Ed.), *Effective parenting strategies literature review.*

Laosa, L. M. (1990). Psychosocial stress, coping and development of Hispanic immigrant children. In F. C. Serafica, A. I. Schuebel, R. K. Russel, P. D. Isaac, & L. Myers (Eds.), *Mental health of ethnic minorities.* New York: Praeger.

Loeber, R., & Dishion, T. (1983). Early predictors of male delinquency: A review. *Psychological Bulletin, 94*(1), 68–99.

Lund, S. R., Johnson, R. P., & Purviens, G. B. (1978). Inhalant abuse among Mexican-Americans of the Southwest. In *Proceedings of the Third National Drug*

Abuse Conference. New York: Marcel Dekker.

Madsen, W. (1964a). The alcoholic agringado. *American Anthropologist, 66*, 355–361.

Madsen, W. (1964b). Value conflicts and folk psychiatry in south Texas. In K. Ari (Ed.), *Magic, faith and healing*. New York: Free Press.

Minuchin, S. (1974). *Families and family therapy*. Cambridge, MA: Harvard University Press.

Moore, J. (1978). *Homeboys*. Philadelphia: Temple University Press.

Morales, A., Fergusen, Y., & Munford, P. R. (1983). The juvenile justice system and minorities. In G. J. Powell (Ed.), *The psychosocial development of minority group children*. New York: Brunner/Mazel.

O'Donnell, J. A., & Clayton, R. R. (1979). Determinants of early marijuana use. In G. M. Beschner & A. S. Friedman (Eds.), *Youth drug abuse*. Lexington, MA: D. C. Heath.

Patterson, G. R. (1982). *Coercive family process*. Eugene, OR: Castalia.

Patterson, G. R. (1986). Performance models for antisocial boys. *American Psychologist, 41*, 432–444.

Patterson, G. R., & Dishion, T. J. (1985). Contributions of families and peers to delinquency. *Criminology, 23*(1), 63–79.

Rio, A., Santisteban, D., & Szapocznik, J. (1990). Treatment approaches for Hispanic drug abusing adolescents. In R. Glick & J. Moore (Eds.), *Drug abuse in Hispanic communities*. New Brunswick, NJ: Rutgers University Press.

Rogler, L. (1984). *Hispanics and criminal justice issues*. Hispanic Research Center, Fordham University, New York.

Rogler, L. H., Malgady, R.G., Costantino, G., & Blumenthal, R. (1987). What do culturally sensitive mental health services mean? The case of Hispanics. *American Psychologist, 42*, 565–570.

Rutter, M. (1979). Protective factors in children's responses to stress and disadvantage. In M. W. Kent & J. E. Rolf (Eds.), *Primary prevention of psychopathology: Vol. 3, Social competence in children* (pp. 49–74). Hanover, NH: University Press of New England.

Santisteban, D. (1979). Toward a conceptual model of drug abuse among Hispanics. In J. Szapocznik (Ed.), *Mental health and drug abuse: An Hispanic assessment of present and future challenges*. Washington, DC: The National Coalition of Hispanic Mental Health and Human Service Organizations (COSSMHO).

Schwartz, I. M. (1984). *The incarceration of Hispanic youth*. Washington, DC: The National Coalition of Hispanic Mental Health and Human Service Organizations (COSSMHO).

Scopetta, M. A., King, O. E., Szapocznik, J., & Tillman, W. (1977). *Ecological structural family therapy with Cuban immigrant families*. Spanish Family Guidance Center, University of Miami, Miami.

Stanton, M. D. (1979). Drugs and the family: A review of the recent literature. *Marriage and Family Review, 2*, 1–10.

Stumphauzer, J. S. (Ed.). (1979). *Progress in behavior therapy with delinquents*. Springfield, IL: Charles C Thomas.

Sue, S., & Zane, N. (1987). The role of culture and cultural techniques in psychotherapy: A critique and reformulation. *American Psychologist, 42*, 37–45.

Szapocznik, J., Foote, F., Perez-Vidal, A., Hervis, O., & Kurtines, W. (1985). *One person family therapy*. Department of Psychiatry, University of Miami, Miami.

Szapocznik, J., & Kurtines, W. (1980). Acculturation, biculturalism and adjustment among Cuban Americans. In A. Padilla (Ed.), *Recent advances in acculturation research: Theory, models, and some new findings*. Boulder, CO: Westview.

Szapocznik, J., & Kurtines, W. (1989). *Breakthroughs in family therapy with drug-*

abusing and problem youth. New York: Springer.

Szapocznik, J., Kurtines, W. M., Foote, F., Perez-Vidal, A., & Hervis, O. (1983). Conjoint versus one person family therapy: Some evidence for the effectiveness of conducting family therapy through one person. *Journal of Consulting and Clinical Psychology, 51,* 889–899.

Szapocznik, J., Kurtines, W. M., Foote, F., Perez-Vidal, A., & Hervis, O. (1986). Conjoint versus one person family therapy: Further evidence for the effectiveness of conducting family therapy through one person. *Journal of Consulting and Clinical Psychology, 54,* 395–397.

Szapocznik, J., Kurtines, W., Perez-Vidal, A., Hervis, O., & Foote, F. (1990). One-person family therapy. In R. A. Wells & V. J. Gianetti (Eds.), *Handbook of brief psychotherapies.* New York: Plenum.

Szapocznik, J., Perez-Vidal, A., Brickman, A., Foote, F. H., Santisteban, D. A., Hervis, O., & Kurtines, W. (1988). Engaging adolescent drug abusers and their families into treatment: A strategic structural systems approach. *Journal of Consulting and Clinical Psychology, 56,* 552–557.

Szapocznik, J., Rio, A., Murray, E., Cohen, R., Scopetta, M., Revis-Vasquez, A., Hervis, O., Posada, V., & Kurtines, W. (1989). Structural family versus psychodynamic child therapy for problematic Hispanic boys. *Journal of Consulting and Clinical Psychology, 57,* 571–578.

Szapocznik, J., Santisteban, D., Rio, A., Perez-Vidal, A., & Kurtines, W. M. (1986). Family effectiveness training (FET) for Hispanic families. In H. P. Lefley & P. B. Pederson (Eds.), *Cross cultural training for mental health professionals.* Springfield, IL: Charles C Thomas.

Szapocznik, J., Scopetta, M. A., & King, O. E. (1978). Theory and practice in matching treatment to the special characteristics and problems of Cuban immigrants. *Journal of Community Psychology, 6,* 112–122.

Szapocznik, J., Scopetta, M. A., Kurtines, W., & Aranalde, M. A. (1978). Theory and measurement of acculturation. *Interamerican Journal of Psychology, 12(2),* 113–130.

Szapocznik, J., & Truss, C. (1978). Intergenerational sources of role conflict in Cuban mothers. In M. Montiel (Ed.), *Hispanic families.* Washington, DC: The National Coalition of Hispanic Mental Health and Human Service Organizations (COSSMHO).

U.S. Department of Commerce, Bureau of the Census. (1986). *Projections of the Hispanic population: 1983–2080.* Current Population Reports, Series P-25, No. 995. Washington, DC: U.S. Government Printing Office.

U.S. Department of Commerce, Bureau of the Census. (1987). *The Hispanic population in the United States: March 1986 and 1987 (Advance Report).* Current Population Reports, Series P-20, No. 416. Washington, DC: U.S. Government Printing Office.

U.S. Department of Commerce, Bureau of the Census. (1988). *The Hispanic population in the United States: 1988 (Advance Report).* Current Population Reports, Series P-25, No. 431. Washington, DC: U.S. Government Printing Office.

Werner, E. E. (1984). Resilient children. *Young children* 40(1), 68–72.

Werner, E. E., & Smith, R. S. (1982). *Vulnerable but invincible: A longitudinal study of resilient children and youth.* New York: McGraw-Hill.